Cloud
Computing

Cloud Computing

Implementation, Management, and Security

John W. Rittinghouse

James F. Ransome

CRC Press
Taylor & Francis Group
Boca Raton   London   New York

CRC Press is an imprint of the
Taylor & Francis Group, an **informa** business

CRC Press
Taylor & Francis Group
6000 Broken Sound Parkway NW, Suite 300
Boca Raton, FL 33487-2742

Visit the Taylor & Francis Web site at
http://www.taylorandfrancis.com

and the CRC Press Web site at
http://www.crcpress.com

Contents

Foreword

While there is no arguing about the staying power of the cloud model and the benefits it can bring to any organization or government, mainstream adoption depends on several key variables falling into alignment that will provide users the reliability, desired outcomes, and levels of trust necessary to truly usher in a "cloud revolution." Until recently, early adopters of cloud computing in the public and private sectors were the catalyst for helping drive technological innovation and increased adoption of cloud-based strategies, moving us closer to this inevitable reality. Today, driven in large part by the financial crisis gripping the global economy, more and more organizations are turning toward cloud computing as a low-cost means of delivering quick-time-to-market solutions for mission-critical operations and services. The benefits of cloud computing are hard to dispute:

1. Reduced implementation and maintenance costs

2. Increased mobility for a global workforce

3. Flexible and scalable infrastructures

4. Quick time to market

5. IT department transformation (focus on innovation vs. maintenance and implementation)

6. "Greening" of the data center

7. Increased availability of high-performance applications to small/medium-sized businesses

Gartner, in a February 2, 2009, press release, posed the question of why, when "the cloud computing market is in a period of excitement, growth and high potential. . . [we] will still require several years and many

changes in the market before cloud computing is a mainstream IT effort"?[1]
In talking with government and industry leaders about this, it became clear
that the individual concerns and variables that were negatively impacting
business leaders' thought processes regarding cloud computing (and therefore preventing what could be even more growth in this market) could be
boiled down to one addressable need: a lack of understanding. Let's take this
case in point: GTRA research showed that the most common concern about
implementing cloud programs was security and privacy, a finding supported
by an IDC study of 244 CIOs on cloud computing, in which 75% of
respondents listed security as their number-one concern.[2] It is true that
moving from architectures that were built for on-premises services and
secured by firewalls and threat-detection systems to mobile environments
with SaaS applications makes previous architectures unsuitable to secure
data effectively. In addition, at a March 2009 FTC meeting discussing cloud
computing security and related privacy issues, it was agreed that data management services might experience failure similar to the current financial
meltdown if further regulation was not implemented. In short, some executives are simply too scared to move forward with cloud initiatives.

However, this concern, while valid, is not insurmountable. Already
there are countless examples of successful cloud computing implementations, from small organizations up to large enterprises that have low risk tol-
erance, such as the U.S. Department of the Navy. The security community
is also coming together through various initiatives aimed at education and
guidance creation. The National Institute of Standards and Technologies
(NIST) is releasing its first guidelines for agencies that want to use cloud
computing in the second half of 2009, and groups such as the Jericho forum
are bringing security executives together to collaborate and deliver solutions.
As with any emerging technology, there exists a learning curve with regard
to security in a cloud environment, but there is no doubt that resources and
case studies exist today to help any organization overcome this.

The same types of pros and cons listed above can be applied to other
concerns facing executives, such as data ownership rights, performance,
and availability. While these are all valid concerns, solutions do exist and
are being fine-tuned every day; the challenge is in bringing executives out
of a state of unknown and fear and giving them the understanding and

---

1.   "Cloud Application Infrastructure Technologies Need Seven Years to Mature," Gartner, Inc.,
     December 2008.
2.   "IT Cloud Services User Study," IDC, Inc., October 2008.

knowledge necessary to make informed, educated decisions regarding their cloud initiatives.

In this book, Drs. Rittinghouse and Ransome do a tremendous job of educating, dispelling myths, and giving detailed examples and steps which will provide the reader with a proper understand of cloud computing, its risks, and how to implement and manage an effective cloud strategy. This is all done is a manner that is reader-friendly but with enough detailed technical language to be complete, and not so much that a nontechnical leader will be lost.

In the Introduction and Chapter 1, Drs. Rittinghouse and Ransome lay the foundation for the reader's proper understanding of cloud computing, detailing its history and evolution and discussing how new technologies such as virtualization played a huge role in the growth and acceptance of cloud computing. Chapter 2 then educates us on the different types of services which can be delivered from the cloud, providing detail on Software-as-a-Service (SaaS), Infrastructure-as-a-Service (IaaS), Platform-as-a-Service (PaaS), Monitoring-as-a-Service (MaaS), and Communication-as-a-Service (CaaS).

Chapter 3 dives into the heart of what it means to build a cloud network, including a look at the roles that service-oriented architecture (SOA and open source software play in the process. Following this, Chapter 4 is dedicated entirely to the topic of virtualization, a critical component of any cloud network and one of the technologies which is a foundation of cloud concepts.

Security and privacy, one of the largest areas of concern for anyone building a cloud network, are covered in Chapters 5 and 6. These chapters look at how federation in the cloud and federated services and applications can be used to increase security, build trust, and mitigate risk. Dr. Ron Ross, a senior computer scientist at NIST, recently said, "You're never going to have complete trust. We don't live in a risk-free environment—we have to manage risk, not avoid it." These chapters give the reader a wealth of guidance, practical applications, and process, which can be used to keep risk at an acceptable level in any cloud network.

Chapter 7 shifts focus to look at common standards in cloud computing, including standards for application development, messaging, and security. Social networking and collaboration is the focus of Chapter 8, in which the authors discuss end-user access to cloud computing (You Tube, Facebook, etc.). Chapter 9, the book's final chapter, discusses in detail how mobile Internet devices react with cloud networks—a topic which is critical now and will only increase in importance as users expect more and more applications to be delivered to their smartphones and other mobile devices.

We feel that completing this book, readers will have a thorough, well-rounded understanding of cloud computing, the knowledge necessary to overcome fears, and will be armed with the guidance necessary to make smart, strategic decisions regarding their cloud initiatives. Ultimately, this book will play a part in ushering in the "cloud revolution" and will help overcome the lack of understanding currently preventing even faster adoption of cloud computing.

Kelly Yocum

Parham Eftekhari

Co-Founders, Government Technology Research Alliance

Kelly Yocum and Parham Eftekhari are the co-founders of the Government Technology Research Alliance (GTRA), an organization that provides government CXO leaders a forum in which to collaborate, strategize, and create innovative solutions for today's most pressing IT needs. Kelly is GTRA's executive director and is responsible for strategic direction, business development, and work with solution and technology providers for the GTRA Government Council. She also serves as the CEO for GOVTek, a collaborative online information resource for government technology executives and industry experts. Kelly was formerly CEO of ConVurge, a business intelligence conference company, where she founded several councils for government technology including SecureGOV, ArchitectureGOV, MobileGOV, and HrGOV, which are currently managed by GTRA. She invented a unique government-to-industry collaboration model, called GTRA Roundtable Meetings, which foster an innovative discussion forum for government and industry experts.

Parham Eftekhari serves as director of research and curriculum development for GTRA, where he is responsible for overseeing all research conducted with senior government technology executives and industry leaders on technology and leadership issues. Parham's areas of expertise include transparency/open government, enterprise architecture, security, virtualization, information sharing, social networking/Web 2.0, knowledge management, green IT, records management, mobility, and cloud computing.

Parham is also responsible for growing GTRA's councils with key government leaders and assisting in the government-to-industry collaboration model. Parham is also vice president of GOVTek, where his primary focus is to oversee the content, research, and resources shared on the site. Parham formerly served as director of technology research for Proactive Worldwide, managing the full life cycle of competitive intelligence, strategic, and market assessment research studies. Together, Parham and Kelly run the semiannual GTRA Council Meeting Symposia, which bring together executive-level decision makers from both the public and private sectors to collaborate, share ideas, and discuss solutions to current challenges. This forum is a unique model for government and technology collaboration in which the concepts of cloud computing and the cloud's value to the next generation of consumers and practitioners in both government and commercial sectors are presented.

Preface

There are lots of books on cloud computing in the market today. This one is not intended for "supergeeks" looking for the next revelation in "geek know-how." In fact, it attempts to present cloud computing in a way that anyone can understand. We do include technical material, but we do so in a way that allows managers and technical people alike to understand what exactly cloud computing is and what it is not. We try to clear up the confusion about current buzzwords such as PaaS, SaaS, etc., and let the reader see how and why the technology has evolved to become "the cloud" as we know and use it today.

In the Introduction we explain what cloud computing is, its characteristics, and the challenges it will face in the future. The biggest challenges that companies will face as they move into the cloud are secure data storage, high-speed access to the Internet, and standardization. Storing large amounts of data in centralized locations while preserving user privacy, security, identity, and their application-specific preferences raises many concerns about data protection. These concerns, in turn, lead to questions about the legal framework that should be implemented for a cloud-oriented environment.

In Chapter 1 we discuss the evolution of cloud computing, including hardware, software, and server virtualization. In order to discuss some of the issues involved in the cloud concept, it is important to place the development of computational technology in a historical context. Looking at the cloud's evolutionary development, and the problems encountered along the way, provides some key reference points to help us understand the challenges that had to be overcome by those who were responsible for the development of the Internet and the World Wide Web. These challenges fell into three primary categories: hardware, software, and virtualization. We discuss how the rules computers use to communicate came about, and how the development of networking and communications protocols helped drive the technology growth we have seen in the last two decades or so. This, in turn, has driven even more changes in protocols and forced the creation of new technologies to mitigate concerns and improve the methods used to communicate over the Internet. The rise of web browsers led to huge growth in use of the Internet and a migration away from the traditional data center toward cloud computing.

In Chapter 2 we discuss the advent of web-based services delivered from the cloud, including Communication-as-a-Service (CaaS), Infrastructure-as-a-Service (IaaS), Monitoring-as-a-Service (MaaS), Platform-as-a-Service (PaaS), and Software-as-a-Service (SaaS). As technology has migrated from the traditional on-premises model to the new cloud model, service offerings have evolved almost daily. We provide some basic exposure to where the technology is today, and we give you a feel for where it will likely be in the not too distant future.

In Chapter 3 we discuss what is required from service providers to make the services described in Chapter 2 available. We describe the basic approach to service-oriented architecture (SOA) as it applies to data center design, how companies can build highly automated private cloud networks that can be managed from a single point, and how server and storage virtualization is used across distributed computing resources. We discuss what it takes to build a cloud network, the evolution from the managed service provider model to cloud computing and SaaS and from single-purpose architectures to multipurpose architectures, the concept and design of data center virtualization, the role and importance of collaboration, SOA as an intermediate step and the basic approach to data center-based SOA, and lastly, the role of open source software in data centers and where and how it is used in the cloud architecture.

In Chapter 4 we provide a virtualization practicum that guides you through a step-by-step process for building a virtualized computing infrastructure using open source software. The beauty of virtualization solutions is that you can run multiple operating systems simultaneously on a single computer. So that you could really understand how powerful that capability is, we show you how to do it for yourself. We show you how to download and install the Sun VirtualBox, how to install and configure it, and how to add a virtual operating environment on top of your existing operating system. In learning the basics of using the Sun xVM VirtualBox, you will also gain knowledge about what virtualization is and how it can be used.

Chapter 5 discusses the importance and relevance of federation, presence, identity, and privacy in cloud computing and the latest challenges, solutions, and potential future for each in the cloud. Building a seamless federated communications capability in a cloud environment, one that is capable of supporting people, devices, information feeds, documents, application interfaces, and other entities, depends on the architecture that is implemented. The solution chosen must be able to find such entities, determine their purpose, and request presence data so that others can interact with them in real time. This process is known as discovery.

The extension of virtualization and virtual machines into the cloud is affecting enterprise security because the traditional enterprise network perimeter is evaporating. In Chapter 6 we identify security as the greatest challenge in cloud computing, particularly with regard to the SaaS environment. Although there is a significant benefit to leveraging cloud computing, security concerns have led some organizations to hesitate to move critical resources to the cloud.

Corporations and individuals are concerned about how security and compliance integrity can be maintained in this new environment. Even more concerning, though, is the corporations that are jumping to cloud computing while being oblivious to the implications of putting critical applications and data in the cloud. Chapter 6 addresses the security concerns of the former and educates the latter. Moving critical applications and sensitive data to a public and shared cloud environment is a major concern for corporations that are moving beyond their data center's network perimeter defense. To alleviate these concerns, a cloud solution provider must ensure that customers can continue to have the same security and privacy controls over their applications and services, provide evidence to these customers that their organization and customers are secure and they can meet their service-level agreements, and show how can they prove compliance to their auditors.

Regardless of how the cloud evolves, it needs some form of standardization so that the market can evolve and thrive. Standards also allow clouds to interoperate and communicate with each other. In Chapter 7 we introduce some of the more common standards in cloud computing. Although we do not analyze each standard in depth, you should gain a feel for how and why each standard is used and, more important, a better understanding of why they evolved. Most current standards evolved from necessity, as individuals took a chance on new innovation. As these innovative techniques became acceptable to users and implementers, more support for the technique ensued. At some point, the innovation began to be considered a "standard," and groups formalized protocols or rules for using it. We discuss the Open Cloud Consortium and the Distributed Management Task Force as examples of cloud-related working groups.

Innovation leading to success in cloud services depends ultimately on acceptance of the application by the user community. In Chapter 8 we present some of the applications that are gaining acceptance among end users. We look at some of the most popular SaaS offerings for consumers and provide an overview of their benefits and why, in our opinion, they are helping to evolve our common understanding of what collaboration and mobility will ultimately mean in our daily lives. We examine five particularly successful SaaS offerings, YouTube, Zimbra, Facebook, Zoho, and DimDim, looking at them from both the user perspective and the developer/implementer perspective. This dual perspective should give you a clear understanding of how such offerings are transforming our concept of computing by making much traditional desktop-type software available from the cloud.

In Chapter 9 we detail the transition from fixed devices connected to the Internet to the new mobile device–empowered Internet. While it is essentially the same Internet, it has become tremendously more accessible, and advances in telephony, coupled with the use of the Internet, have led to some very compelling, powerful offerings. In this chapter we provide an overview of the more common offerings and how their widespread use will affect the cloud computing world. When more than 90% of your user base depends on mobile devices for common applications such as email, contacts, and media streaming or sharing, you cannot take the same approach as you used with statically connected Internet devices such as laptops and desktop PCs. It is a brave, new cloud-based world we are entering.

We hope that what you take away from reading this book is knowledge that separates hype from reality in talking about cloud computing. It seems that everyone you ask has a different answer. Most of the time, each answer you hear is based on one person's experience with the cloud or with his or her desire to capitalize on the cloud for profit. Our intent is to present the cloud as an evolving, changing entity that does so out of demand from the Internet community itself. The technologies that are used in the cloud often give rise to new uses. For example, 10 years ago, you needed custom applications to watch video, the right codec had to be used for the right software, etc. It was more trouble than watching the video was worth. Today, there is a *de facto* standard. Look at how YouTube has come about as a result of such innovation. After you read this book, you will know about the cloud, but not from the perspective of any one source; you will know from the perspective of how technological innovation has actually made it what it is.

Introduction

The purpose of this book is to clear up some of the mystery surrounding the topic of cloud computing. In order to understand how computing has evolved, one must understand the evolution of computing from a historical perspective, focusing primarily on those advances that led to the development of cloud computing, such as the transition from mainframes to desktops, laptops, mobile devices, and on to the cloud. We will also need to discuss in some detail the key components that are critical to make the cloud computing paradigm feasible with the technology available today. We will cover some of the standards that are used or are proposed for use in the cloud computing model, since standardization is crucial to achieving widespread acceptance of cloud computing. We will also discuss the means used to manage effectively the infrastructure for cloud computing. Significant legal considerations in properly protecting user data and mitigating corporate liability will also be covered. Finally, we will discuss what some of the more successful cloud vendors have done and how their achievements have helped the cloud model evolve.

Over the last five decades, businesses that use computing resources have learned to contend with a vast array of buzzwords. Much of this *geek-speak* or marketing vapor, over time, has been guilty of making promises that often are never kept. Some promises, to be sure, have been delivered, although others have drifted into oblivion. When it comes to offering technology in a *pay-as-you-use* services model, most information technology (IT) professionals have heard it all—from allocated resource management to grid computing, to on-demand computing and software-as-a-service (SaaS), to utility computing. A new buzzword, *cloud computing,* is presently in vogue in the marketplace, and it is generating all sorts of confusion about what it actually represents.

What Is the Cloud?

The term *cloud* has been used historically as a metaphor for the Internet. This usage was originally derived from its common depiction in network diagrams as an outline of a cloud, used to represent the transport of data across carrier backbones (which owned the cloud) to an endpoint location on the other side of the cloud. This concept dates back as early as 1961, when Professor John McCarthy suggested that computer time-sharing technology might lead to a future where computing power and even specific applications might be sold through a utility-type business model.[1] This idea became very popular in the late 1960s, but by the mid-1970s the idea faded away when it became clear that the IT-related technologies of the day were unable to sustain such a futuristic computing model. However, since the turn of the millennium, the concept has been revitalized. It was during this time of revitalization that the term *cloud computing* began to emerge in technology circles.

The Emergence of Cloud Computing

Utility computing can be defined as the provision of computational and storage resources as a metered service, similar to those provided by a traditional public utility company. This, of course, is not a new idea. This form of computing is growing in popularity, however, as companies have begun to extend the model to a cloud computing paradigm providing virtual servers that IT departments and users can access on demand. Early enterprise adopters used utility computing mainly for non-mission-critical needs, but that is quickly changing as trust and reliability issues are resolved.

Some people think cloud computing is the next big thing in the world of IT. Others believe it is just another variation of the utility computing model that has been repackaged in this decade as something new and cool. However, it is not just the buzzword "cloud computing" that is causing confusion among the masses. Currently, with so few cloud computing vendors actually practicing this form of technology and also almost every analyst from every research organization in the country defining the term differently, the meaning of the term has become very nebulous. Even among those who think they understand it, definitions vary, and most of those definitions are hazy at best. To clear the haze and make some sense of the new

---

1.   http://computinginthecloud.wordpress.com/2008/09/25/utility-cloud-computingflashback-
      to-1961-prof-john-mccarthy, retrieved 5 Jan 2009.

concept, this book will attempt to help you understand just what cloud computing really means, how disruptive to your business it may become in the future, and what its advantages and disadvantages are.

As we said previously, the term *the cloud* is often used as a metaphor for the Internet and has become a familiar cliché. However, when "the cloud" is combined with "computing," it causes a lot of confusion. Market research analysts and technology vendors alike tend to define cloud computing very narrowly, as a new type of utility computing that basically uses virtual servers that have been made available to third parties via the Internet. Others tend to define the term using a very broad, all-encompassing application of the virtual computing platform. They contend that anything beyond the firewall perimeter is in the cloud. A more tempered view of cloud computing considers it the delivery of computational resources from a location other than the one from which you are computing.

The Global Nature of the Cloud

The cloud sees no borders and thus has made the world a much smaller place. The Internet is global in scope but respects only established communication paths. People from everywhere now have access to other people from anywhere else. Globalization of computing assets may be the biggest contribution the cloud has made to date. For this reason, the cloud is the subject of many complex geopolitical issues. Cloud vendors must satisfy myriad regulatory concerns in order to deliver cloud services to a global market. When the Internet was in its infancy, many people believed cyberspace was a distinct environment that needed laws specific to itself. University computing centers and the ARPANET were, for a time, the encapsulated environments where the Internet existed. It took a while to get business to warm up to the idea.

Cloud computing is still in its infancy. There is a hodge-podge of providers, both large and small, delivering a wide variety of cloud-based services. For example, there are full-blown applications, support services, mail-filtering services, storage services, etc. IT practitioners have learned to contend with some of the many cloud-based services out of necessity as business needs dictated. However, cloud computing aggregators and integrators are already emerging, offering packages of products and services as a single entry point into the cloud.

The concept of cloud computing becomes much more understandable when one begins to think about what modern IT environments always require—the means to increase capacity or add capabilities to their infra-structure dynamically, without investing money in the purchase of new infrastructure, all the while without needing to conduct training for new personnel and without the need for licensing new software. Given a solution to the aforementioned needs, cloud computing models that encompass a subscription-based or pay-per-use paradigm provide a service that can be used over the Internet and extends an IT shop's existing capabilities. Many users have found that this approach provides a return on investment that IT managers are more than willing to accept.

Cloud-Based Service Offerings

Cloud computing may be viewed as a resource available as a service for vir-tual data centers, but cloud computing and virtual data centers are not the same. For example, consider Amazon's S3 Storage Service. This is a data storage service designed for use across the Internet (i.e., the cloud). It is designed to make web-scale computing easier for developers. According to Amazon:

> Amazon S3 provides a simple web services interface that can be used to store and retrieve any amount of data, at any time, from anywhere on the web. It gives any developer access to the same highly scalable, reliable, fast, inexpensive data storage infrastructure that Amazon uses to run its own global network of web sites. The service aims to maximize benefits of scale and to pass those benefits on to developers.[2]

Amazon.com has played a vital role in the development of cloud com-puting. In modernizing its data centers after the dot-com bubble burst in 2001, it discovered that the new cloud architecture it had implemented resulted in some very significant internal efficiency improvements. By pro-viding access to its systems for third-party users on a utility computing basis, via Amazon Web Services, introduced in 2002, a revolution of sorts began. Amazon Web Services began implementing its model by renting computing cycles as a service outside a given user's domain, wherever on the planet that domain might be located. This approach modernized a style of computing whereby IT-related capabilities could be provided "as a service"

---

2.   http://aws.amazon.com/s3, retrieved 5 Jan 2009.

to users. By allowing their users to access technology-enabled services "in the cloud," without any need for knowledge of, expertise with, or control over how the technology infrastructure that supports those services worked, Amazon shifted the approach to computing radically. This approach transformed cloud computing into a paradigm whereby data is permanently stored in remote servers accessible via the Internet and cached temporarily on client devices that may include desktops, tablet computers, notebooks, hand-held devices, mobile phones, etc., and is often called *Software as a Service* (SaaS).

SaaS is a type of cloud computing that delivers applications through a browser to thousands of customers using a multiuser architecture. The focus for SaaS is on the end user as opposed to managed services (described below). For the customer, there are no up-front investment costs in servers or software licensing. For the service provider, with just one product to maintain, costs are relatively low compared to the costs incurred with a conventional hosting model. Salesforce.com[3] is by far the best-known example of SaaS computing among enterprise applications. Salesforce.com was founded in 1999 by former Oracle executive Marc Benioff, who pioneered the concept of delivering enterprise applications via a simple web site. Nowdays, SaaS is also commonly used for enterprise resource planning and human resource applications. Another example is Google Apps, which provides online access via a web browser to the most common office and business applications used today, all the while keeping the software and user data stored on Google servers. A decade ago, no one could have predicted the sudden rise of SaaS applications such as these.

Managed service providers (MSPs) offer one of the oldest forms of cloud computing. Basically, a managed service is an application that is accessible to an organization's IT infrastructure rather than to end users. Services include virus scanning for email, antispam services such as Postini,[4] desktop management services such as those offered by CenterBeam[5] or Everdream,[6] and

---

3.   http://www.salesforce.com , retrieved 5 Jan 2009.
4.   In September 2007, Google acquired Postini, recognized as a global leader in on-demand communications security and compliance solutions. This is further evidence of the aggregation of cloud service providers.
5.   CenterBeam delivers services over the Internet using a SaaS model.
6.   In November 2007, Dell signed an agreement to acquire Everdream, a leading provider of SaaS solutions for remote service management. The planned acquisition was a key component in Dell's strategy of enabling customers to simplify IT. Everdream's capabilities complement those provided by the recently acquired SilverBack Technologies, further enabling end-to-end remote management of customers' IT environments.

application performance monitoring. Managed security services that are delivered by third-party providers also fall into this category.

Platform-as-a-Service (PaaS) is yet another variation of SaaS. Sometimes referred to simply as web services in the cloud, PaaS is closely related to SaaS but delivers a platform from which to work rather than an application to work with. These service providers offer application programming interfaces (APIs) that enable developers to exploit functionality over the Internet, rather than delivering full-blown applications. This variation of cloud computing delivers development environments to programmers, analysts, and software engineers as a service. A general model is implemented under which developers build applications designed to run on the provider's infrastructure and which are delivered to users in via an Internet browser. The main drawback to this approach is that these services are limited by the vendor's design and capabilities. This means a compromise between freedom to develop code that does something other than what the provider can provide and application predictability, performance, and integration.

An example of this model is the Google App Engine. According to Google, "Google App Engine makes it easy to build an application that runs reliably, even under heavy load and with large amounts of data."[7] The Google App Engine environment includes the following features

- Dynamic web serving, with full support for common web technologies
- Persistent storage with queries, sorting, and transactions
- Automatic scaling and load balancing
- APIs for authenticating users and sending email using Google Accounts
- A fully featured local development environment that simulates Google App Engine on your computer

Currently, Google App Engine applications are implemented using the Python programming language. The runtime environment includes the full Python language and most of the Python standard library. For extremely lightweight development, cloud-based mashup platforms (Ajax modules that are assembled in code) abound, such as Yahoo Pipes or Dapper.net.

---

7.   http://code.google.com/appengine/docs/whatisgoogleappengine.html, retrieved 5 Jan 2009.

Grid Computing or Cloud Computing?

Grid computing is often confused with cloud computing. Grid computing is a form of distributed computing that implements a *virtual supercomputer* made up of a cluster of networked or Internetworked computers acting in unison to perform very large tasks. Many cloud computing deployments today are powered by grid computing implementations and are billed like utilities, but cloud computing can and should be seen as an evolved next step away from the grid utility model. There is an ever-growing list of providers that have successfully used cloud architectures with little or no centralized infrastructure or billing systems, such as the peer-to-peer network BitTorrent and the volunteer computing initiative SETI@home.[8]

Service commerce platforms are yet another variation of SaaS and MSPs. This type of cloud computing service provides a centralized service hub that users interact with. Currently, the most often used application of this platform is found in financial trading environments or systems that allow users to order things such as travel or personal services from a common platform (e.g., Expedia.com or Hotels.com), which then coordinates pricing and service delivery within the specifications set by the user.

Is the Cloud Model Reliable?

The majority of today's cloud computing infrastructure consists of time-tested and highly reliable services built on servers with varying levels of virtualized technologies, which are delivered via large data centers operating under service-level agreements that require 99.99% or better uptime. Commercial offerings have evolved to meet the quality-of-service requirements of customers and typically offer such service-level agreements to their customers. From users' perspective, the cloud appears as a single point of access for all their computing needs. These cloud-based services are accessible anywhere in the world, as long as an Internet connection is available. Open standards and open-source software have also been significant factors in the growth of cloud computing, topics we will discuss in more depth later.

---

8. SETI@home is a scientific experiment that uses Internet-connected computers in the Search for Extraterrestrial Intelligence (SETI). For more information, see http://www.seti.org.

Benefits of Using a Cloud Model

Because customers generally do not own the infrastructure used in cloud computing environments, they can forgo capital expenditure and consume resources as a service by just paying for what they use. Many cloud computing offerings have adopted the utility computing and billing model described above, while others bill on a subscription basis. By sharing computing power among multiple users, utilization rates are generally greatly improved, because cloud computing servers are not sitting dormant for lack of use. This factor alone can reduce infrastructure costs significantly and accelerate the speed of applications development.

A beneficial side effect of using this model is that computer capacity increases dramatically, since customers do not have to engineer their applications for peak times, when processing loads are greatest. Adoption of the cloud computing model has also been enabled because of the greater availability of increased high-speed bandwidth. With greater enablement, though, there are other issues one must consider, especially legal ones.

What About Legal Issues When Using Cloud Models?

Recently there have been some efforts to create and unify the legal environment specific to the cloud. For example, the United States–European Union Safe Harbor Act provides a seven-point framework of requirements for U.S. companies that may use data from other parts of the world, namely, the European Union. This framework sets forth how companies can participate and certify their compliance and is defined in detail on the U.S. Department of Commerce and Federal Trade Commission web sites. In summary, the agreement allows most U.S. corporations to certify that they have joined a self-regulatory organization that adheres to the following seven Safe Harbor Principles or has implemented its own privacy policies that conform with these principles:

1.   Notify individuals about the purposes for which information is collected and used.

2.   Give individuals the choice of whether their information can be disclosed to a third party.

3.   Ensure that if it transfers personal information to a third party, that third party also provides the same level of privacy protection.

4. Allow individuals access to their personal information.

5. Take reasonable security precautions to protect collected data from loss, misuse, or disclosure.

6. Take reasonable steps to ensure the integrity of the data collected.;

7. Have in place an adequate enforcement mechanism.

Major service providers such as Amazon Web Services cater to a global marketplace, typically the United States, Japan, and the European Union, by deploying local infrastructure at those locales and allowing customers to select availability zones. However, there are still concerns about security and privacy at both the individual and governmental levels. Of major concern is the USA PATRIOT Act and the Electronic Communications Privacy Act's Stored Communications Act. The USA PATRIOT Act, more commonly known as the Patriot Act, is a controversial Act of Congress that U.S. President George W. Bush signed into law on October 26, 2001. The contrived acronym stands for "Uniting and Strengthening America by Providing Appropriate Tools Required to Intercept and Obstruct Terrorism Act of 2001" (Public Law P.L. 107-56). The Act expanded the definition of terrorism to include domestic terrorism, thus enlarging the number of activities to which the USA PATRIOT Act's law enforcement powers could be applied. It increased law enforcement agencies' ability to surveil telephone, email communications, medical, financial, and other records and increased the range of discretion for law enforcement and immigration authorities when detaining and deporting immigrants suspected of terrorism-related acts. It lessened the restrictions on foreign intelligence gathering within the United States. Furthermore, it expanded the Secretary of the Treasury's authority to regulate financial transactions involving foreign individuals and businesses.

The Electronic Communications Privacy Act's Stored Communications Act is defined in the U.S. Code, Title 18, Part I, Chapter 121, § 2701, Unlawful Access to Stored Communications. Offenses committed under this act include intentional access without authorization to a facility through which an electronic communication service is provided or intentionally exceeding an authorization to access that facility in order to obtain, alter, or prevent authorized access to a wire or electronic communication while it is in electronic storage in such a system. Persons convicted under this Act can be punished if the offense is committed for purposes of commercial advantage, malicious destruction or damage, or private commercial gain, or in furtherance of any criminal or tortious act in violation of the Constitution or laws of the United States or any state by a fine or imprisonment or both for not more than five years in the case of a first offense. For a second or subsequent offense, the penalties stiffen to fine or imprisonment for not more than 10 years, or both.

What Are the Key Characteristics of Cloud Computing?

There are several key characteristics of a cloud computing environment. Service offerings are most often made available to specific consumers and small businesses that see the benefit of use because their capital expenditure is minimized. This serves to lower barriers to entry in the marketplace, since the infrastructure used to provide these offerings is owned by the cloud service provider and need not be purchased by the customer. Because users are not tied to a specific device (they need only the ability to access the Internet) and because the Internet allows for location independence, use of the cloud enables cloud computing service providers' customers to access cloud-enabled systems regardless of where they may be located or what device they choose to use.

Multitenancy[9] enables sharing of resources and costs among a large pool of users. Chief benefits to a multitenancy approach include:

- Centralization of infrastructure and lower costs
- Increased peak-load capacity
- Efficiency improvements for systems that are often underutilized
- Dynamic allocation of CPU, storage, and network bandwidth
- Consistent performance that is monitored by the provider of the service

Reliability is often enhanced in cloud computing environments because service providers utilize multiple redundant sites. This is attractive to enter-

---

9.   http://en.wikipedia.org/wiki/Multitenancy, retrieved 5 Jan 2009. Multitenancy refers to a principle in software architecture where a single instance of the software runs on a SaaS vendor's servers, serving multiple client organizations (tenants).

prises for business continuity and disaster recovery reasons. The drawback, however, is that IT managers can do very little when an outage occurs.

Another benefit that makes cloud services more reliable is that scalability can vary dynamically based on changing user demands. Because the service provider manages the necessary infrastructure, security often is vastly improved. As a result of data centralization, there is an increased focus on protecting customer resources maintained by the service provider. To assure customers that their data is safe, cloud providers are quick to invest in dedicated security staff. This is largely seen as beneficial but has also raised concerns about a user's loss of control over sensitive data. Access to data is usually logged, but accessing the audit logs can be difficult or even impossible for the customer.

Data centers, computers, and the entire associated infrastructure needed to support cloud computing are major consumers of energy. Sustainability of the cloud computing model is achieved by leveraging improvements in resource utilization and implementation of more energy-efficient systems. In 2007, Google, IBM, and a number of universities began working on a large-scale cloud computing research project. By the summer of 2008, quite a few cloud computing events had been scheduled. The first annual conference on cloud computing was scheduled to be hosted online April 20–24, 2009. According to the official web site:

> This conference is the world's premier cloud computing event, covering research, development and innovations in the world of cloud computing. The program reflects the highest level of accomplishments in the cloud computing community, while the invited presentations feature an exceptional lineup of speakers. The panels, workshops, and tutorials are selected to cover a range of the hottest topics in cloud computing.[10]

It may seem that all the world is raving about the potential of the cloud computing model, but most business leaders are likely asking: "What is the market opportunity for this technology and what is the future potential for long-term utilization of it?" Meaningful research and data are difficult to find at this point, but the potential uses for cloud computing models are wide. Ultimately, cloud computing is likely to bring supercomputing capa-

---

10.   http://cloudslam09.com, retireved 5 Jan 09.

bilities to the masses. Yahoo, Google, Microsoft, IBM, and others are engaged in the creation of online services to give their users even better access to data to aid in daily life issues such as health care, finance, insurance, etc.

Challenges for the Cloud

The biggest challenges these companies face are secure data storage, high-speed access to the Internet, and standardization. Storing large amounts of data that is oriented around user privacy, identity, and application-specific preferences in centralized locations raises many concerns about data protection. These concerns, in turn, give rise to questions regarding the legal framework that should be implemented for a cloud-oriented environment. Another challenge to the cloud computing model is the fact that broadband penetration in the United States remains far behind that of many other countries in Europe and Asia. Cloud computing is untenable without high-speed connections (both wired and wireless). Unless broadband speeds are available, cloud computing services cannot be made widely accessible. Finally, technical standards used for implementation of the various computer systems and applications necessary to make cloud computing work have still not been completely defined, publicly reviewed, and ratified by an oversight body. Even the consortiums that are forming need to get past that hurdle at some point, and until that happens, progress on new products will likely move at a snail's pace.

Aside from the challenges discussed in the previous paragraph, the reliability of cloud computing has recently been a controversial topic in technology circles. Because of the public availability of a cloud environment, problems that occur in the cloud tend to receive lots of public exposure. Unlike problems that occur in enterprise environments, which often can be contained without publicity, even when only a few cloud computing users have problems, it makes headlines.

In October 2008, Google published an article online that discussed the lessons learned from hosting over a million business customers in the cloud computing model.[11] Google's personnel measure availability as the average uptime per user based on server-side error rates. They believe this reliability metric allows a true side-by-side comparison with other solutions. Their

---

11.   Matthew Glotzbach, Product Management Director, Google Enterprise, "What We Learned from 1 Million Businesses in the Cloud," http://googleblog.blogspot.com/2008/10/what-we-learned-from-1-million.html, 30 Oct 2008.

measurements are made for every server request for every user, every moment of every day, and even a single millisecond delay is logged. Google analyzed data collected over the previous year and discovered that their Gmail application was available to everyone more than 99.9% of the time.

One might ask how a 99.9% reliability metric compares to conventional approaches used for business email. According to the research firm Radicati Group,[12] companies with on-premises email solutions averaged from 30 to 60 minutes of unscheduled downtime and an additional 36 to 90 minutes of planned downtime per month, compared to 10 to 15 minutes of downtime with Gmail. Based on analysis of these findings, Google claims that for unplanned outages, Gmail is twice as reliable as a Novell GroupWise solution and four times more reliable than a Microsoft Exchange-based solution, both of which require companies to maintain an internal infrastructure themselves. It stands to reason that higher reliability will translate to higher employee productivity. Google discovered that Gmail is more than four times as reliable as the Novell GroupWise solution and 10 times more reliable than an Exchange-based solution when you factor in planned outages inherent in on-premises messaging platforms.

Based on these findings, Google was confident enough to announce publicly in October 2008 that the 99.9% service-level agreement offered to their Premier Edition customers using Gmail would be extended to Google Calendar, Google Docs, Google Sites, and Google Talk. Since more than a million businesses use Google Apps to run their businesses, Google has made a series of commitments to improve communications with customers during any outages and to make all issues visible and transparent through open user groups. Since Google itself runs on its Google Apps platform, the commitment they have made has teeth, and I am a strong advocate of "eating your own dog food." Google leads the industry in evolving the cloud computing model to become a part of what is being called Web 3.0—the next generation of Internet.[13]

In the following chapters, we will discuss the evolution of computing from a historical perspective, focusing primarily on those advances that led to the development of cloud computing. We will discuss in detail some of the more critical components that are necessary to make the cloud com-

---

12.   The Radicati Group, 2008, "Corporate IT Survey—Messaging & Collaboration, 2008–2009," http://www.marketwatch.com/news/story/The-Radicati-Group-Releases-New/story.aspx?guid=%7B80D6388A-731C-457F-9156-F783B3E3C720%7D, retrieved 12 Feb 2009.

13.   http://en.wikipedia.org/wiki/Web_3.0, retrieved 5 Jan 2009.

puting paradigm feasible. Standardization is a crucial factor in gaining widespread adoption of the cloud computing model, and there are many different standards that need to be finalized before cloud computing becomes a mainstream method of computing for the masses. This book will look at those various standards based on the use and implementation issues surrounding cloud computing. Management of the infrastructure that is maintained by cloud computing service providers will also be discussed. As with any IT, there are legal considerations that must be addressed to properly protect user data and mitigate corporate liability, and we will cover some of the more significant legal issues and even some of the philosophical issues that will most likely not be resolved without adoption of a legal framework. Finally, this book will take a hard look at some of the cloud computing vendors that have had significant success and examine what they have done and how their achievements have helped to shape cloud computing.

Chapter 1

The Evolution of Cloud Computing

1.1 Chapter Overview

It is important to understand the evolution of computing in order to get an appreciation of how we got into the cloud environment. Looking at the evolution of the computing hardware itself, from the first generation to the current (fourth) generation of computers, shows how we got from there to here. The hardware, however, was only part of the evolutionary process. As hardware evolved, so did software. As networking evolved, so did the rules for how computers communicate. The development of such rules, or protocols, also helped drive the evolution of Internet software.

Establishing a common protocol for the Internet led directly to rapid growth in the number of users online. This has driven technologists to make even more changes in current protocols and to create new ones. Today, we talk about the use of IPv6 (Internet Protocol version 6) to mitigate addressing concerns and for improving the methods we use to communicate over the Internet. Over time, our ability to build a common interface to the Internet has evolved with the improvements in hardware and software. Using web browsers has led to a steady migration away from the traditional data center model to a cloud-based model. Using technologies such as server virtualization, parallel processing, vector processing, symmetric multiprocessing, and massively parallel processing has fueled radical change. Let's take a look at how this happened, so we can begin to understand more about the cloud.

In order to discuss some of the issues of the cloud concept, it is important to place the development of computational technology in a historical context. Looking at the Internet cloud's evolutionary development,[1] and the problems encountered along the way, provides some key reference points to help us understand the challenges that had to be overcome to develop the Internet and the World Wide Web (WWW) today. These challenges fell into two primary areas, hardware and software. We will look first at the hardware side.

1.2   Hardware Evolution

Our lives today would be different, and probably difficult, without the benefits of modern computers. Computerization has permeated nearly every facet of our personal and professional lives. Computer evolution has been both rapid and fascinating. The first step along the evolutionary path of computers occurred in 1930, when binary arithmetic was developed and became the foundation of computer processing technology, terminology, and programming languages. Calculating devices date back to at least as early as 1642, when a device that could mechanically add numbers was invented. Adding devices evolved from the abacus. It was a significant milestone in the history of computers. In 1939, the Berry brothers invented an electronic computer capable of operating digitally. Computations were performed using vacuum-tube technology.

In 1941, the introduction of Konrad Zuse's Z3 at the German Laboratory for Aviation in Berlin was one of the most significant events in the evolution of computers because this machine supported both floating-point and binary arithmetic. Because it was a "Turing-complete" device,[2] it is considered to be the very first computer that was fully operational. A programming language is considered Turing-complete if it falls into the same computational class as a Turing machine, meaning that it can perform any calculation a universal Turing machine can perform. This is especially significant because, under the Church-Turing thesis,[3] a Turing machine is the embodiment of the intuitive notion of an algorithm. Over the course of the next two years, computer prototypes were built to decode secret German messages by the U.S. Army.

---

1.   Paul Wallis, "A Brief History of Cloud Computing: Is the Cloud There Yet? A Look at the Cloud's Forerunners and the Problems They Encountered," http://soa.sys-con.com/node/581838, 22 Aug 2008, retrieved 7 Jan 2009.
2.   According to the online encyclopedia Wikipedia, "A computational system that can compute every Turing-computable function is called Turing-complete (or Turing-powerful). Alternatively, such a system is one that can simulate a universal Turing machine." http://en.wikipedia.org/wiki/Turing_complete, retrieved 17 Mar 2009.
3.   http://esolangs.org/wiki/Church-Turing_thesis, retrieved 10 Jan 2009.

1.2.1   First-Generation Computers

The first generation of modern computers can be traced to 1943, when the Mark I and Colossus computers (see Figures 1.1 and 1.2) were developed,[4] albeit for quite different purposes. With financial backing from IBM (then International Business Machines Corporation), the Mark I was designed and developed at Harvard University. It was a general-purpose electrome-chanical programmable computer. Colossus, on the other hand, was an elec-tronic computer built in Britain at the end 1943. Colossus was the world's first programmable, digital, electronic, computing device. First-generation computers were built using hard-wired circuits and vacuum tubes (thermi-onic valves). Data was stored using paper punch cards. Colossus was used in secret during World War II to help decipher teleprinter messages encrypted by German forces using the Lorenz SZ40/42 machine. British code breakers referred to encrypted German teleprinter traffic as "Fish" and called the SZ40/42 machine and its traffic "Tunny."[5]

To accomplish its deciphering task, Colossus compared two data streams read at high speed from a paper tape. Colossus evaluated one data stream representing the encrypted "Tunny," counting each match that was discovered based on a programmable Boolean function. A comparison with the other data stream was then made. The second data stream was generated internally and designed to be an electronic simulation of the

The Harvard Mark I

Figure 1.1   The Harvard Mark I computer. (Image from www.columbia.edu/acis/ history/mark1.html, retrieved 9 Jan 2009.)

---

4.   http://trillian.randomstuff.org.uk/~stephen/history, retrieved 5 Jan 2009.
5.   http://en.wikipedia.org/wiki/Colossus_computer, retrieved 7 Jan 2009.

Figure 1.2   The British-developed Colossus computer. (Image from www.computerhistory.org, retrieved 9 Jan 2009.)

Lorenz SZ40/42 as it ranged through various trial settings. If the match count for a setting was above a predetermined threshold, that data match would be sent as character output to an electric typewriter.

1.2.2   Second-Generation Computers

Another general-purpose computer of this era was ENIAC (Electronic Numerical Integrator and Computer, shown in Figure 1.3), which was built in 1946. This was the first Turing-complete, digital computer capable of being reprogrammed to solve a full range of computing problems,[6] although earlier machines had been built with some of these properties. ENIAC's original purpose was to calculate artillery firing tables for the U.S. Army's Ballistic Research Laboratory. ENIAC contained 18,000 thermionic valves, weighed over 60,000 pounds, and consumed 25 kilowatts of electrical power per hour. ENIAC was capable of performing 100,000 calculations a second. Within a year after its completion, however, the invention of the transistor meant that the inefficient thermionic valves could be replaced with smaller, more reliable components, thus marking another major step in the history of computing.

---

6.   Joel Shurkin, Engines of the Mind: The Evolution of the Computer from Mainframes to Microprocessors, New York: W. W. Norton, 1996.

Figure 1.3   The ENIAC computer. (Image from www.mrsec.wisc.edu/.../computer/
eniac.html, retrieved 9 Jan 2009.)

Transistorized computers marked the advent of second-generation computers, which dominated in the late 1950s and early 1960s. Despite using transistors and printed circuits, these computers were still bulky and expensive. They were therefore used mainly by universities and government agencies.

The integrated circuit or microchip was developed by Jack St. Claire Kilby, an achievement for which he received the Nobel Prize in Physics in 2000.[7] In congratulating him, U.S. President Bill Clinton wrote, "You can take pride in the knowledge that your work will help to improve lives for generations to come." It was a relatively simple device that Mr. Kilby showed to a handful of co-workers gathered in the semiconductor lab at Texas Instruments more than half a century ago. It was just a transistor and a few other components on a slice of germanium. Little did this group realize that Kilby's invention was about to revolutionize the electronics industry.

1.2.3   Third-Generation Computers

Kilby's invention started an explosion in third-generation computers. Even though the first integrated circuit was produced in September 1958,

7.   http://www.ti.com/corp/docs/kilbyctr/jackstclair.shtml, retrieved 7 Jan 2009.

Figure 1.4   The Intel 4004 processor. (Image from www.thg.ru/cpu/20051118/
index.html, retrieved 9 Jan 2009.)

microchips were not used in computers until 1963. While mainframe computers like the IBM 360 increased storage and processing capabilities even further, the integrated circuit allowed the development of minicomputers that began to bring computing into many smaller businesses. Large-scale integration of circuits led to the development of very small processing units, the next step along the evolutionary trail of computing. In November 1971, Intel released the world's first commercial microprocessor, the Intel 4004 (Figure 1.4). The 4004 was the first complete CPU on one chip and became the first commercially available microprocessor. It was possible because of the development of new silicon gate technology that enabled engineers to integrate a much greater number of transistors on a chip that would perform at a much faster speed. This development enabled the rise of the fourth-generation computer platforms.

1.2.4   Fourth-Generation Computers

The fourth-generation computers that were being developed at this time utilized a microprocessor that put the computer's processing capabilities on a single integrated circuit chip. By combining random access memory (RAM), developed by Intel, fourth-generation computers were faster than ever before and had much smaller footprints. The 4004 processor was capable of "only" 60,000 instructions per second. As technology progressed, however, new processors brought even more speed and computing capability to users. The microprocessors that evolved from the 4004 allowed manufacturers to begin developing personal computers small enough and cheap enough to be purchased by the general public. The first commercially available personal computer was the MITS Altair 8800, released at the end of 1974. What followed was a flurry of other personal computers to market, such as the Apple I and II, the Commodore PET, the

VIC-20, the Commodore 64, and eventually the original IBM PC in 1981. The PC era had begun in earnest by the mid-1980s. During this time, the IBM PC and IBM PC compatibles, the Commodore Amiga, and the Atari ST computers were the most prevalent PC platforms available to the public. Computer manufacturers produced various models of IBM PC compatibles. Even though microprocessing power, memory and data storage capacities have increased by many orders of magnitude since the invention of the 4004 processor, the technology for large-scale integration (LSI) or very-large-scale integration (VLSI) microchips has not changed all that much. For this reason, most of today's computers still fall into the category of fourth-generation computers.

1.3   Internet Software Evolution

The Internet is named after the Internet Protocol, the standard communications protocol used by every computer on the Internet. The conceptual foundation for creation of the Internet was significantly developed by three individuals. The first, Vannevar Bush,[8] wrote a visionary description of the potential uses for information technology with his description of an automated library system named MEMEX (see Figure 1.5). Bush introduced the concept of the MEMEX in the 1930s as a microfilm-based "device in which an individual stores all his books, records, and communications, and which is mechanized so that it may be consulted with exceeding speed and flexibility."[9]

Figure 1.5   Vannevar Bush's MEMEX. (Image from www.icesi.edu.co/ blogs_estudiantes/luisaulestia, retrieved 9 Jan 2009.)

8.   http://en.wikipedia.org/wiki/Vannevar_Bush, retrieved 7 Jan 2009.
9.   http://www.livinginternet.com/i/ii_summary.htm, retrieved 7 Jan 2009.

After thinking about the potential of augmented memory for several years, Bush wrote an essay entitled "As We May Think" in 1936. It was finally published in July 1945 in the *Atlantic Monthly*. In the article, Bush predicted: "Wholly new forms of encyclopedias will appear, ready made with a mesh of associative trails running through them, ready to be dropped into the MEMEX and there amplified."[10] In September 1945, *Life* magazine published a condensed version of "As We May Think" that was accompanied by several graphic illustrations showing what a MEMEX machine might look like, along with its companion devices.

The second individual to have a profound effect in shaping the Internet was Norbert Wiener. Wiener was an early pioneer in the study of stochastic and noise processes. His work in stochastic and noise processes was relevant to electronic engineering, communication, and control systems.[11] He also founded the field of cybernetics. This field of study formalized notions of feedback and influenced research in many other fields, such as engineering, systems control, computer science, biology, philosophy, etc. His work in cybernetics inspired future researchers to focus on extending human capabilities with technology. Influenced by Wiener, Marshall McLuhan put forth the idea of a *global village* that was interconnected by an electronic nervous system as part of our popular culture.

In 1957, the Soviet Union launched the first satellite, *Sputnik I*, prompting U.S. President Dwight Eisenhower to create the Advanced Research Projects Agency (ARPA) agency to regain the technological lead in the arms race. ARPA (renamed DARPA, the Defense Advanced Research Projects Agency, in 1972) appointed J. C. R. Licklider to head the new Information Processing Techniques Office (IPTO). Licklider was given a mandate to further the research of the SAGE system. The SAGE system (see Figure 1.6) was a continental air-defense network commissioned by the U.S. military and designed to help protect the United States against a space-based nuclear attack. SAGE stood for Semi-Automatic Ground Environment.[12] SAGE was the most ambitious computer project ever undertaken at the time, and it required over 800 programmers and the technical resources of some of America's largest corporations. SAGE was started in the 1950s and became operational by 1963. It remained in continuous operation for over 20 years, until 1983.

---

10.   http://www.theatlantic.com/doc/194507/bush, retrieved 7 Jan 2009.
11.   http://en.wikipedia.org/wiki/Norbert_Wiener, retrieved 7 Jan 2009.
12.   http://www.computermuseum.li/Testpage/IBM-SAGE-computer.htm, retrieved 7 Jan 2009.

Figure 1.6   The SAGE system. (Image from USAF Archives, retrieved from http://history.sandiego.edu/GEN/recording/images5/PDRM0380.jpg.)

While working at ITPO, Licklider evangelized the potential benefits of a country-wide communications network. His chief contribution to the development of the Internet was his ideas, not specific inventions. He foresaw the need for networked computers with easy user interfaces. His ideas foretold of graphical computing, point-and-click interfaces, digital libraries, e-commerce, online banking, and software that would exist on a network and migrate to wherever it was needed. Licklider worked for several years at ARPA, where he set the stage for the creation of the ARPANET. He also worked at Bolt Beranek and Newman (BBN), the company that supplied the first computers connected on the ARPANET.

After he had left ARPA, Licklider succeeded in convincing his replacement to hire a man named Lawrence Roberts, believing that Roberts was just the person to implement Licklider's vision of the future network computing environment. Roberts led the development of the network. His efforts were based on a novel idea of "packet switching" that had been developed by Paul Baran while working at RAND Corporation. The idea for a common interface to the ARPANET was first suggested in Ann Arbor, Michigan, by Wesley Clark at an ARPANET design session set up by Lawrence Roberts in April 1967. Roberts's implementation plan called for each site that was to connect to the ARPANET to write the software necessary to connect its computer to the network. To the attendees, this approach seemed like a lot of work. There were so many different kinds of computers and operating systems in use throughout the DARPA community that every piece of code would have to be individually written, tested, implemented, and maintained. Clark told Roberts that he thought the design was "bass-ackwards."[13]

After the meeting, Roberts stayed behind and listened as Clark elaborated on his concept to deploy a minicomputer called an Interface Message Processor (IMP, see Figure 1.7) at each site. The IMP would handle the interface to the ARPANET network. The physical layer, the data link layer, and the network layer protocols used internally on the ARPANET were implemented on this IMP. Using this approach, each site would only have to write one interface to the commonly deployed IMP. The host at each site connected itself to the IMP using another type of interface that had different physical, data link, and network layer specifications. These were specified by the Host/IMP Protocol in BBN Report 1822.[14]

So, as it turned out, the first networking protocol that was used on the ARPANET was the Network Control Program (NCP). The NCP provided the middle layers of a protocol stack running on an ARPANET-connected host computer.[15] The NCP managed the connections and flow control among the various processes running on different ARPANET host computers. An application layer, built on top of the NCP, provided services such as email and file transfer. These applications used the NCP to handle connections to other host computers.

A minicomputer was created specifically to realize the design of the Interface Message Processor. This approach provided a system-independent interface to the ARPANET that could be used by any computer system. Because of this approach, the Internet architecture was an open architecture from the very beginning. The Interface Message Processor interface for the ARPANET went live in early October 1969. The implementation of the architecture is depicted in Figure 1.8.

---

13.   http://www.urbandictionary.com/define.php?term=Bass+Ackwards defined this as "The art and science of hurtling blindly in the wrong direction with no sense of the impending doom about to be inflicted on one's sorry ass. Usually applied to procedures, processes, or theories based on faulty logic, or faulty personnel." Retrieved 8 Jan 2009.

14.   Frank Heart, Robert Kahn, Severo Ornstein, William Crowther, and David Walden, "The Interface Message Processor for the ARPA Computer Network," Proc. 1970 Spring Joint Computer Conference 36:551–567, AFIPS, 1970.

15.   http://www.answers.com/topic/network-control-program, retrieved 8 Jan 2009.

Figure 1.7   An Interface Message Processor. (Image from luni.net/wp-content/
uploads/2007/02/bbn-imp.jpg, retrieved 9 Jan 2009.)

IMP Architecture

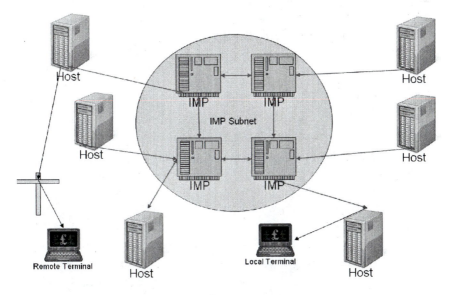

Figure 1.8   Overview of the IMP architecture.

1.3.1   Establishing a Common Protocol for the Internet

Since the lower-level protocol layers were provided by the IMP host interface, the NCP essentially provided a transport layer consisting of the ARPANET Host-to-Host Protocol (AHHP) and the Initial Connection Protocol (ICP). The AHHP specified how to transmit a unidirectional, flow-controlled data stream between two hosts. The ICP specified how to establish a bidirectional pair of data streams between a pair of connected host processes. Application protocols such as File Transfer Protocol (FTP), used for file transfers, and Simple Mail Transfer Protocol (SMTP), used for sending email, accessed network services through an interface to the top layer of the NCP. On January 1, 1983, known as Flag Day, NCP was rendered obsolete when the ARPANET changed its core networking protocols from NCP to the more flexible and powerful TCP/IP protocol suite, marking the start of the Internet as we know it today.

It was actually Robert Kahn and Vinton Cerf who built on what was learned with NCP to develop the TCP/IP networking protocol we use today. TCP/IP quickly became the most widely used network protocol in the world. The Internet's open nature and use of the more efficient TCP/IP protocol became the cornerstone of an internetworking design that has become the most widely used network protocol in the world. The history of TCP/IP reflects an interdependent design. Development of this protocol was conducted by many people. Over time, there evolved four increasingly better versions of TCP/IP (TCP v1, TCP v2, a split into TCP v3 and IP v3, and TCP v4 and IPv4). Today, IPv4 is the standard protocol, but it is in the process of being replaced by IPv6, which is described later in this chapter.

The TCP/IP protocol was deployed to the ARPANET, but not all sites were all that willing to convert to the new protocol. To force the matter to a head, the TCP/IP team turned off the NCP network channel numbers on the ARPANET IMPs twice. The first time they turned it off for a full day in mid-1982, so that only sites using TCP/IP could still operate. The second time, later that fall, they disabled NCP again for two days. The full switchover to TCP/IP happened on January 1, 1983, without much hassle. Even after that, however, there were still a few ARPANET sites that were down for as long as three months while their systems were retrofitted to use the new protocol. In 1984, the U.S. Department of Defense made TCP/IP the standard for all military computer networking, which gave it a high profile and stable funding. By 1990, the ARPANET was retired and transferred to the NSFNET. The NSFNET was soon connected to the CSNET, which linked universities around North America, and then to the EUnet, which connected research facilities in Europe. Thanks in part to the National Science Foundation's enlightened management, and fueled by the growing popularity of the web, the use of the Internet exploded after 1990, prompting the U.S. government to transfer management to independent organizations starting in 1995.

1.3.2   Evolution of Ipv6

The amazing growth of the Internet throughout the 1990s caused a vast reduction in the number of free IP addresses available under IPv4. IPv4 was never designed to scale to global levels. To increase available address space, it had to process data packets that were larger (i.e., that contained more bits of data). This resulted in a longer IP address and that caused problems for existing hardware and software. Solving those problems required the design, development, and implementation of a new architecture and new hardware to support it. It also required changes to all of the TCP/IP routing software. After examining a number of proposals, the Internet Engineering Task Force (IETF) settled on IPv6, which was released in January 1995 as RFC 1752. Ipv6 is sometimes called the Next Generation Internet Protocol (IPNG) or TCP/IP v6. Following release of the RFP, a number of organizations began working toward making the new protocol the *de facto* standard. Fast-forward nearly a decade later, and by 2004, IPv6 was widely available from industry as an integrated TCP/IP protocol and was supported by most new Internet networking equipment.

1.3.3   Finding a Common Method to Communicate Using the Internet Protocol

In the 1960s, twenty years after Vannevar Bush proposed MEMEX, the word *hypertext* was coined by Ted Nelson. Ted Nelson was one of the major visionaries of the coming hypertext revolution. He knew that the technology of his time could never handle the explosive growth of information that was proliferating across the planet. Nelson popularized the hypertext concept, but it was Douglas Engelbart who developed the first working hypertext systems. At the end of World War II, Douglas Engelbart was a 20-year-old U.S. Navy radar technician in the Philippines. One day, in a Red Cross library, he picked up a copy of the *Atlantic Monthly* dated July 1945. He happened to come across Vannevar Bush's article about the MEMEX automated library system and was strongly influenced by this vision of the future of information technology. Sixteen years later, Engelbart published his own version of Bush's vision in a paper prepared for the Air Force Office of Scientific Research and Development. In Englebart's paper, "Augmenting Human Intellect: A Conceptual Framework," he described an advanced electronic information system:

> Most of the structuring forms I'll show you stem from the simple capability of being able to establish arbitrary linkages between different substructures, and of directing the computer subsequently to display a set of linked substructures with any relative positioning we might designate among the different substructures. You can designate as many different kinds of links as you wish, so that you can specify different display or manipulative treatment for the different types.[16]

Engelbart joined Stanford Research Institute in 1962. His first project was *Augment,* and its purpose was to develop computer tools to augment human capabilities. Part of this effort required that he developed the mouse, the graphical user interface (GUI), and the first working hypertext system, named NLS (derived from o**N**-**L**ine **S**ystem). NLS was designed to cross-reference research papers for sharing among geographically distributed researchers. NLS provided groupware capabilities, screen sharing among remote users, and reference links for moving between sentences within a research paper and from one research paper to another. Engelbart's NLS system was chosen as the second node on the ARPANET, giving him a role in the invention of the Internet as well as the World Wide Web.

In the 1980s, a precursor to the web as we know it today was developed in Europe by Tim Berners-Lee and Robert Cailliau. Its popularity skyrocketed, in large part because Apple Computer delivered its HyperCard product free with every Macintosh bought at that time. In 1987, the effects of hypertext rippled through the industrial community. HyperCard was the first hypertext editing system available to the general public, and it caught on very quickly. In the 1990s, Marc Andreessen and a team at the National Center for Supercomputer Applications (NCSA), a research institute at the University of Illinois, developed the Mosaic and Netscape browsers. A technology revolution few saw coming was in its infancy at this point in time.

---

16.   Douglas Engelbart, "Augmenting Human Intellect: A Conceptual Framework," in a report for the Air Force Office of Scientific Research and Development, October 1962.

1.3.4   Building a Common Interface to the Internet

While Marc Andreessen and the NCSA team were working on their browsers, Robert Cailliau at CERN independently proposed a project to develop a hypertext system. He joined forces with Berners-Lee to get the web initiative into high gear. Cailliau rewrote his original proposal and lobbied CERN management for funding for programmers. He and Berners-Lee worked on papers and presentations in collaboration, and Cailliau helped run the very first WWW conference.

In the fall of 1990, Berners-Lee developed the first web browser (Figure 1.9) featuring an integrated editor that could create hypertext documents. He installed the application on his and Cailliau's computers, and they both began communicating via the world's first web server, at info.cern.ch, on December 25, 1990.

A few months later, in August 1991, Berners-Lee posted a notice on a newsgroup called alt.hypertext that provided information about where one could download the web server (Figure 1.10) and browser. Once this information hit the newsgroup, new web servers began appearing all over the world almost immediately.

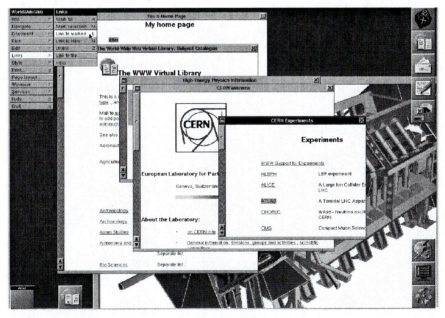

Figure 1.9   The first web browser, created by Tim Berners-Lee. (Image from www.tranquileye.com/cyber/index.html, retrieved 9 Jan 2009.)

Figure 1.10   Tim Berners-Lee's first web server.

Following this initial success, Berners-Lee enhanced the server and browser by adding support for the FTP protocol. This made a wide range of existing FTP directories and Usenet newsgroups instantly accessible via a web page displayed in his browser. He also added a Telnet server on info.cern.ch, making a simple line browser available to anyone with a Telnet client.

The first public demonstration of Berners-Lee's web server was at a conference called Hypertext 91. This web server came to be known as CERN httpd (short for hypertext transfer protocol daemon), and work in it continued until July 1996. Before work stopped on the CERN httpd, Berners-Lee managed to get CERN to provide a certification on April 30, 1993, that the web technology and program code was in the public domain so that anyone could use and improve it. This was an important decision that helped the web to grow to enormous proportions.

In 1992, Joseph Hardin and Dave Thompson were working at the NCSA. When Hardin and Thompson heard about Berners-Lee's work, they downloaded the Viola WWW browser and demonstrated it to NCSA's Software Design Group by connecting to the web server at CERN over the Internet.[17] The Software Design Group was impressed by what they saw. Two students from the group, Marc Andreessen and Eric Bina, began work on a browser version for X-Windows on Unix computers, first released as version 0.5 on January 23, 1993 (Figure 1.11). Within a week, Andreeson's release message was forwarded to various newsgroups by Berners-Lee. This generated a huge swell in the user base and subsequent redistribution ensued, creating a wider awareness of the product. Working together to support the product, Bina provided expert coding support while Andreessen

17.   Marc Andreessen, NCSA Mosaic Technical Summary, 20 Feb 1993.

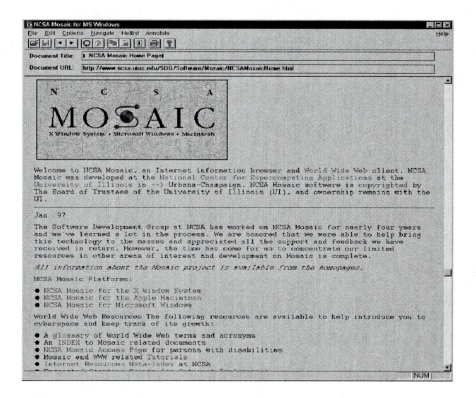

Figure 1.11   The original NCSA Mosaic browser. (Image from http://www.nsf.gov/
od/lpa/news/03/images/mosaic.6beta.jpg.)

provided excellent customer support. They monitored the newsgroups continuously to ensure that they knew about and could fix any bugs reported
and make the desired enhancements pointed out by the user base.

Mosaic was the first widely popular web browser available to the general public. It helped spread use and knowledge of the web across the world.
Mosaic provided support for graphics, sound, and video clips. An early version of Mosaic introduced forms support, enabling many powerful new uses
and applications. Innovations including the use of bookmarks and history
files were added. Mosaic became even more popular, helping further the
growth of the World Wide Web. In mid-1994, after Andreessen had gradu-
ated from the University of Illinois, Silicon Graphics founder Jim Clark col-
laborated with Andreessen to found Mosaic Communications, which was
later renamed Netscape Communications.

In October 1994, Netscape released the first beta version of its browser,
Mozilla 0.96b, over the Internet. The final version, named Mozilla 1.0, was

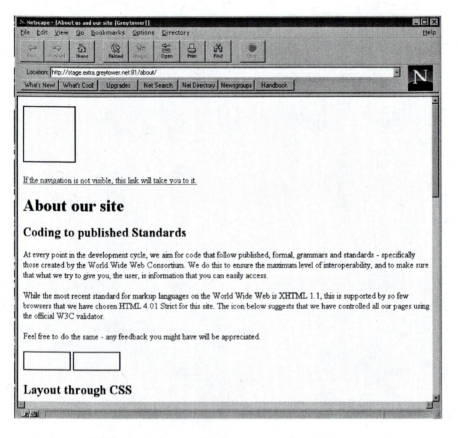

Figure 1.12   The original Netscape browser. (Image from http://
browser.netscape.com/downloads/archive.)

released in December 1994. It became the very first commercial web browser. The Mosaic programming team then developed another web browser, which they named Netscape Navigator. Netscape Navigator was later renamed Netscape Communicator, then renamed back to just Netscape. See Figure 1.12.

During this period, Microsoft was not asleep at the wheel. Bill Gates realized that the WWW was the future and focused vast resources to begin developing a product to compete with Netscape. In 1995, Microsoft hosted an Internet Strategy Day[18] and announced its commitment to adding Internet capabilities to all its products. In fulfillment of that announcement, Microsoft Internet Explorer arrived as both a graphical Web browser and the name for a set of technologies.

18.   http://www.microsoft.com/windows/WinHistoryIE.mspx, retrieved 8 Jan 2009.

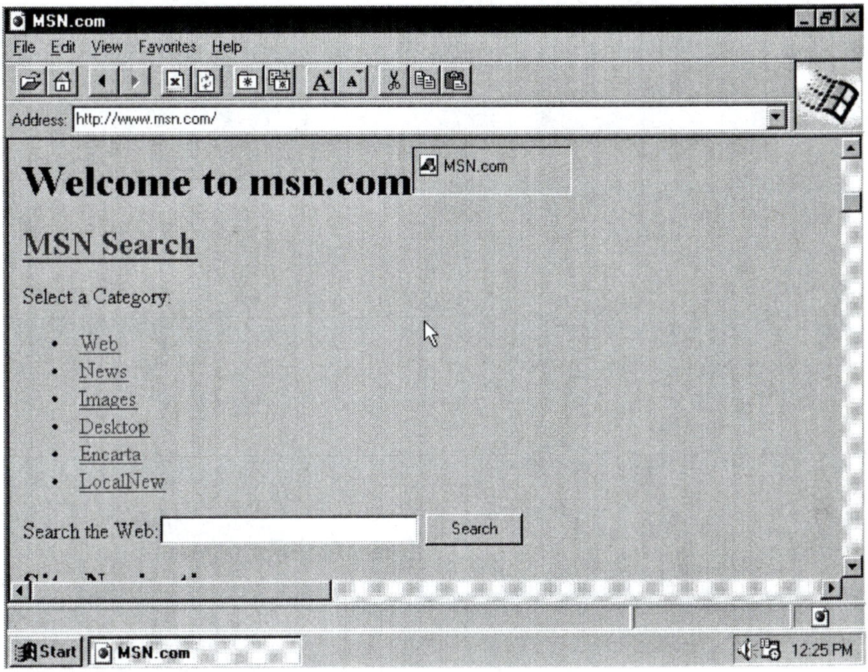

Figure 1.13   Internet Explorer version 1.0. (Image from http://www.microsoft.com/ library/media/1033/windows/IE/images/community/columns/ old_ie.gif, retrieved 9 Jan 2009.)

In July 1995, Microsoft released the Windows 95 operating system, which included built-in support for dial-up networking and TCP/IP, two key technologies for connecting a PC to the Internet. It also included an add-on to the operating system called Internet Explorer 1.0 (Figure 1.13). When Windows 95 with Internet Explorer debuted, the WWW became accessible to a great many more people. Internet Explorer technology originally shipped as the Internet Jumpstart Kit in Microsoft Plus! for Windows 95.

One of the key factors in the success of Internet Explorer was that it eliminated the need for cumbersome manual installation that was required by many of the existing shareware browsers. Users embraced the "do-it-for-me" installation model provided by Microsoft, and browser loyalty went out the window. The Netscape browser led in user and market share until Microsoft released Internet Explorer, but the latter product took the market lead in 1999. This was due mainly to its distribution advantage, because it was included in every version of Microsoft Windows. The browser wars had begun, and the battlefield was the Internet. In response to Microsoft's move,

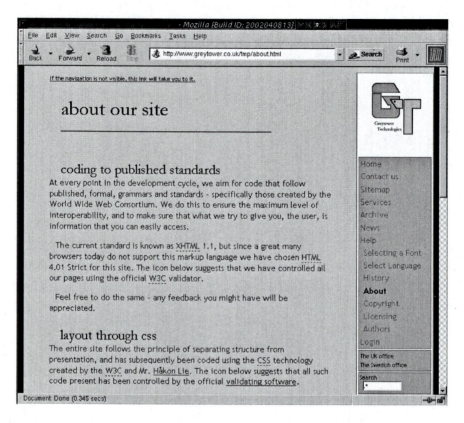

Figure 1.14   The open source version of Netscape, named Mozilla. (Image from http://browser.netscape.com/downloads/archive.)

Netscape decided in 2002 to release a free, open source software version of Netscape named Mozilla (which was the internal name for the old Netscape browser; see Figure 1.14). Mozilla has steadily gained market share, particularly on non-Windows platforms such as Linux, largely because of its open source foundation. Mozilla Firefox, released in November 2004, became very popular almost immediately.

1.3.5   The Appearance of Cloud Formations—From One Computer to a Grid of Many

Two decades ago, computers were clustered together to form a single larger computer in order to simulate a supercomputer and harness greater processing power. This technique was common and was used by many IT departments. *Clustering*, as it was called, allowed one to configure computers using special protocols so they could "talk" to each other. The purpose was to balance the computational load across several machines, divvying up units of work and spreading it across multiple processors. To the user, it made little difference which CPU executed an application. Cluster management software ensured that the CPU with the most available processing capability at that time was used to run the code. A key to efficient cluster management was engineering where the data was to be held. This process became known as *data residency.* Computers in the cluster were usually physically connected to magnetic disks that stored and retrieved a data while the CPUs performed input/output (I/O) processes quickly and efficiently.

In the early 1990s, Ian Foster and Carl Kesselman presented their concept of "The Grid." They used an analogy to the electricity grid, where users could plug in and use a (metered) utility service. They reasoned that if companies cannot generate their own power, it would be reasonable to assume they would purchase that service from a third party capable of providing a steady electricity supply. So, they asked, "Why can't the same apply to computing resources?" If one node could plug itself into a grid of computers and pay only for the resources it used, it would be a more cost-effective solution for companies than buying and managing their own infrastructure. Grid computing expands on the techniques used in clustered computing models, where multiple independent clusters appear to act like a grid simply because they are not all located within the same domain.[19]

A major obstacle to overcome in the migration from a clustering model to grid computing was data residency. Because of the distributed nature of a grid, computational nodes could be anywhere in the world. Paul Wallis explained the data residency issue for a grid model like this:

> It was fine having all that CPU power available, but the data on which the CPU performed its operations could be thousands of miles away, causing a delay (latency) between data fetch and execution. CPUs need to be fed and watered with different volumes of data depending on the tasks they are processing. Running a data-intensive process with disparate data sources can create a bottleneck in the I/O, causing the CPU to run inefficiently, and affecting economic viability.[20]

---

19.   Paul Wallis, "Keystones and Rivets," http://it.toolbox.com/blogs/keystones-and-rivets/understanding-cloud-computing-22611, retrieved 2 Jan 2009.

20.   Ibid.

The issues of storage management, migration of data, and security provisioning were key to any proposed solution in order for a grid model to succeed. A toolkit called Globus[21] was created to solve these issues, but the infrastructure hardware available still has not progressed to a level where true grid computing can be wholly achieved.

The Globus Toolkit is an open source software toolkit used for building grid systems and applications. It is being developed and maintained by the Globus Alliance[22] and many others all over the world. The Globus Alliance has grown into community of organizations and individuals developing fundamental technologies to support the grid model. The toolkit provided by Globus allows people to share computing power, databases, instruments, and other online tools securely across corporate, institutional, and geographic boundaries without sacrificing local autonomy.

The cloud is helping to further propagate the grid computing model. Cloud-resident entities such as data centers have taken the concepts of grid computing and bundled them into service offerings that appeal to other entities that do not want the burden of infrastructure but do want the capabilities hosted from those data centers. One of the most well known of the new cloud service providers is Amazon's S3 (Simple Storage Service) third-party storage solution. Amazon S3 is storage for the Internet. According to the Amazon S3 website,[23] it provides a simple web services interface that can be used to store and retrieve any amount of data, at any time, from anywhere on the web. It gives any developer access to the same highly scalable, reliable, fast, inexpensive data storage infrastructure that Amazon uses to run its own global network of web sites. The service aims to maximize benefits of scale and to pass those benefits on to developers.

In 2002, EMC offered a Content Addressable Storage (CAS) solution called Centera as yet another cloud-based data storage service that competes with Amazon's offering. EMC's product creates a global network of data centers, each with massive storage capabilities. When a user creates a document, the application server sends it to the Centera storage system. The storage system then returns a unique content address to the server. The unique address allows the system to verify the integrity of the documents whenever a user moves or copies them. From that point, the application can request the document by submitting the address. Duplicates of documents

---

21.   The reader is encouraged to visit http://globus.org/toolkit for more information.
22.   http://www.globus.org, retrieved 6 Jan 2009.
23.   The reader is encouraged to visit http://aws.amazon.com/s3.

are saved only once under the same address, leading to reduced storage requirements. Centera then retrieves the document regardless of where it may be physically located.

EMC's Centera product takes the sensible approach that no one can afford the risk of placing all of their data in one place, so the data is distributed around the globe. Their cloud will monitor data usage and automatically move data around in order to load-balance data requests and better manage the flow of Internet traffic. Centera is constantly self-tuning to react automatically to surges in demand.   The Centera architecture functions as a cluster that automatically configures itself upon installation. The system also handles fail-over, load balancing, and failure notification.

There are some drawbacks to these cloud-based solutoins, however. An example is a recent problem at Amazon S3. They suffered a "massive" outage in February 2008, which served to highlight the risks involved with adopting such cloud-based service offerings. Amazon's technical representative from the Web Services Team commented publicly with the following press release:

> Early this morning, at 3:30am PST, we started seeing elevated levels of authenticated requests from multiple users in one of our locations. While we carefully monitor our overall request volumes and these remained within normal ranges, we had not been monitoring the proportion of authenticated requests. Importantly, these cryptographic requests consume more resources per call than other request types. Shortly before 4:00am PST, we began to see several other users significantly increase their volume of authenticated calls. The last of these pushed the authentication service over its maximum capacity before we could complete putting new capacity in place.
>
> In addition to processing authenticated requests, the authentication service also performs account validation on every request Amazon S3 handles. This caused Amazon S3 to be unable to process any requests in that location, beginning at 4:31am PST. By 6:48am PST, we had moved enough capacity online to resolve the issue.
>
> As we said earlier today, though we're proud of our uptime track record over the past two years with this service, any amount of downtime is unacceptable. As part of the post mortem for this event, we have identified a set of short-term actions as well as longer

term improvements. We are taking immediate action on the following: (a) improving our monitoring of the proportion of authenticated requests; (b) further increasing our authentication service capacity; and (c) adding additional defensive measures around the authenticated calls. Additionally, we've begun work on a service health dashboard, and expect to release that shortly.

Sincerely,

The Amazon Web Services Team

The message above clearly points out the lesson one should take from this particular incident: *caveat emptor,* which is Latin for "Let the buyer beware."

1.4   Server Virtualization

Virtualization is a method of running multiple independent virtual operating systems on a single physical computer.[24] This approach maximizes the return on investment for the computer. The term was coined in the 1960s in reference to a virtual machine (sometimes called a pseudo-machine). The creation and management of virtual machines has often been called *platform virtualization.* Platform virtualization is performed on a given computer (hardware platform) by software called a control program. The control program creates a simulated environment, a virtual computer, which enables the device to use hosted software specific to the virtual environment, sometimes called guest software.

The guest software, which is often itself a complete operating system, runs just as if it were installed on a stand-alone computer. Frequently, more than one virtual machine is able to be simulated on a single physical computer, their number being limited only by the host device's physical hardware resources. Because the guest software often requires access to specific peripheral devices in order to function, the virtualized platform must support guest interfaces to those devices. Examples of such devices are the hard disk drive, CD-ROM, DVD, and network interface card. Virtualization technology is a way of reducing the majority of hardware acquisition and maintenance costs, which can result in significant savings for any company.

---

24.   George Ou, "Introduction to Server Virtualization," http://articles.techrepublic.com.com/5100-10878_11-6074941.html, retrieved 6 Jan 2009.

1.4.1   Parallel Processing

Parallel processing is performed by the simultaneous execution of program instructions that have been allocated across multiple processors with the objective of running a program in less time.[25] On the earliest computers, a user could run only one program at a time. This being the case, a computation-intensive program that took X minutes to run, using a tape system for data I/O that took X minutes to run, would take a total of X + X minutes to execute. To improve performance, early forms of parallel processing were developed to allow interleaved execution of both programs simultaneously. The computer would start an I/O operation (which is typically measured in milliseconds), and while it was waiting for the I/O operation to complete, it would execute the processor-intensive program (measured in nanoseconds). The total execution time for the two jobs combined became only slightly longer than the X minutes required for the I/O operations to complete.

The next advancement in parallel processing was multiprogramming. In a multiprogramming system, multiple programs submitted by users are each allowed to use the processor for a short time, each taking turns and having exclusive time with the processor in order to execute instructions. This approach is known as "round-robin scheduling" (RR scheduling). It is one of the oldest, simplest, fairest, and most widely used scheduling algorithms, designed especially for time-sharing systems.[26]

In RR scheduling, a small unit of time called a time slice (or quantum) is defined. All executable processes are held in a circular queue. The time slice is defined based on the number of executable processes that are in the queue. For example, if there are five user processes held in the queue and the time slice allocated for the queue to execute in total is 1 second, each user process is allocated 200 milliseconds of process execution time on the CPU before the scheduler begins moving to the next process in the queue. The CPU scheduler manages this queue, allocating the CPU to each process for a time interval of one time slice. New processes are always added to the end of the queue. The CPU scheduler picks the first process from the queue, sets its timer to interrupt the process after the expiration of the timer, and then dispatches the next process in the queue. The process whose time has expired is placed at the end of the queue. If a process is still running at the end of a time slice, the CPU is interrupted and the process goes to the end

25.   http://searchdatacenter.techtarget.com/sDefinition/0,,sid80_gci212747,00.html, retrieved 10 Jan 2009.

26.   http://choices.cs.uiuc.edu/~f-kon/RoundRobin/node1.html, retrieved 10 Jan 2009.

of the queue. If the process finishes before the end of the time-slice, it releases the CPU voluntarily. In either case, the CPU scheduler assigns the CPU to the next process in the queue. Every time a process is granted the CPU, a context switch occurs, which adds overhead to the process execution time. To users it appears that all of the programs are executing at the same time.

Resource contention problems often arose in these early systems. Explicit requests for resources led to a condition known as deadlock. Competition for resources on machines with no tie-breaking instructions led to the critical section routine. Contention occurs when several processes request access to the same resource. In order to detect deadlock situations, a counter for each processor keeps track of the number of consecutive requests from a process that have been rejected. Once that number reaches a predetermined threshold, a state machine that inhibits other processes from making requests to the main store is initiated until the deadlocked process is successful in gaining access to the resource.

1.4.2   Vector Processing

The next step in the evolution of parallel processing was the introduction of multiprocessing. Here, two or more processors share a common workload. The earliest versions of multiprocessing were designed as a master/slave model, where one processor (the master) was responsible for all of the tasks to be performed and it only off-loaded tasks to the other processor (the slave) when the master processor determined, based on a predetermined threshold, that work could be shifted to increase performance. This arrangement was necessary because it was not then understood how to program the machines so they could cooperate in managing the resources of the system.

Vector processing was developed to increase processing performance by operating in a multitasking manner. Matrix operations were added to computers to allow a single instruction to manipulate two arrays of numbers performing arithmetic operations. This was valuable in certain types of applications in which data occurred in the form of vectors or matrices. In applications with less well-formed data, vector processing was less valuable.

1.4.3   Symmetric Multiprocessing Systems

The next advancement was the development of symmetric multiprocessing systems (SMP) to address the problem of resource management in master/ slave models. In SMP systems, each processor is equally capable and responsible for managing the workflow as it passes through the system. The primary goal is to achieve *sequential consistency,* in other words, to make SMP systems appear to be exactly the same as a single-processor, multiprogramming platform. Engineers discovered that system performance could be increased nearly 10–20% by executing some instructions out of order. However, programmers had to deal with the increased complexity and cope with a situation where two or more programs might read and write the same operands simultaneously. This difficulty, however, is limited to a very few programmers, because it only occurs in rare circumstances. To this day, the question of how SMP machines should behave when accessing shared data remains unresolved.

Data propagation time increases in proportion to the number of processors added to SMP systems. After a certain number (usually somewhere around 40 to 50 processors), performance benefits gained by using even more processors do not justify the additional expense of adding such processors. To solve the problem of long data propagation times, message passing systems were created. In these systems, programs that share data send messages to each other to announce that particular operands have been assigned a new value. Instead of a global message announcing an operand's new value, the message is communicated only to those areas that need to know the change. There is a network designed to support the transfer of messages between applications. This allows a great number processors (as many as several thousand) to work in tandem in a system. These systems are highly scalable and are called massively parallel processing (MPP) systems.

1.4.4   Massively Parallel Processing Systems

Massive parallel processing is used in computer architecture circles to refer to a computer system with many independent arithmetic units or entire microprocessors, which run in parallel.[27] "Massive" connotes hundreds if not thousands of such units. In this form of computing, all the processing elements are interconnected to act as one very large computer. This approach is in contrast to a distributed computing model, where massive numbers of separate computers are used to solve a single problem (such as in the SETI project, mentioned previously). Early examples of MPP systems were the Distributed Array Processor, the Goodyear MPP, the Connection Machine, and the Ultracomputer. In data mining, there is a need to perform multiple searches of a static database. The earliest massively parallel

---

27.   http://en.wikipedia.org/wiki/Massive_parallel_processing, retrieved 10 Jan 2009.

processing systems all used serial computers as individual processing units in order to maximize the number of units available for a given size and cost. Single-chip implementations of massively parallel processor arrays are becoming ever more cost effective due to the advancements in integrated-circuit technology.

An example of the use of MPP can be found in the field of artificial intelligence. For example, a chess application must analyze the outcomes of many possible alternatives and formulate the best course of action to take. Another example can be found in scientific environments, where certain simulations (such as molecular modeling) and complex mathematical problems can be split apart and each part processed simultaneously. Parallel data query (PDQ) is a technique used in business. This technique divides very large data stores into pieces based on various algorithms. Rather than searching sequentially through an entire database to resolve a query, 26 CPUs might be used simultaneously to perform a sequential search, each CPU individually evaluating a letter of the alphabet. MPP machines are not easy to program, but for certain applications, such as data mining, they are the best solution.

1.5   Chapter Summary

In this chapter, we stressed the importance of knowing about the evolution of computing in order to get an appreciation of how we got into the cloud environment. Examining the history of computing hardware and software helps us to understand why we are standing on the shoulders of giants. We discussed how the rules computers use to communicate came about, and how the development of networking and communications protocols has helped drive the Internet technology growth we have seen in the last 20-plus years. This, in turn, has driven even more changes in protocols and forced the creation of new technologies to mitigate addressing concerns and improve the methods used to communicate over the Internet. The use of web browsers has led to huge Internet growth and a migration away from the traditional data center. In the next chapter, we will begin to examine how services offered to Internet users has also evolved and changed the way business is done.

Chapter 2

Web Services Delivered from the Cloud

2.1 Chapter Overview

In this chapter we will examine some of the web services delivered from the cloud. We will take a look at Communication-as-a-Service (CaaS) and explain some of the advantages of using CaaS. Infrastructure is also a service in cloud land, and there are many variants on how infrastructure is managed in cloud environments. When vendors outsource Infrastructure-as-a-Service (IaaS), it relies heavily on modern on-demand computing technology and high-speed networking. We will look at some vendors who provide Software-as-a-Service (SaaS), such as Amazon.com with their elastic cloud platform, and foray into the implementation issues, the characteristics, benefits, and architectural maturity level of the service. Outsourced hardware environments (called platforms) are available as Platforms-as-a-Service (PaaS), and we will look at Mosso (Rackspace) and examine key characteristics of their PaaS implementation.

As technology migrates from the traditional on-premise model to the new cloud model, service offerings evolve almost daily. Our intent in this chapter is to provide some basic exposure to where the field is currently from the perspective of the technology and give you a feel for where it will be in the not-too-distant future.

Web service offerings often have a number of common characteristics, such as a low barrier to entry, where services are offered specifically for consumers and small business entities. Often, little or no capital expenditure for infrastructure is required from the customer. While massive scalability is common with these types of offerings, it not always necessary. Many cloud vendors have yet to achieve massive scalability because their user base generally does not require it. Multitenancy enables cost and resource sharing across the (often vast) user base. Finally, device and location independence enables users to access systems regardless of where they are or what device they are using. Now, let's examine some of the more common web service offerings.

2.2 Communication-as-a-Service (CaaS)

CaaS is an outsourced enterprise communications solution. Providers of this type of cloud-based solution (known as CaaS vendors) are responsible for the management of hardware and software required for delivering Voice over IP (VoIP) services, Instant Messaging (IM), and video conferencing capabilities to their customers. This model began its evolutionary process from within the telecommunications (Telco) industry, not unlike how the SaaS model arose from the software delivery services sector. CaaS vendors are responsible for all of the hardware and software management consumed by their user base. CaaS vendors typically offer guaranteed quality of service (QoS) under a service-level agreement (SLA).

A CaaS model allows a CaaS provider's business customers to selectively deploy communications features and services throughout their company on a pay-as-you-go basis for service(s) used. CaaS is designed on a utility-like pricing model that provides users with comprehensive, flexible, and (usually) simple-to-understand service plans. According to Gartner,[1] the CaaS market is expected to total $2.3 billion in 2011, representing a compound annual growth rate of more than 105% for the period.

CaaS service offerings are often bundled and may include integrated access to traditional voice (or VoIP) and data, advanced unified communications functionality such as video calling, web collaboration, chat, real-time presence and unified messaging, a handset, local and long-distance voice services, voice mail, advanced calling features (such as caller ID, three-way and conference calling, etc.) and advanced PBX functionality. A CaaS solution includes redundant switching, network, POP and circuit diversity, customer premises equipment redundancy, and WAN fail-over that specifically addresses the needs of their customers. All VoIP transport components are located in geographically diverse, secure data centers for high availability and survivability.

CaaS offers flexibility and scalability that small and medium-sized business might not otherwise be able to afford. CaaS service providers are usually prepared to handle peak loads for their customers by providing services

---

1. Gartner Press Release, "Gartner Forecasts Worldwide Communications-as-a-Service Revenue to Total $252 Million in 2007," August 2007, retrieved 13 Jan 2009.

capable of allowing more capacity, devices, modes or area coverage as their customer demand necessitates. Network capacity and feature sets can be changed dynamically, so functionality keeps pace with consumer demand and provider-owned resources are not wasted. From the service provider customer's perspective, there is very little to virtually no risk of the service becoming obsolete, since the provider's responsibility is to perform periodic upgrades or replacements of hardware and software to keep the platform technologically current.

CaaS requires little to no management oversight from customers. It eliminates the business customer's need for any capital investment in infrastructure, and it eliminates expense for ongoing maintenance and operations overhead for infrastructure. With a CaaS solution, customers are able to leverage enterprise-class communication services without having to build a premises-based solution of their own. This allows those customers to reallocate budget and personnel resources to where their business can best use them.

2.2.1   Advantages of CaaS

From the handset found on each employee's desk to the PC-based software client on employee laptops, to the VoIP private backbone, and all modes in between, every component in a CaaS solution is managed 24/7 by the CaaS vendor. As we said previously, the expense of managing a carrier-grade data center is shared across the vendor's customer base, making it more economical for businesses to implement CaaS than to build their own VoIP network. Let's look as some of the advantages of a hosted approach for CaaS.

Hosted and Managed Solutions

Remote management of infrastructure services provided by third parties once seemed an unacceptable situation to most companies. However, over the past decade, with enhanced technology, networking, and software, the attitude has changed. This is, in part, due to cost savings achieved in using those services. However, unlike the "one-off" services offered by specialist providers, CaaS delivers a complete communications solution that is entirely managed by a single vendor. Along with features such as VoIP and unified communications, the integration of core PBX features with advanced functionality is managed by one vendor, who is responsible for all of the integration and delivery of services to users.

2.2.2 Fully Integrated, Enterprise-Class Unified Communications

With CaaS, the vendor provides voice and data access and manages LAN/WAN, security, routers, email, voice mail, and data storage. By managing the LAN/WAN, the vendor can guarantee consistent quality of service from a user's desktop across the network and back. Advanced unified communications features that are most often a part of a standard CaaS deployment include:

- Chat
- Multimedia conferencing
- Microsoft Outlook integration
- Real-time presence
- "Soft" phones (software-based telephones)
- Video calling
- Unified messaging and mobility

Providers are constantly offering new enhancements (in both performance and features) to their CaaS services. The development process and subsequent introduction of new features in applications is much faster, easier, and more economical than ever before. This is, in large part, because the service provider is doing work that benefits many end users across the provider's scalable platform infrastructure. Because many end users of the provider's service ultimately share this cost (which, from their perspective, is miniscule compared to shouldering the burden alone), services can be offered to individual customers at a cost that is attractive to them.

No Capital Expenses Needed

When business outsource their unified communications needs to a CaaS service provider, the provider supplies a complete solution that fits the company's exact needs. Customers pay a fee (usually billed monthly) for what they use. Customers are not required to purchase equipment, so there is no capital outlay. Bundled in these types of services are ongoing maintenance and upgrade costs, which are incurred by the service provider. The use of CaaS services allows companies the ability to collaborate across any workspace. Advanced collaboration tools are now used to create high-quality, secure, adaptive work spaces throughout any organization. This allows a company's workers, partners, vendors, and customers to communicate and collaborate more effectively. Better communication allows organizations to adapt quickly to market changes and to build competitive advantage. CaaS can also accelerate decision making within an organization. Innovative unified communications capabilities (such as presence, instant messaging, and rich media services) help ensure that information quickly reaches whoever needs it.

Flexible Capacity and Feature Set

When customers outsource communications services to a CaaS provider, they pay for the features they need when they need them. The service provider can distribute the cost services and delivery across a large customer base. As previously stated, this makes the use of shared feature functionality more economical for customers to implement. Economies of scale allow service providers enough flexibility that they are not tied to a single vendor investment. They are able to leverage best-of-breed providers such as Avaya, Cisco, Juniper, Microsoft, Nortel and ShoreTel more economically than any independent enterprise.

No Risk of Obsolescence

Rapid technology advances, predicted long ago and known as Moore's law,[2] have brought about product obsolescence in increasingly shorter periods of time. Moore's law describes a trend he recognized that has held true since the beginning of the use of integrated circuits (ICs) in computing hardware. Since the invention of the integrated circuit in 1958, the number of transistors that can be placed inexpensively on an integrated circuit has increased exponentially, doubling approximately every two years.

Unlike IC components, the average life cycles for PBXs and key communications equipment and systems range anywhere from five to 10 years. With the constant introduction of newer models for all sorts of technology (PCs, cell phones, video software and hardware, etc.), these types of products now face much shorter life cycles, sometimes as short as a single year. CaaS vendors must absorb this burden for the user by continuously upgrading the equipment in their offerings to meet changing demands in the marketplace.

---

2.   Gordon E. Moore, "Cramming More Components onto Integrated Circuits," Electronics Magazine, 4, 1965, retrieved 1 Jan 2009.

No Facilities and Engineering Costs Incurred

CaaS providers host all of the equipment needed to provide their services to their customers, virtually eliminating the need for customers to maintain data center space and facilities. There is no extra expense for the constant power consumption that such a facility would demand. Customers receive the benefit of multiple carrier-grade data centers with full redundancy—and it's all included in the monthly payment.

Guaranteed Business Continuity

If a catastrophic event occurred at your business's physical location, would your company disaster recovery plan allow your business to continue operating without a break? If your business experienced a serious or extended communications outage, how long could your company survive? For most businesses, the answer is "not long." Distributing risk by using geographically dispersed data centers has become the norm today. It mitigates risk and allows companies in a location hit by a catastrophic event to recover as soon as possible. This process is implemented by CaaS providers because most companies don't even contemplate voice continuity if catastrophe strikes. Unlike data continuity, eliminating single points of failure for a voice network is usually cost-prohibitive because of the large scale and management complexity of the project. With a CaaS solution, multiple levels of redundancy are built into the system, with no single point of failure.

2.3   Infrastructure-as-a-Service (IaaS)

According to the online reference Wikipedia, Infrastructure-as-a-Service (IaaS) is the delivery of computer infrastructure (typically a platform virtualization environment) as a service.[3] IaaS leverages significant technology, services, and data center investments to deliver IT as a service to customers. Unlike traditional outsourcing, which requires extensive due diligence, negotiations ad infinitum, and complex, lengthy contract vehicles, IaaS is centered around a model of service delivery that provisions a predefined, standardized infrastructure specifically optimized for the customer's applications. Simplified statements of work and à la carte service-level choices make it easy to tailor a solution to a customer's specific application requirements. IaaS providers manage the transition and hosting of selected applications on their infrastructure. Customers maintain ownership and

---

3.   http://en.wikipedia.org/wiki/Infrastructure_as_a_Service, retrieved 11 Jan 2009.

management of their application(s) while off-loading hosting operations and infrastructure management to the IaaS provider. Provider-owned implementations typically include the following layered components:

- Computer hardware (typically set up as a grid for massive horizontal scalability)
- Computer network (including routers, firewalls, load balancing, etc.)
- Internet connectivity (often on OC 192 backbones[4])
- Platform virtualization environment for running client-specified virtual machines
- Service-level agreements
- Utility computing billing

Rather than purchasing data center space, servers, software, network equipment, etc., IaaS customers essentially rent those resources as a fully outsourced service. Usually, the service is billed on a monthly basis, just like a utility company bills customers. The customer is charged only for resources consumed. The chief benefits of using this type of outsourced service include:

- Ready access to a preconfigured environment that is generally ITIL-based[5] (The Information Technology Infrastructure Library [ITIL] is a customized framework of best practices designed to promote quality computing services in the IT sector.)
- Use of the latest technology for infrastructure equipment
- Secured, "sand-boxed" (protected and insulated) computing platforms that are usually security monitored for breaches
- Reduced risk by having off-site resources maintained by third parties
- Ability to manage service-demand peaks and valleys
- Lower costs that allow expensing service costs instead of making capital investments

---

4.   An Optical Carrier (OC) 192 transmission line is capable of transferring 9.95 gigabits of data per second.
5.   Jan Van Bon, The Guide to IT Service Management, Vol. I, New York: Addison-Wesley, 2002, p. 131.

- Reduced time, cost, and complexity in adding new features or capabilities

2.3.1   Modern On-Demand Computing

On-demand computing is an increasingly popular enterprise model in which computing resources are made available to the user as needed.[6] Computing resources that are maintained on a user's site are becoming fewer and fewer, while those made available by a service provider are on the rise. The on-demand model evolved to overcome the challenge of being able to meet fluctuating resource demands efficiently. Because demand for computing resources can vary drastically from one time to another, maintaining sufficient resources to meet peak requirements can be costly. Overengineering a solution can be just as adverse as a situation where the enterprise cuts costs by maintaining only minimal computing resources, resulting in insufficient resources to meet peak load requirements. Concepts such as clustered computing, grid computing, utility computing, etc., may all seem very similar to the concept of on-demand computing, but they can be better understood if one thinks of them as building blocks

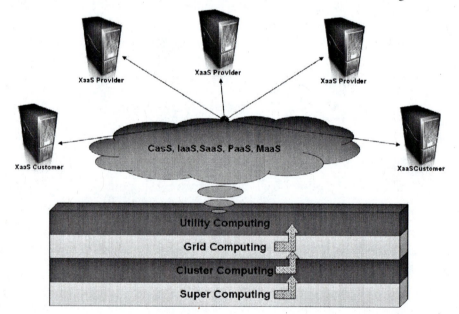

Figure 2.1   Building blocks to the cloud

---

6.   http://searchdatacenter.techtarget.com/sDefinition/0,,sid80_gci903730,00.html#, retrieved 15 Jan 2009.

that evolved over time and with techno-evolution to achieve the modern cloud computing model we think of and use today (see Figure 2.1).

One example we will examine is Amazon's Elastic Compute Cloud (Amazon EC2). This is a web service that provides resizable computing capacity in the cloud. It is designed to make web-scale computing easier for developers and offers many advantages to customers:

- It's web service interface allows customers to obtain and configure capacity with minimal effort.

- It provides users with complete control of their (leased) computing resources and lets them run on a proven computing environment.

- It reduces the time required to obtain and boot new server instances to minutes, allowing customers to quickly scale capacity as their computing demands dictate.

- It changes the economics of computing by allowing clients to pay only for capacity they actually use.

- It provides developers the tools needed to build failure-resilient applications and isolate themselves from common failure scenarios.

2.3.2   Amazon's Elastic Cloud

Amazon EC2 presents a true virtual computing environment, allowing clients to use a web-based interface to obtain and manage services needed to launch one or more instances of a variety of operating systems (OSs). Clients can load the OS environments with their customized applications. They can manage their network's access permissions and run as many or as few systems as needed. In order to use Amazon EC2, clients first need to create an Amazon Machine Image (AMI). This image contains the applications, libraries, data, and associated configuration settings used in the virtual computing environment. Amazon EC2 offers the use of preconfigured images built with templates to get up and running immediately. Once users have defined and configured their AMI, they use the Amazon EC2 tools provided for storing the AMI by uploading the AMI into Amazon S3. Amazon S3 is a repository that provides safe, reliable, and fast access to a client AMI. Before clients can use the AMI, they must use the Amazon EC2 web service to configure security and network access.

Using Amazon EC2 to Run Instances

During configuration, users choose which instance type(s) and operating system they want to use. Available instance types come in two distinct categories, Standard or High-CPU instances. Most applications are best suited for Standard instances, which come in small, large, and extra-large instance platforms. High-CPU instances have proportionally more CPU resources than random-access memory (RAM) and are well suited for compute-intensive applications. With the High-CPU instances, there are medium and extra large platforms to choose from. After determining which instance to use, clients can start, terminate, and monitor as many instances of their AMI as needed by using web service Application Programming Interfaces (APIs) or a wide variety of other management tools that are provided with the service. Users are able to choose whether they want to run in multiple locations, use static IP endpoints, or attach persistent block storage to any of their instances, and they pay only for resources actually consumed. They can also choose from a library of globally available AMIs that provide useful instances. For example, if all that is needed is a basic Linux server, clients can choose one of the standard Linux distribution AMIs.

2.3.3   Amazon EC2 Service Characteristics

There are quite a few characteristics of the EC2 service that provide significant benefits to an enterprise. First of all, Amazon EC2 provides financial benefits. Because of Amazon's massive scale and large customer base, it is an inexpensive alternative to many other possible solutions. The costs incurred to set up and run an operation are shared over many customers, making the overall cost to any single customer much lower than almost any other alternative. Customers pay a very low rate for the compute capacity they actually consume. Security is also provided through Amazon EC2 web service interfaces. These allow users to configure firewall settings that control network access to and between groups of instances. Amazon EC2 offers a highly reliable environment where replacement instances can be rapidly provisioned.

When one compares this solution to the significant up-front expenditures traditionally required to purchase and maintain hardware, either in-house or hosted, the decision to outsource is not hard to make. Outsourced solutions like EC2 free customers from many of the complexities of capacity planning and allow clients to move from large capital investments and fixed costs to smaller, variable, expensed costs. This approach removes the need to overbuy and overbuild capacity to handle periodic traffic spikes. The EC2 service runs within Amazon's proven, secure, and reliable network infrastructure and data center locations.

Dynamic Scalability

Amazon EC2 enables users to increase or decrease capacity in a few minutes. Users can invoke a single instance, hundreds of instances, or even thousands of instances simultaneously. Of course, because this is all controlled with web service APIs, an application can automatically scale itself up or down depending on its needs. This type of dynamic scalability is very attractive to enterprise customers because it allows them to meet their customers' demands without having to overbuild their infrastructure.

Full Control of Instances

Users have complete control of their instances. They have root access to each instance and can interact with them as one would with any machine. Instances can be rebooted remotely using web service APIs. Users also have access to console output of their instances. Once users have set up their account and uploaded their AMI to the Amazon S3 service, they just need to boot that instance. It is possible to start an AMI on any number of instances (or any type) by calling the *RunInstances* API that is provided by Amazon.

Configuration Flexibility

Configuration settings can vary widely among users. They have the choice of multiple instance types, operating systems, and software packages. Amazon EC2 allows them to select a configuration of memory, CPU, and instance storage that is optimal for their choice of operating system and application. For example, a user's choice of operating systems may also include numerous Linux distributions, Microsoft Windows Server, and even an OpenSolaris environment, all running on virtual servers.

Integration with Other Amazon Web Services

Amazon EC2 works in conjunction with a variety of other Amazon web services. For example, Amazon Simple Storage Service (Amazon S3), Amazon SimpleDB, Amazon Simple Queue Service (Amazon SQS), and Amazon CloudFront are all integrated to provide a complete solution for computing, query processing, and storage across a wide range of applications.

Amazon S3 provides a web services interface that allows users to store and retrieve any amount of data from the Internet at any time, anywhere. It gives developers direct access to the same highly scalable, reliable, fast, inexpensive data storage infrastructure Amazon uses to run its own global network of web sites. The S3 service aims to maximize benefits of scale and to pass those benefits on to developers.

Amazon SimpleDB is another web-based service, designed for running queries on structured data stored with the Amazon Simple Storage Service (Amazon S3) in real time. This service works in conjunction with the Amazon Elastic Compute Cloud (Amazon EC2) to provide users the capability to store, process, and query data sets within the cloud environment. These services are designed to make web-scale computing easier and more cost-effective for developers. Traditionally, this type of functionality was provided using a clustered relational database that requires a sizable investment. Implementations of this nature brought on more complexity and often required the services of a database administer to maintain it.

By comparison to traditional approaches, Amazon SimpleDB is easy to use and provides the core functionality of a database (e.g., real-time lookup and simple querying of structured data) without inheriting the operational complexity involved in traditional implementations. Amazon SimpleDB requires no schema, automatically indexes data, and provides a simple API for data storage and access. This eliminates the need for customers to perform tasks such as data modeling, index maintenance, and performance tuning.

Amazon Simple Queue Service (Amazon SQS) is a reliable, scalable, hosted queue for storing messages as they pass between computers. Using Amazon SQS, developers can move data between distributed components of applications that perform different tasks without losing messages or requiring 100% availability for each component. Amazon SQS works by exposing Amazon's web-scale messaging infrastructure as a service. Any computer connected to the Internet can add or read messages without the need for having any installed software or special firewall configurations. Components of applications using Amazon SQS can run independently and do not need to be on the same network, developed with the same technologies, or running at the same time.

Amazon CloudFront is a web service for content delivery. It integrates with other Amazon web services to distribute content to end users with low latency and high data transfer speeds. Amazon CloudFront delivers content using a global network of edge locations. Requests for objects are automatically routed to the nearest edge server, so content is delivered with the best possible performance. An edge server receives a request from the user's computer and makes a connection to another computer called the origin server, where the application resides. When the origin server fulfills the request, it sends the application's data back to the edge server, which, in turn, forwards the data to the client computer that made the request.

Reliable and Resilient Performance

Amazon Elastic Block Store (EBS) is yet another Amazon EC2 feature that provides users powerful features to build failure-resilient applications. Amazon EBS offers persistent storage for Amazon EC2 instances. Amazon EBS volumes provide "off-instance" storage that persists independently from the life of any instance. Amazon EBS volumes are highly available, highly reliable data shares that can be attached to a running Amazon EC2 instance and are exposed to the instance as standard block devices. Amazon EBS volumes are automatically replicated on the back end. The service provides users with the ability to create point-in-time snapshots of their data volumes, which are stored using the Amazon S3 service. These snapshots can be used as a starting point for new Amazon EBS volumes and can protect data indefinitely.

Support for Use in Geographically Disparate Locations

Amazon EC2 provides users with the ability to place one or more instances in multiple locations. Amazon EC2 locations are composed of Regions (such as North America and Europe) and Availability Zones. Regions consist of one or more Availability Zones, are geographically dispersed, and are in separate geographic areas or countries. Availability Zones are distinct locations that are engineered to be insulated from failures in other Availability Zones and provide inexpensive, low-latency network connectivity to other Availability Zones in the same Region.[7] For example, the North America Region may be split into the following Availability Zones: Northeast, East, SouthEast, NorthCentral, Central, SouthCentral, NorthWest, West, SouthWest, etc. By launching instances in any one or more of the separate Availability Zones, you can insulate your applications from a single point of failure. Amazon EC2 has a service-level agreement that commits to a 99.95% uptime availability for each Amazon EC2 Region. Amazon EC2 is currently available in two regions, the United States and Europe.

---

7.   http://developer.amazonwebservices.com/connect/entry.jspa?externalID=1347, retrieved 16 Jan 2009.

Elastic IP Addressing

Elastic IP (EIP) addresses are static IP addresses designed for dynamic cloud computing. An Elastic IP address is associated with your account and not with a particular instance, and you control that address until you choose explicitly to release it. Unlike traditional static IP addresses, however, EIP addresses allow you to mask instance or Availability Zone failures by programmatically remapping your public IP addresses to any instance in your account. Rather than waiting on a technician to reconfigure or replace your host, or waiting for DNS to propagate to all of your customers, Amazon EC2 enables you to work around problems that occur with client instances or client software by quickly remapping their EIP address to another running instance. A significant feature of Elastic IP addressing is that each IP address can be reassigned to a different instance when needed. Now, let's review how the Elastic IPs work with Amazon EC2 services.

First of all, Amazon allows users to allocate up to five Elastic IP addresses per account (which is the default). Each EIP can be assigned to a single instance. When this reassignment occurs, it replaces the normal dynamic IP address used by that instance. By default, each instance starts with a dynamic IP address that is allocated upon startup. Since each instance can have only one external IP address, the instance starts out using the default dynamic IP address. If the EIP in use is assigned to a different instance, a new dynamic IP address is allocated to the vacated address of that instance. Assigning or reassigning an IP to an instance requires only a few minutes. The limitation of designating a single IP at a time is due to the way Network Address Translation (NAT) works. Each instance is mapped to an internal IP address and is also assigned an external (public) address. The public address is mapped to the internal address using Network Address Translation tables (hence, NAT). If two external IP addresses happen to be translated to the same internal IP address, all inbound traffic (in the form of data packets) would arrive without any issues. However, assigning outgoing packets to an external IP address would be very difficult because a determination of which external IP address to use could not be made. This is why implementors have built in the limitation of having only a single external IP address per instance at any one time.

2.3.4 Mosso (Rackspace)

Mosso, a direct competitor of Amazon's EC2 service, is a web application hosting service and cloud platform provider that bills on a utility computing basis. Mosso was launched in February 2008 and is owned and operated by Rackspace, a web hosting provider that has been around for some time. Most new hosting platforms require custom code and architecture to make an application work. What makes Mosso different is that it has been designed to run an application with very little or no modifications. The Mosso platform is built on existing web standards and powered by proven technologies. Customers reap the benefits of a scalable platform for free. They spend no time coding custom APIs or building data schemas. Mosso has also branched out into cloud storage and cloud infrastructure.

Mosso Cloud Servers and Files

Mosso Cloud Servers (MCS) came into being from the acquisition of a company called Slicehost by Rackspace. Slicehost was designed to enable deployment of multiple cloud servers instantly. In essence, it touts capability for the creation of advanced, high-availability architectures. In order to create a full-service offering, Rackspace also acquired another company, JungleDisk. JungleDisk was an online backup service. By integrating JungleDisk's backup features with virtual servers that Slicehost provides, Mosso, in effect, created a new service to compete with Amazon's EC2. Mosso claims that these "cloud sites" are the fastest way for scustomer to put their site in the cloud. Cloud sites are capable of running Windows or Linux applications across banks of servers numbering in the hundreds.

Mosso's *Cloud Files* provide unlimited storage for content by using a partnership formed with Limelight Networks. This partnership allows Mosso to offer its customers a content delivery network (CDN). With CDN services, servers are placed around the world and, depending on where you are located, you get served via the closest or most appropriate server. CDNs cut down on the hops back and forth to handle a request. The chief benefit of using CDN is a scalable, dynamic storage platform that offers a metered service by which customers pay only for what they use. Customers can manage files through a web-based control panel or programmatically through an API.

Integrated backups with the CDN offering implemented in the Mosso services platform began in earnest with Jungle Disk version 2.5 in early 2009. Jungle Disk 2.5 is a major upgrade, adding a number of highly requested features to its portfolio. Highlights of the new version include running as a background service. The background service will keep running even if the Jungle Disk Monitor is logged out or closed. Users do not have to be logged into the service for automatic backups to be performed. There is native file system support on both 32-bit and 64-bit versions of Windows (Windows 2000, XP, Vista, 2003 and 2008), and Linux. A new download resume capability has been added for moving large files and performing restore operations. A time-slice restore interface was also added, allowing restoration of files from any given point-in-time where a snapshot was taken. Finally, it supports automatic updates on Windows (built-in) and Macintosh (using Sparkle).

2.4   Monitoring-as-a-Service (MaaS)

Monitoring-as-a-Service (MaaS) is the outsourced provisioning of security, primarily on business platforms that leverage the Internet to conduct business.[8] MaaS has become increasingly popular over the last decade. Since the advent of cloud computing, its popularity has, grown even more. Security monitoring involves protecting an enterprise or government client from cyber threats. A security team plays a crucial role in securing and maintaining the confidentiality, integrity, and availability of IT assets. However, time and resource constraints limit security operations and their effectiveness for most companies. This requires constant vigilance over the security infrastructure and critical information assets.

Many industry regulations require organizations to monitor their security environment, server logs, and other information assets to ensure the integrity of these systems. However, conducting effective security monitoring can be a daunting task because it requires advanced technology, skilled security experts, and scalable processes—none of which come cheap. MaaS security monitoring services offer real-time, 24/7 monitoring and nearly immediate incident response across a security infrastructure—they help to protect critical information assets of their customers. Prior to the advent of electronic security systems, security monitoring and response were heavily dependent on human resources and human capabilities, which also limited the accuracy and effectiveness of monitoring efforts. Over the past two decades, the adoption of information technology into facility security systems, and their ability to be connected to security operations centers (SOCs) via corporate networks, has significantly changed that picture. This means two important things: (1) The total cost of ownership (TCO) for traditional SOCs is much higher than for a modern-technology SOC; and (2)

---

8.   http://en.wikipedia.org/wiki/Monitoring_as_a_service, retrieved 14 Jan 2009.

achieving lower security operations costs and higher security effectiveness means that modern SOC architecture must use security and IT technology to address security risks.

2.4.1 Protection Against Internal and External Threats

SOC-based security monitoring services can improve the effectiveness of a customer security infrastructure by actively analyzing logs and alerts from infrastructure devices around the clock and in real time. Monitoring teams correlate information from various security devices to provide security analysts with the data they need to eliminate false positives[9] and respond to true threats against the enterprise. Having consistent access to the skills needed to maintain the level of service an organization requires for enterprise-level monitoring is a huge issue. The information security team can assess system performance on a periodically recurring basis and provide recommendations for improvements as needed. Typical services provided by many MaaS vendors are described below.

Early Detection

An early detection service detects and reports new security vulnerabilities shortly after they appear. Generally, the threats are correlated with third-party sources, and an alert or report is issued to customers. This report is usually sent by email to the person designated by the company. Security vulnerability reports, aside from containing a detailed description of the vulnerability and the platforms affected, also include information on the impact the exploitation of this vulnerability would have on the systems or applications previously selected by the company receiving the report. Most often, the report also indicates specific actions to be taken to minimize the effect of the vulnerability, if that is known.

Platform, Control, and Services Monitoring

Platform, control, and services monitoring is often implemented as a dashboard interface[10] and makes it possible to know the operational status of the platform being monitored at any time. It is accessible from a web interface, making remote access possible. Each operational element that is monitored usually provides an operational status indicator, always taking into account

---

9.   A false positive is an event that is picked up by an intrusion detection system and perceived as an attack but that in reality is not.
10.   A dashboard is a floating, semitransparent window that provides contextual access to commonly used tools in a software program.

the critical impact of each element. This service aids in determining which elements may be operating at or near capacity or beyond the limits of established parameters. By detecting and identifying such problems, preventive measures can be taken to prevent loss of service.

Intelligent Log Centralization and Analysis

Intelligent log centralization and analysis is a monitoring solution based mainly on the correlation and matching of log entries. Such analysis helps to establish a baseline of operational performance and provides an index of security threat. Alarms can be raised in the event an incident moves the established baseline parameters beyond a stipulated threshold. These types of sophisticated tools are used by a team of security experts who are responsible for incident response once such a threshold has been crossed and the threat has generated an alarm or warning picked up by security analysts monitoring the systems.

Vulnerabilities Detection and Management

Vulnerabilities detection and management enables automated verification and management of the security level of information systems. The service periodically performs a series of automated tests for the purpose of identifying system weaknesses that may be exposed over the Internet, including the possibility of unauthorized access to administrative services, the existence of services that have not been updated, the detection of vulnerabilities such as phishing, etc. The service performs periodic follow-up of tasks performed by security professionals managing information systems security and provides reports that can be used to implement a plan for continuous improvement of the system's security level.

Continuous System Patching/Upgrade and Fortification

Security posture is enhanced with continuous system patching and upgrading of systems and application software. New patches, updates, and service packs for the equipment's operating system are necessary to maintain adequate security levels and support new versions of installed products. Keeping abreast of all the changes to all the software and hardware requires a committed effort to stay informed and to communicate gaps in security that can appear in installed systems and applications.

Intervention, Forensics, and Help Desk Services

Quick intervention when a threat is detected is crucial to mitigating the effects of a threat. This requires security engineers with ample knowledge in the various technologies and with the ability to support applications as well as infrastructures on a 24/7 basis. MaaS platforms routinely provide this service to their customers. When a detected threat is analyzed, it often requires forensic analysis to determine what it is, how much effort it will take to fix the problem, and what effects are likely to be seen. When problems are encountered, the first thing customers tend to do is pick up the phone. Help desk services provide assistance on questions or issues about the operation of running systems. This service includes assistance in writing failure reports, managing operating problems, etc.

2.4.2   Delivering Business Value

Some consider balancing the overall economic impact of any build-versus-buy decision as a more significant measure than simply calculating a return on investment (ROI). The key cost categories that are most often associated with MaaS are (1) service fees for security event monitoring for all firewalls and intrusion detection devices, servers, and routers; (2) internal account maintenance and administration costs; and (3) preplanning and development costs.

Based on the total cost of ownership, whenever a customer evaluates the option of an in-house security information monitoring team and infrastructure compared to outsourcing to a service provider, it does not take long to realize that establishing and maintaining an in-house capability is not as attractive as outsourcing the service to a provider with an existing infrastructure. Having an in-house security operations center forces a company to deal with issues such as staff attrition, scheduling, around the clock operations, etc.

Losses incurred from external and internal incidents are extremely significant, as evidenced by a regular stream of high-profile cases in the news. The generally accepted method of valuing the risk of losses from external and internal incidents is to look at the amount of a potential loss, assume a frequency of loss, and estimate a probability for incurring the loss. Although this method is not perfect, it provides a means for tracking information security metrics. Risk is used as a filter to capture uncertainty about varying cost and benefit estimates. If a risk-adjusted ROI demonstrates a compelling business case, it raises confidence that the investment is likely to succeed because the risks that threaten the project have been considered and quantified. Flexibility represents an investment in additional capacity or agility today that can be turned into future business benefits at some additional cost. This provides an organization with the ability to engage in future initiatives, but not the obligation to do so. The value of flexibility is unique to each organization, and willingness to measure its value varies from company to company.

2.4.3   Real-Time Log Monitoring Enables Compliance

Security monitoring services can also help customers comply with industry regulations by automating the collection and reporting of specific events of interest, such as log-in failures. Regulations and industry guidelines often require log monitoring of critical servers to ensure the integrity of confidential data. MaaS providers' security monitoring services automate this time-consuming process.

2.5   Platform-as-a-Service (PaaS)

Cloud computing has evolved to include platforms for building and running custom web-based applications, a concept known as Platform-as-a-Service. PaaS is an outgrowth of the SaaS application delivery model. The PaaS model makes all of the facilities required to support the complete life cycle of building and delivering web applications and services entirely available from the Internet, all with no software downloads or installation for developers, IT managers, or end users. Unlike the IaaS model, where developers may create a specific operating system instance with home-grown applications running, PaaS developers are concerned only with web-based development and generally do not care what operating system is used. PaaS services allow users to focus on innovation rather than complex infrastructure. Organizations can redirect a significant portion of their budgets to creating applications that provide real business value instead of worrying about all the infrastructure issues in a roll-your-own delivery model. The PaaS model is thus driving a new era of mass innovation. Now, developers around the world can access unlimited computing power. Anyone with an Internet connection can build powerful applications and easily deploy them to users globally.

2.5.1   The Traditional On-Premises Model

The traditional approach of building and running on-premises applications has always been complex, expensive, and risky. Building your own solution has never offered any guarantee of success. Each application was designed to meet specific business requirements. Each solution required a specific set of hardware, an operating system, a database, often a middleware package, email and web servers, etc. Once the hardware and software environment was created, a team of developers had to navigate complex programming development platforms to build their applications. Additionally, a team of network, database, and system management experts was needed to keep everything up and running. Inevitably, a business requirement would force the developers to make a change to the application. The changed application then required new test cycles before being distributed. Large companies often needed specialized facilities to house their data centers. Enormous amounts of electricity also were needed to power the servers as well as to keep the systems cool. Finally, all of this required use of fail-over sites to mirror the data center so that information could be replicated in case of a disaster. Old days, old ways—now, let's fly into the silver lining of todays cloud.

2.5.2   The New Cloud Model

PaaS offers a faster, more cost-effective model for application development and delivery. PaaS provides all the infrastructure needed to run applications over the Internet. Such is the case with companies such as Amazon.com, eBay, Google, iTunes, and YouTube. The new cloud model has made it possible to deliver such new capabilities to new markets via the web browsers. PaaS is based on a metering or subscription model, so users pay only for what they use. PaaS offerings include workflow facilities for application design, application development, testing, deployment, and hosting, as well as application services such as virtual offices, team collaboration, database integration, security, scalability, storage, persistence, state management, dashboard instrumentation, etc.

2.5.3   Key Characteristics of PaaS

Chief characteristics of PaaS include services to develop, test, deploy, host, and manage applications to support the application development life cycle. Web-based user interface creation tools typically provide some level of support to simplify the creation of user interfaces, based either on common standards such as HTML and JavaScript or on other, proprietary technologies. Supporting a multitenant architecture helps to remove developer concerns regarding the use of the application by many concurrent users. PaaS providers often include services for concurrency management, scalability, fail-over and security. Another characteristic is the integration with web services and databases. Support for Simple Object Access Protocol (SOAP) and other interfaces allows PaaS offerings to create combinations of web services (called mashups) as well as having the ability to access databases and reuse services maintained inside private networks. The ability to form and share code with ad-hoc, predefined, or distributed teams greatly enhances the productivity of PaaS offerings. Integrated PaaS offerings provide an opportunity for developers to have much greater insight into the inner workings of their applications and the behavior of their users by implementing dashboard-like tools to view the inner workings based on measurements such as performance, number of concurrent accesses, etc. Some PaaS offerings leverage this instrumentation to enable pay-per-use billing models.

2.6   Software-as-a-Service (SaaS)

The traditional model of software distribution, in which software is purchased for and installed on personal computers, is sometimes referred to as Software-as-a-Product. Software-as-a-Service is a software distribution model in which applications are hosted by a vendor or service provider and made available to customers over a network, typically the Internet. SaaS is becoming an increasingly prevalent delivery model as underlying technologies that support web services and service-oriented architecture (SOA) mature and new developmental approaches become popular. SaaS is also often associated with a pay-as-you-go subscription licensing model. Meanwhile, broadband service has become increasingly available to support user access from more areas around the world.

The huge strides made by Internet Service Providers (ISPs) to increase bandwidth, and the constant introduction of ever more powerful microprocessors coupled with inexpensive data storage devices, is providing a huge platform for designing, deploying, and using software across all areas of business and personal computing. SaaS applications also must be able to interact with other data and other applications in an equally wide variety of environments and platforms. SaaS is closely related to other service delivery models we have described. IDC identifies two slightly different delivery models for SaaS.[11] The hosted application management model is similar to an Application Service Provider (ASP) model. Here, an ASP hosts commercially available software for customers and delivers it over the Internet. The other model is a software on demand model where the provider gives customers network-based access to a single copy of an application created specifically for SaaS distribution. IDC predicted that SaaS would make up 30% of the software market by 2007 and would be worth $10.7 billion by the end of 2009.[12]

SaaS is most often implemented to provide business software functionality to enterprise customers at a low cost while allowing those customers to obtain the same benefits of commercially licensed, internally operated software without the associated complexity of installation, management, support, licensing, and high initial cost.[13] Most customers have little interest in the how or why of software implementation, deployment, etc., but all have a need to use software in their work. Many types of software are well suited to the SaaS model (e.g., accounting, customer relationship management, email software, human resources, IT security, IT service management, video conferencing, web analytics, web content management). The distinction between SaaS and earlier applications delivered over the Internet is that SaaS solutions were developed specifically to work within a web browser. The architecture of SaaS-based applications is specifically designed to support many concurrent users (multitenancy) at once. This is a big difference from the traditional client/server or application service provider (ASP)-based solutions that cater to a contained audience. SaaS providers, on the other hand, leverage enormous economies of scale in the deployment, management, support, and maintenance of their offerings.

2.6.1   SaaS Implementation Issues

Many types of software components and applications frameworks may be employed in the development of SaaS applications. Using new technology found in these modern components and application frameworks can drastically reduce the time to market and cost of converting a traditional on-premises product into a SaaS solution. According to Microsoft,[14] SaaS architectures can be classified into one of four maturity levels whose key

11.   "Software as a Service Threatens Partner Revenue and Profit Streams, New Partners Emerging, IDC Research Shows," from http://www.idc.com/getdoc.jsp?containerId=prUS20884007, 20 Sep 2007, retrieved 16 Jan 2009.
12.   Ibid.
13.   http://en.wikipedia.org/wiki/Software_as_a_service, retrieved 11 Jan 2009.
14.   http://www.microsoft.com/serviceproviders/saas/saasplatform.mspx, retrieved 14 Jan 2009.

attributes are ease of configuration, multitenant efficiency, and scalability. Each level is distinguished from the previous one by the addition of one of these three attributes. The levels described by Microsoft are as follows.

- **SaaS Architectural Maturity Level 1—Ad-Hoc/Custom.** The first level of maturity is actually no maturity at all. Each customer has a unique, customized version of the hosted application. The application runs its own instance on the host's servers. Migrating a traditional non-networked or client-server application to this level of SaaS maturity typically requires the least development effort and reduces operating costs by consolidating server hardware and administration.

- **SaaS Architectural Maturity Level 2—Configurability.** The second level of SaaS maturity provides greater program flexibility through configuration metadata. At this level, many customers can use separate instances of the same application. This allows a vendor to meet the varying needs of each customer by using detailed configuration options. It also allows the vendor to ease the maintenance burden by being able to update a common code base.

- **SaaS Architectural Maturity Level 3—Multitenant Efficiency.** The third maturity level adds multitenancy to the second level. This results in a single program instance that has the capability to serve all of the vendor's customers. This approach enables more efficient use of server resources without any apparent difference to the end user, but ultimately this level is limited in its ability to scale massively.

- **SaaS Architectural Maturity Level 4—Scalable.** At the fourth SaaS maturity level, scalability is added by using a multitiered architecture. This architecture is capable of supporting a load-balanced farm of identical application instances running on a variable number of servers, sometimes in the hundreds or even thousands. System capacity can be dynamically increased or decreased to match load demand by adding or removing servers, with no need for further alteration of application software architecture.

2.6.2   Key Characteristics of SaaS

Deploying applications in a service-oriented architecture is a more complex problem than is usually encountered in traditional models of software deployment. As a result, SaaS applications are generally priced based on the number of users that can have access to the service. There are often additional fees for the use of help desk services, extra bandwidth, and storage. SaaS revenue streams to the vendor are usually lower initially than traditional software license fees. However, the trade-off for lower license fees is a monthly recurring revenue stream, which is viewed by most corporate CFOs as a more predictable gauge of how the business is faring quarter to quarter. These monthly recurring charges are viewed much like maintenance fees for licensed software.[15] The key characteristics of SaaS software are the following:

- Network-based management and access to commercially available software from central locations rather than at each customer's site, enabling customers to access applications remotely via the Internet.

- Application delivery from a one-to-many model (single-instance, multitenant architecture), as opposed to a traditional one-to-one model.

- Centralized enhancement and patch updating that obviates any need for downloading and installing by a user. SaaS is often used in conjunction with a larger network of communications and collaboration software, sometimes as a plug-in to a PaaS architecture.

2.6.3 Benefits of the SaaS Model

Application deployment cycles inside companies can take years, consume massive resources, and yield unsatisfactory results. Although the initial decision to relinquish control is a difficult one, it is one that can lead to improved efficiency, lower risk, and a generous return on investment.[16] An increasing number of companies want to use the SaaS model for corporate applications such as customer relationship management and those that fall under the Sarbanes-Oxley Act compliance umbrella (e.g., financial recording and human resources). The SaaS model helps enterprises ensure that all locations are using the correct application version and, therefore, that the

15. Erin Traudt and Amy Konary, "2005 Software as a Service Taxonomy and Research Guide," IDC, http://www.idc.com/getdoc.jsp?containerId=33453&pageType=PRINT-FRIENDLY#33453-S-0001, retrieved 11 Jan 2009.

16. http://searchnetworking.techtarget.com/generic/0,295582,sid7_gci1164670,00.html, retrieved 18 Jan 2009.

format of the data being recorded and conveyed is consistent, compatible, and accurate. By placing the responsibility for an application onto the doorstep of a SaaS provider, enterprises can reduce administration and management burdens they would otherwise have for their own corporate applications. SaaS also helps to increase the availability of applications to global locations. SaaS also ensures that all application transactions are logged for compliance purposes. The benefits of SaaS to the customer are very clear:

- Streamlined administration
- Automated update and patch management services
- Data compatibility across the enterprise (all users have the same version of software)
- Facilitated, enterprise-wide collaboration
- Global accessibility

As we have pointed out previously, server virtualization can be used in SaaS architectures, either in place of or in addition to multitenancy. A major benefit of platform virtualization is that it can increase a system's capacity without any need for additional programming. Conversely, a huge amount of programming may be required in order to construct more efficient, multitenant applications. The effect of combining multitenancy and platform virtualization into a SaaS solution provides greater flexibility and performance to the end user. In this chapter, we have discussed how the computing world has moved from stand-alone, dedicated computing to client/ network computing and on into the cloud for remote computing. The advent of web-based services has given rise to a variety of service offerings, sometimes known collectively as XaaS. We covered these service models, focusing on the type of service provided to the customer (i.e., communications, infrastructure, monitoring, outsourced platforms, and software). In the next chapter, we will take a look at what is required from the service provider's perspective to make these services available.

2.7   Chapter Summary

In this chapter we have examined the various types of web services delivered from the cloud. Having the ability to leverage reusable software components across a network has great appeal to implementors. Today, the most common and successful example of cloud computing is SaaS, but other functions, including communication, infrastructure, and platforms, are also core components of cloud computing. Because of the extremely low barriers to entry, offerings have been made available to consumers and small businesses as well as mid-sized and large enterprises. This is a key differentiator from many service-oriented architecture (SAO) offerings, which will be covered next.

In the next chapter we will learn how companies build highly automated private cloud networks that can be managed from a single point. We will discuss how server and storage virtualization is used across distributed computing resources. We will describe in basic terms how cloud infrastructure is built. We will provide an overview of the basic approach to SOA as it applies to data center design. And we will examine the role and use of open source software in data centers. Understanding the use and importance of collaboration technologies in cloud computing architectures is fundamental to understanding how requirements of the cloud have evolved.

Chapter 3

Building Cloud Networks

3.1 Chapter Overview

In previous chapters we have explained what cloud computing is. In this chapter, we will describe what it takes to build a cloud network. You will learn how and why companies build these highly automated private cloud networks providing resources that can be managed from a single point. We will discuss the significant reliance of cloud computing architectures on server and storage virtualization as a layer between applications and distributed computing resources. You will learn the basics of how flexible cloud computing networks such as those modeled after public providers such as Google and Amazon are built, and how they interconnect with corporate IT private clouds designed as service-oriented architectures (SOAs). We provide an overview of how SOA is used as an intermediary step for cloud computing and the basic approach to SOA as it applies to data center design. We then describe the role and use of open source software in data centers. The use and importance of collaboration technologies in cloud computing architectures is also discussed. Last and most important, you will gain an understanding of how the engine of cloud computing will drive the future of infrastructure and operations design.

Ten years ago, no one could have predicted that the cloud (both hardware and software) would become the next big thing in the computing world. IT automation has evolved out of business needs expressed by customers to infrastructure management and administrators. There has never been a grand unified plan to automate the IT industry. Each provider, responding to the needs of individual customers, has been busily building technology solutions to handle repetitive tasks, respond to events, and produce predictable outcomes given certain conditions. All the while this evolutionary process was occurring, it was presumed that the cost of not doing it would be higher than just getting it done.[1] The solutions provided to meet customer needs involved both hardware and software innovation and, as those solutions emerged, they gave rise to another generation of innovation, improving on the foundation before it. Thus the effects of Moore's law[2] seem to prevail even for cloud evolution.

From the military use of TCP/IP in the 1960s and 1970s to the development and emergence of the browser on the Internet in the late 1980s and early 1990s, we have witnessed growth at a rate similar to what Gordon Moore had predicted in 1965: essentially, a doubling of capability approximately every two years. We saw the emergence of network security in the mid/late 1990s (again, as a response to a need), and we saw the birth of performance and traffic optimization in the late 1990s/early 2000s, as the growth of the Internet necessitated optimization and higher-performance solutions. According to Greg Ness, the result has been "a renaissance of sorts in the network hardware industry, as enterprises installed successive foundations of specialized gear dedicated to the secure and efficient transport of an ever increasing population of packets, protocols and services."[3] Welcome to the world that has been called Infrastructure1.0 (I-1.0).

The evolution of the basic entity we call I-1.0 is precisely the niche area that made successful companies such as Cisco, F5 Networks, Juniper, and Riverbed. I-1.0 established and maintained routes of connectivity between a globally scaled user base constantly deploying increasingly powerful and ever more capable network devices. I-1.0's impact on productivity and commerce have been as important to civilization as the development of transoceanic shipping, paved roads, railway systems, electricity, and air travel. I-1.0 has created and shifted wealth and accelerated technological advancement on a huge number of fronts in countless fields of endeavor. There simply has been no historical precedent to match the impact that I-1.0 has had on our world. However, at this point in its evolution, the greatest threat to the I-1.0 world is the advent of even greater factors of change and complexity as technology continues to evolve. What once was an almost exclusive domain of firmware and hardware has now evolved to require much more intelligent and sophisticated software necessary for interfacing with, administering, configuring, and managing that hardware. By providing such sophisticated interfaces to firmware/hardware-configured devices, it marked

1.   James Urquhart, http://blogs.cisco.com/datacenter/comments/
     the_network_the_final_frontier_for_cloud_computing, retrieved 5 Feb 09.
2.   http://www.intel.com/technology/mooreslaw/index.htm, retrieved 6 Feb 09.
3.   Greg Ness, http://gregness.wordpress.com/2008/10/13/clouds-networks-and-recessions,
     retrieved 5 Feb 09.

the beginning of the emergence of virtualization. When companies such as VMware, Microsoft, and Citrix announced plans to move their offerings into mainstream production data centers such as Exodus Communications, the turning point for I-1.0 became even more evident. The I-1.0 infrastructure world was on its way into the cold, dark halls of history.

As the chasm between I-1.0 and the increasingly sophisticated software packages widened, it became evident that the software could ultimately drive the emergence of a more dynamic and resilient network. This network became even more empowered by the addition of application-layer innovations and the integration of static infrastructure with enhanced management and connectivity intelligence. The evolving network systems had become more dynamic and created new problems that software was unprepared to contend with. This gave rise to a new area, virtualization security (VirtSec, which once again, arose out of necessity), and marked the beginning of an even greater realization that the static infrastructure built over the previous quarter of a century was not adequate for supporting dynamic systems or for avoiding the impact that malevolent actions would have on such dynamic networking paradigms. The recognition that new solutions had to be developed became apparent when the first virus hit back in the 1970s (The Creeper virus was first detected on ARPANET, the forerunner of the Internet, in the early 1970s[4]). No one realized at the time that this single problem would create an entire industry. As we have discussed, the driving force for all such technological innovation has been need. For the cloud, the biggest evolutionary jump began with managed service providers (MSPs) and their motivation to satisfy and retain customers paying monthly recurring fees.

3.2   The Evolution from the MSP Model to Cloud Computing and Software-as-a-Service

If you think about how cloud computing really evolved, it won't take long to realize that the first iteration of cloud computing can probably be traced back to the days of frame relay networks. Organizations with frame relay were essentially singular clouds that were interconnected to other frame relay-connected organizations using a carrier/provider to transport data communications between the two entities. Everyone within the frame network sharing a common Private Virtual Connection (PVC) could share

---

4.   http://en.wikipedia.org/wiki/Computer_virus, retrieved 6 Feb 09.

their data with everyone else on the same PVC. To go outside their cloud and connect to another cloud, users had to rely on the I-1.0 infrastructure's routers and switches along the way to connect the dots between the clouds. The endpoint for this route between the clouds and the I-1.0 pathway was a demarcation point between the cloud and the provider's customer. Where the dots ended between the clouds (i.e., the endpoints) was where access was controlled by I-1.0 devices such as gateways, proxies, and firewalls on the customer's premises.

From customers' perspective, this endpoint was known as the main point of entry (MPOE) and marked their authorized pathway into their internal networking infrastructure. By having applications use specific protocols to transport data (e.g., Simple Mail Transfer Protocol [SMTP] for sending mail or File Transfer Protocol [FTP] for moving files from one location to another), applications behind the MPOE could accept or reject traffic passing over the network and allow email and file transfer to occur with little to no impedance from the network infrastructure or their administrators. Specialized applications (developed out of necessity to satisfy specific business needs) often required a client/server implementation using specific portals created through the firewall to allow their traffic protocols to proceed unhindered and often required special administrative setup before they could work properly. While some of this may still hold, that was, for the most part, how it was done "old school." Things have changed considerably since that model was considered state of the art. However state of the art it was, it was difficult to manage and expensive. Because organizations did not want to deal with the complexities of managing I-1.0 infrastructure, a cottage industry was born to do just that.

3.2.1   From Single-Purpose Architectures to Multipurpose Architectures

In the early days of MSPs, the providers would actually go onto customer sites and perform their services on customer-owned premises. Over time, these MSPs specialized in implementation of infrastructure and quickly figured out ways to build out data centers and sell those capabilities off in small chunks commonly known as monthly recurring services, in addition to the basic fees charged for ping, power, and pipe (PPP). *Ping* refers to the ability to have a live Internet connection, *power* is obvious enough, and *pipe* refers to the amount of data throughput that a customer is willing to pay for. Generally, the PPP part of the charge was built into the provider's monthly service fee in addition to their service offerings. Common services provided by MSPs include remote network, desktop and security monitoring, incident response, patch management, and remote data backup, as well as technical support. An advantage for customers using an MSP is that by purchasing a defined set of services, MSPs bill a flat or near-fixed monthly fee, which benefits customers by having a predictable IT cost to budget for over time. Step forward to today and we find that many MSPs now provide their services remotely over the Internet rather than having to sell data center space and services or perform on-site client visits (which is time-consuming and expensive).

3.2.2   Data Center Virtualization

From the evolutionary growth of the MSP field, coupled with the leaps made in Internet and networking technology over the past 10 years, we have come to a point where infrastructure has become almost secondary to the services offered on such infrastructure. By allowing the infrastructure to be virtualized and shared across many customers, the providers have changed their business model to provide remotely managed services at lower costs, making it attractive to their customers. These X-as-a-Service models (XaaS) are continually growing and evolving, as we are currently standing at the forefront of a new era of computing service driven by a huge surge in demand by both enterprises and individuals. Software-as-a-Service (SaaS, and other [X]aaS offerings such as IaaS, MaaS, and PaaS) can be seen as a subset or segment of the cloud computing market that is growing all the time. One IDC report indicated that cloud computing spending will increase from $16 billion in 2008 to $42 billion in 2012.[5] Is there little wonder there is incentive for consumers to pursue cloud computing and SaaS?

Typically, cloud computing has been viewed as a broad array of Internet Protocol (IP) services (generally using an application called a Web browser as the main interface) in order to allow users to obtain a specific set of functional capabilities on a "pay for use" basis. Previously, obtaining such services required tremendous hardware/software investments and professional skills that were required in hosting environments such as Exodus Communications, Cable & Wireless, SAVVIS, and Digital Island. From an enterprise customer perspective, the biggest advantages of cloud computing and

---

5.   Roger Smith, "IDC Says IT Cloud Services to Reach $42 Billion by 2012," http://www.informationweek.com/blog/main/archives/2008/10/idc_says_it_clo.html, October 2008, retrieved 6 Feb 2009.

SaaS over the traditional hosting environment are that cloud computing is an I-1.0 response to a business need to find a reasonable substitute for using expensive out-sourced data centers. Also, SaaS is a "pay as you go" model that evolved as an alternative to using classical (more expensive) software licensing solutions.

The cloud evolved from the roots of managed service provider environments and data centers and is a critical element of next-generation data centers when compared to the MSPs they evolved from. Today, customers no longer care where the data is physically stored or where servers are physically located, as they will only use and pay for them when they need them. What drives customer decision making today is lower cost, higher performance and productivity, and currency of solutions.

3.3   The Cloud Data Center

Unlike the MSP or hosting model, the cloud can offer customers the flexibility to specify the exact amount of computing power, data, or applications they need to satisfy their business requirements. Because customers don't need to invest capital to have these services, what we have today is a reliable and cost-effective alternative to what has been available in the past. Today, customers are able to connect to the cloud without installing software or buying specific hardware. A big reason for their desire to use the cloud is the availability of collaborative services. *Collaboration is the opiate of the masses in "cloud land."*

3.4   Collaboration

Collaboration is a very natural experience that humans have been engaging in for thousands of years. Up until the 1970s, most businesses embraced collaboration through a management style called "management by walking around." This was facilitated by corporate styles in which people tended to be working together in the same place. In the 1960s and 1970s the "head office/branch office" model emerged as companies grew in size. These introduced time and distance into business processes, but the productivity gap was minimized because branch offices tended to be autonomous and people could still easily connect with one another.

Since then, the workforce has become increasingly distributed. This has accelerated as globalization has taken hold. In the last 30 years, tools such as voice mail and email have tried to close the gap by facilitating communications in real and nonreal (sometimes, even unreal) time. However, an increasing remote workforce coupled with the variable nature of a team (including contractors, suppliers, and customers) has meant that the productivity gap is also quickly growing. Distance and time slow down decision making and have the adverse effect of impeding innovation. Existing technology models are failing to keep up. Part of this failure has been introduced by the rapidly evolving workspace.

When we talk about the workspace, we talk about the wide variety of tools and systems that people need to do their jobs. It is the range of devices from mobile phones to IP phones, laptop computers, and even job-specific tools such as inventory scanners or process controllers. It is about the operating systems that power those tools. And it's about accessibility, as workspaces constantly change—from the home to the car, from the car to the office or to the factory floor, even to the hotel room.

Intelligent networks are used to unify not only the elements of the workspace, but also to unify workspaces among groups of users. People need to connect, communicate, and collaborate to ensure that everyone can be included in decision making. Only architectures that embrace the ever-changing workspace can enable collaboration, and only the network can ensure that the collaboration experience is universally available to all. The role of the network has been critical in driving productivity innovations. In fact, the network has fueled each of the IT-driven productivity shifts over the last 30 years.

While IBM, Microsoft, and Apple were making computing power available to all, it wasn't until the emergence of the IP network that people could connect easily from one machine and person to another. This network gave rise to both the Internet and to IP telephony. IP telephony dramatically changed the economics of communications, making corporate globalization financially feasible. IP telephony gave rise to unified communications and the ability to blend together many forms of communications including text, video, and voice. And while unified communications have enabled business transformation, it is collaboration that will close the productivity gap by overcoming the barriers of distance and time, speeding up business, and accelerating innovations by enabling the inclusion of people, anywhere.

Today's leading-edge collaboration portfolio solutions, FaceBook and Google, capture the best of two very different worlds, offering speed, ubiquity, and flexibility. Cloud-based solutions offer widely adopted standards used by legions of developers. It is where innovation happens rapidly and on a large scale. Most applications are offered as subscription services, available on demand and hosted in distant data centers in "the cloud." The enterprise world offers certainty of availability, security, reliability, and manageability. The enterprise experience is all about consistency. It also carries with it the legacy of proprietary toolsets and slower innovation cycles. It is a world that, for reasons of compliance, is usually hosted on-premises under tight controls and purchased through a capital budget. A portfolio of products can be built to enable the best of two worlds, the speed and flexibility of the consumer world and the certainty of the enterprise world.

Collaboration is not just about technology. Collaboration is the platform for business, but to achieve it, customers must focus on three important areas. First, customers need to develop a corporate culture that is inclusive and fosters collaboration. Second, business processes need to be adapted and modified to relax command and control and embrace boards and councils to set business priorities and make decisions. Finally, customers need to leverage technologies that can help overcome the barriers of distance and time and changing workforces.

If collaboration is the platform for business, the network is the platform for collaboration. Unlike vendor-specific collaboration suites, the next-generation portfolio is designed to ensure that all collaboration applications operate better. Whether it is WaaS (Wide-Area Application Service) optimizing application performance, or connecting Microsoft Office Communicator to the corporate voice network, the foundation ensures the delivery of the collaborative experience by enabling people and systems to connect securely and reliably. On top of the network connections, three solutions are deployed to support and enable the collaborative experience. These solutions are unified communications that enable people to communicate, video that adds context to communications, and Web 2.0 applications that deliver an open model to unify communications capabilities with existing infrastructure and business applications.

Unified communications enable people to communicate across the intelligent network. It incorporates best-of-breed applications such as IP telephony, contact centers, conferencing, and unified messaging. Video adds context to communication so that people can communicate more clearly and more quickly. The intelligent network assures that video can be available and useful from mobile devices and at the desktop. Web 2.0 applications provide rich collaboration applications to enable the rapid development and deployment of third-party solutions that integrate network services, communications, and video capabilities with business applications and infrastructure.

Customers should be able to choose to deploy applications depending on their business need rather than because of a technological limitation. Increasingly, customers can deploy applications on demand or on-premises. Partners also manage customer-provided equipment as well as hosted systems. With the intelligent network as the platform, customers can also choose to deploy some applications on demand, with others on-premises, and be assured that they will interoperate.

3.4.1   Why Collaboration?

Several evolutionary forces are leading companies and organizations to collaborate. The global nature of the workforce and business opportunities has created global projects with teams that are increasingly decentralized. Knowledge workers, vendors, and clients are increasingly global in nature. The global scope of business has resulted in global competition, a need for innovation, and a demand for greatly shortened development cycles on a scale unknown to previous generations. Competition is driving innovation cycles faster than ever to maximize time to market and achieve cost savings through economies of scale. This demand for a greatly reduced innovation cycle has also driven the need for industry-wide initiatives and multiparty global collaboration. Perhaps John Chambers, CEO and chairman of Cisco Systems, put it best in a 2007 blog post:

> Collaboration is the future. It is about what we can do together. And collaboration within and between firms worldwide is accelerating. It is enabled by technology and a change in behavior. Global, cross-functional teams create a virtual boundary-free workspace, collaborating across time zones to capture new opportunities created with customers and suppliers around the world. Investments in unified communications help people work together more efficiently. In particular, collaborative, information search and communications technologies fuel productivity by giving employees ready access to relevant information. Companies are flatter and more decentralized.[6]

6.   John Chambers, "Ushering in a New Era of Collaboration," http://blogs.cisco.com/collaboration/2007/10, 10 Oct 2007, retrieved 8 Feb 2009.

Collaboration solutions can help you address your business imperatives. Collaboration can save you money to invest in the future by allowing
you to intelligently reduce costs to fund investments for improvement and
focus on profitability and capital efficiency without reducing the bottom
line. It can also help you unlock employee potential by providing them a
vehicle by which they can work harder, smarter, and faster, ultimately doing
more with less by leveraging their collaborative network. With it you can
drive true customer intimacy by allowing your customers to be involved in
your decision process and truly embrace your ideas, personalize and customize your solutions to match customer needs, empower your customers to get
answers quickly and easily, all without dedicating more resources. Even further, it can give you the opportunity to be much closer to key customers to
ensure that they are getting the best service possible.

Collaboration gives you the ability to distance yourself from competitors because you now have a cost-effective, efficient, and timely way to make
your partners an integral part of your business processes; make better use of
your ecosystem to drive deeper and faster innovation and productivity; and
collaborate with partners to generate a higher quality and quantity of leads.
Ultimately, what all of these things point to is a transition to a borderless
enterprise where your business is inclusive of your entire ecosystem, so it is
no longer constrained by distance, time, or other inefficiencies of business
processes. Currently there is a major inflection point that is changing the
way we work, the way our employees work, the way our partners work, and
the way our customers work. There is a tremendous opportunity for businesses to move with unprecedented speed and alter the economics of their
market. Depending on a number of variables in the industry you're in, and
how big your organization is, there are trends that are affecting businesses in
any combination of the points made above.

Collaboration isn't just about being able to communicate better. It is
ultimately about enabling multiple organizations and individuals working
together to achieve a common goal. It depends heavily on effective communication, the wisdom of crowds, the open exchange and analysis of ideas,
and the execution of those ideas. In a business context, execution means
business processes, and the better you are able to collaborate on those processes, the better you will be able to generate stronger business results and
break away from your competitors.

These trends are creating some pretty heavy demands on businesses and
organizations. From stock prices to job uncertainty to supplier viability, the

global economic environment is raising both concerns and opportunities for businesses today. Stricken by the crisis on Wall Street, executives are doing everything they can to keep stock prices up. They are worried about keeping their people employed, happy and motivated because they cannot afford a drop in productivity, nor can they afford to lose their best people to competitors. They are thinking about new ways to create customer loyalty and customer satisfaction. They are also hungry to find ways to do more with less. How can they deliver the same or a better level of quality to their customers with potentially fewer resources, and at a lower cost?

Collaboration is also about opportunity. Businesses are looking for new and innovative ways to work with their partners and supply chains, deal with globalization, enter new markets, enhance products and services, unlock new business models. At the end of the day, whether they are in "survival mode," "opportunistic mode," or both, businesses want to act on what's happening out there—and they want to act fast in order to break away from their competitors.

So what choices do current IT departments have when it comes to enabling collaboration in their company and with their partners and customers? They want to serve the needs of their constituencies, but they typically find themselves regularly saying "no." They have a responsibility to the organization to maintain the integrity of the network, and to keep their focus on things like compliance, backup and disaster recovery strategies, security, intellectual property protection, quality of service, and scalability.

They face questions from users such as "Why am I limited to 80 MB storage on the company email system that I rely on to do business when I can get gigabytes of free email and voicemail storage from Google or Yahoo?" While Internet applications are updated on three- to six-month innovation cycles, enterprise software is updated at a much slower pace. Today it's virtually impossible to imagine what your workers might need three to five years from now. Look at how much the world has changed in the last five years. A few years ago, Google was "just a search engine," and we were not all sharing videos on YouTube, or updating our profiles on Facebook or MySpace. But you can't just have your users bringing their own solutions into the organization, because they may not meet your standards for security, compliance, and other IT requirements. As today's college students join the workforce, the disparity and the expectation for better answers grows even more pronounced.

The intent of collaboration is to enable the best of both worlds: web-speed innovation and a robust network foundation. New types of conversations are occurring in corporate board rooms and management meetings, and these conversations are no longer happening in siloed functional teams, but in a collaborative team environment where multiple functions and interests are represented. Enabling these collaborative conversations is more than systems and technology. It actually starts with your corporate culture, and it should be inclusive and encourage collaborative decision making. It's also not just about your own culture; your collaborative culture should extend externally as well as to your customers, partners, and supply chain. How do you include all these elements in your decision-making processes? Are you as transparent with them as you can be? How consistently do you interact with them to make them feel that they are a part of your culture? Once you have a collaborative culture, you will have the strong user base through which to collaboration-enable the processes in which people work.

All business processes should include collaborative capabilities so that they are not negatively impacted by the restrictions we see affecting processes today: time, distance, latency. At any point in a business process, whether internal or external, you should be able to connect with the information and/or expertise you need in order to get things done. This is especially true with customer-facing processes. As consumers, we always want to be able to talk directly to a person at any time if we have a question. Of course, this is all enabled by the tools and technology that are available to us today. Collaboration technology has evolved to a point where it is no longer just about being able to communicate more effectively; it is now at a point where you can drive real business benefits, transform the way business gets done, and, in many cases, unlock entirely new business models and/or new routes to market. As you look at the key business imperatives to focus on, it is important to consider the changes and/or investments you can make on any of these levels (short-term or long-term) to deliver the value you are looking for. Let's take a look at some examples now.

Customer Intimacy

When we talk about customer intimacy, we are really talking about making yourself available to communicate with them frequently in order to better understand their challenges, goals, and needs; ensuring that you are delivering what they need, in the way they need it; and including them in the decision-making processes. And just as there are a number of solutions that can improve the employee experience, your vendor should offer several solutions that can do the same for the customer experience, including an increase in the frequency, timeliness, and quality of customer meetings; improvement in the sales success rate, reduced sales cycle time, improved and more frequent customer engagements that can lead to uncovering new and deeper opportunities, and increasing your level of communication up-levels and your relationship as a business partner, not just as a vendor.

Extending Your Reach to Support Customers Anywhere and at Any Time

You can extend your reach to support customers anywhere and at any time by promoting a collaborative culture through the use of collaborative technologies such as Wikis or blogs. Enabling customers to voice their questions, concerns, opinions, and ideas via simple web 2.0 tools such as Wikis or blogs gives them a voice and contributes tremendous feedback, ideas, and information to your business and "innovation engine." These collaborative technologies can also be used to promote employee participation to drive innovation and self-service and increase employee morale, which is key to productivity. In turn, this can yield higher customer satisfaction and loyalty in branch locations. It is really more about driving a collaborative culture than anything else. This culture is created by initiatives that promote participation in these tools, which are easier to implement and use than most executives believe. A Wiki can be a self-regulated setup for any operating system and can become one of the most helpful and information-rich resources in a company, even if the department does not support that particular operation system or have anything to do with the Wiki itself.

Save to Invest

Organizations are doing many things to cut costs to free up money to invest in the future through the use of collaborative technologies such as telepresence, unified communications, and IP-connected real estate. Telepresence has vastly simplified the way virtual collaboration takes place, currently offering the most realistic meeting experience and an alternative to traveling for face-to-face meetings with customers, suppliers, and staff as well as other essential partners. Most important, it yields significant reductions in travel costs, improved business productivity, and elimination of travel-induced stress. Consolidation and centralization of communications infrastructure and resources resulting from moving away from legacy communication systems to IP-based unified communications and management systems can result in drastic reductions in PBX lease costs, maintenance costs, and management costs.

Mobility costs can be controlled by routing mobile long-distance calls over the Enterprise IP network. A unified communications solution allows users to place a call while they are on the public mobile network, but the call is originated and carried from the customer's communications manager cluster. In other words, now your customers can leverage a unified communications manager to manage mobile calls, offering the same cost-reduction benefits that Voice over IP (VoIP) did for land-line long-distance calls. Real estate, energy, and utility expenses can be cut by enabling remote and connected workforce through IP-connected real estate solutions. These collaborative technology solutions provide the ability to conduct in-person meetings without traveling, reduce sales cycles, significantly increase global travel savings, and increase productivity. Even better, many of these technologies can pay for themselves within a year because of their significant cost savings. Most important, these savings free up hard-earned company revenue to invest elsewhere as needed.

The opportunity is there to drive tremendous growth and productivity with new collaborations tools and composite applications, but it presents great challenges for IT. Collaboration is challenging, not only from an IT perspective but also from a political and a security perspective. It takes a holistic approach—not just throwing technology at the problem but rather an optimized blend of people, process, and technology. To fill this need, the service-oriented architecture was developed and SOA-based infrastructures were created to enable people to collaborate more effectively.

The service-oriented infrastructure is the foundation of an overall service-oriented architecture. An important part in this is the human interface and the impact of new technologies that arrived with Web 2.0. The benefits include the way IT systems are presented to the user. Service-oriented architectures have become an intermediate step in the evolution to cloud computing.

3.5   Service-Oriented Architectures as a Step Toward Cloud Computing

An SOA involves policies, principles, and a framework that illustrate how network services can be leveraged by enterprise applications to achieve desired business outcomes. These outcomes include enabling the business capabilities to be provided and consumed as a set of services. SOA is thus an architectural style that encourages the creation of coupled business services. The "services" in SOA are business services. For example, updating a customer's service-level agreement is a business service, updating a record in a database is not. A service is a unit of work done by a service provider to achieve desired end results for a service consumer.

An SOA solution consists of a linked set of business services that realize an end-to-end business process. At a high level, SOA can be viewed as enabling improved management control, visibility, and metrics for business processes, allowing business process integration with a holistic view of business processes, creating a new capability to create composite solutions, exposing granular business activities as services, and allowing reuse of existing application assets. Differentiating between SOA and cloud computing can be confusing because they overlap in some areas but are fundamentally different. SOA delivers web services from applications to other programs, whereas the cloud is about delivering software services to end users and running code. Thus the cloud-versus-SOA debate is like comparing apples and oranges.[7]

A couple of areas that SOA has brought to the table have been mostly ignored in the rapid evolution to cloud computing. The first is governance. Although governance is not always implemented well in with SOA, it is a fundamental part of the architecture and has been generally ignored in cloud computing. The control and implementation of policies is a business imperative that must be met before there is general adoption of cloud computing by the enterprise. SOA is derived from an architecture and a methodology. Since cloud computing is typically driven from the view of business resources that are needed, there is a tendency to ignore the architecture. The second area that SOA brings to cloud computing is an end-to-end architectural approach.

Cloud service providers such as Amazon, TheWebService, Force.com, and others have evolved from the typically poorly designed SOA service models and have done a pretty good job in architecting and delivering their services. Another evolutionary step that cloud computing has taken from the SOA model is to architect and design services into the cloud so that it can expand and be accessed as needed. Expanding services in an SOA is typically a difficult and expensive process.

---

7.   Rich Seeley, "Is Microsoft Dissing SOA Just to PUSH Azure Cloud Computing?," http://searchsoa.techtarget.com/news/article/0,289142,sid26_gci1337378,00.html, 31 Oct 2008, retrieved 9 Feb 09.

SOA has evolved into a crucial element of cloud computing as an approach to enable the sharing of IT infrastructures in which large pools of computer systems are linked together to provide IT services. Virtual resources and computing assets are accessed through the cloud, including not only externally hosted services but also those provided globally by companies. This provides the basis for the next generation of enterprise data centers which, like the Internet, will provide extreme scalability and fast access to networked users. This is why cloud computing can be used across an entire range of activities—a big advantage over grid computing, which distributes IT only for a specific task.

Placing information, services, and processes outside the enterprise without a clear strategy is not productive. A process, architecture, and methodology using SOA and for leveraging cloud computing is used. As part of the enterprise architecture, SOA provides the framework for using cloud computing resources. In this context, SOA provides the evolutionary step to cloud computing by creating the necessary interfaces from the IT infrastructure to the cloud outside the enterprise. Cloud computing essentially becomes an extension of SOA. Services and processes may be run inside or outside the enterprise, as required by the business. By connecting the enterprise to a web platform or cloud, businesses can take advantage of Internet-delivered resources that provide access to prebuilt processes, services, and platforms delivered as a service, when and where needed, to reduce overhead costs. We have discussed SOA as an evolutionary step because you don't move to cloud computing from SOA or replace SOA with cloud computing but rather use SOA to enable cloud computing or as a transit point to cloud computing. SOA as an enterprise architecture is the intermediate step toward cloud computing.

3.6   Basic Approach to a Data Center-Based SOA

A service-oriented architecture is essentially a collection of services. A service is, in essence, a function that is well defined, self-contained, and does not depend on the context or state of other services. Services most often reflect logical business activities. Some means of connecting services to each other is needed, so services communicate with each other, have an interface, and are message-oriented. The communication between services may involve simple data passing or may require two or more services coordinating an activity. The services generally communicate using standard protocols, which allows for broad interoperability. SOA encompasses legacy systems and processes, so the effectiveness of existing investments is preserved. New services can be added or created without affecting existing services.

Service-oriented architectures are not new. The first service-oriented architectures are usually considered to be the Distributed Component Object Model (DCOM) or Object Request Brokers (ORBs), which were based on the Common Object Requesting Broker Architecture (CORBA) specification. The introduction of SOA provides a platform for technology and business units to meet business requirements of the modern enterprise. With SOA, your organization can use existing application systems to a greater extent and may respond faster to change requests. These benefits are attributed to several critical elements of SOA:

1.   Free-standing, independent components
2.   Combined by loose coupling
3.   Message (XML)-based instead of API-based
4.   Physical location, etc., not important

3.6.1   Planning for Capacity

It is important to create a capacity plan for an SOA architecture. To accomplish this, it is necessary to set up an initial infrastructure and establish a baseline of capacity. Just setting up the initial infrastructure can be a challenge. That should be based on known capacity requirements and vendor recommendations for software and hardware. Once the infrastructure is set up, it is necessary to establish a set of processing patterns. These patterns will be used to test capacity and should include a mix of simple, medium, and complex patterns. They need to cover typical SOA designs and should exercise all the components within the SOA infrastructure.

3.6.2   Planning for Availability

Availability planning includes performing a business impact analysis (BIA) and developing and implementing a written availability plan. The goal is to ensure that system administrators adequately understand the criticality of a system and implement appropriate safeguards to protect it. This requires proper planning and analysis at each stage of the systems development life cycle (SDLC). A BIA is the first step in the availability planning process. A BIA provides the necessary information for a administrator to fully understand and protect systems. This process should fully characterize system requirements, processes, and interdependencies that will determine the availability requirements and priorities. Once this is done, a written availability plan is created. It should define the overall availability objectives and establish the organizational framework and responsibilities for personnel. Management should be included in the process of developing availability structure, objectives, roles, and responsibilities to support the development of a successful plan.

3.6.3 Planning for SOA Security

The foundations of SOA security are well known and are already widely used in the IT industry. SOA practitioners have come to realize they also must understand these foundations in order to provide adequate security for the systems being developed. The foundations include public key infrastructure (PKI), the common security authentication method Kerberos, XML (Extensible Markup Language) encryption, and XML digital signatures. Three main areas of concern are widely accepted as part of the SOA security arena. First, message-level security provides the ability to ensure that security requirements are met in an SOA environment, where transport-level security is inadequate because transactions are no longer point-to-point in SOA. Second, Security-as-a-Service provides the ability to implement security requirements for services. Third, declarative and policy-based security provides the ability to implement security requirements that are transparent to security administrators and can be used to quickly implement emerging new security requirements for services that implement new business functionalities.

Message-Level Security

The OASIS set of WS-Security standards addresses message-level security concerns. These standards are supported by key vendors including IBM, Microsoft, and Oracle. The standards provide a model describing how to manage and authenticate message exchanges between parties (including security context exchange) as well as establishing and deriving session keys. The standards recommend a Web service endpoint policy describing the capabilities and constraints of the security and other business policies on intermediaries and endpoints including required security tokens, supported encryption algorithms, and privacy rules. Furthermore, a federated trust model describing how to manage and broker the trust relationships in a heterogeneous federated environment, including support for federated identities, is described. The standards include a Web service trust model that describes a framework for trust models that enables Web services to operate securely. There is also an authorization model describing how to manage authorization data and authorization policies. Finally, the standards include a Web service privacy model describing how to enable Web services and requesters to state subject privacy preferences and organizational privacy practice statements.

Security-as-a-Service

Security-as-a-Service can be accomplished by collecting an inventory of service security requirements throughout the enterprise architecture (EA) and specifying the set of discrete security services that will be needed for the enterprise. Next, the organization must complete the process of designing and implementing these security services as services themselves. Often, a toolkit approach can help specify the set of typical security services that may be used to provide most of the requirements and accelerate the establishment of Security-as-a-Service in an organization.

Declarative and Policy-Based Security

Implementation of declarative and policy-based security requires tools and techniques for use at the enterprise management level and at the service level. These tools and techniques should provide transparency for security administrators, policy enforcement, and policy monitoring. When policy violations are detected, alerts should be issued. Traceability of such violations, both for data and users, should be included as a critical element.

3.7 The Role of Open Source Software in Data Centers

The Open Source Initiative uses the Open Source Definition to determine whether a software license can truly be considered open source. The definition is based on the Debian Free Software Guidelines,[8] written and adapted primarily by Bruce Perens.[9] Under Perens's definition, the term *open source* broadly describes a general type of software license that makes source code available to the public without significant copyright restrictions. The principles defined say nothing about trademark or patent use and require no cooperation to ensure that any common audit or release regime applies to

---

8. Bruce Perens, "Debian's 'Social Contract' with the Free Software Community," http://lists.debian.org/debian-announce/debian-announce-1997/msg00017.html, retrieved 08 Feb 2009.

9. Bruce Perens, "The Open Source Definition," http://opensource.org/docs/osd, 1999, retrieved 08 Feb 2009.

any derived works. It is considered as an explicit "feature" of open source that it may put no restrictions on the use or distribution by any organization or user. It forbids this, in principle, to guarantee continued access to derived works even by the major original contributors.

Over the past decade, open source software has come of age. There has always been a demand for software that is free, reliable, and available to anyone for modification to suit individual needs. Open source distributions such as Red Hat, OpenSuSE, and BSD, coupled with open source applications such as Apache, MySQL, and scores of others have long been used to power databases, web, email, and file servers. However, something that has as much impact as the applications used in a data center has caused many implementors to hesitate to adopt open source software—until now. Recently, more than just a few users have become strong advocates that open source can and does work in the data center environment. In an online article, Robert Wiseman, chief technology officer at Sabre Holdings (a travel marketing and distribution technology company in Southlake, Texas, that uses open source software on over 5,000 servers) stated: .

> It's true that with open-source products, users generally forfeit the security of professional support teams to help resolve their problems quickly. But in our environment, we almost always purchase support for our open-source products from high-quality vendors. This, of course, reduces some of the cost advantages of using open source, but the advantages are big enough that there's still plenty left over, and the security we get from a service contract lets us sleep better at night.[10]

Sabre Holdings uses an enterprise service bus for message transformation, routing, and other tasks. An enterprise service bus (ESB) refers to a software architecture construct that is typically implemented by technologies seen as a type of middleware infrastructure. ESBs are usually based on recognized standards and provide fundamental services for complex architectures via an event-driven and standards-based messaging engine (called the bus since it transforms and transports the messages across the architecture).

---

10.   Julie Sartain, "Open-Source Software in the Data Center—There Is a Place for It, but It Won't Do Everything," http://www.computerworld.com/action/article.do?command=viewArticleBasic&articleId=9057879 (Computerworld, 25 Jan 2008), retrieved 08 Feb 2009.

One example of open source ESB, Apache Synapse, is an easy-to-use and lightweight ESB that offers a wide range of management, routing, and transformation capabilities. With support for HTTP, SOAP, SMTP, JMS, FTP, and file system transports, it is considered quite versatile and can be applied in a wide variety of environments. It supports standards such as WS-Addressing, Web Services Security (WSS), Web Services Reliable Messaging (WSRM), efficient binary attachments (MTOM/XOP), as well as key transformation standards such as XSLT, XPath, and XQuery. Synapse supports a number of useful functions out of the box, without programming, but it also can be extended using popular programming languages such as Java, JavaScript, Ruby, and Groovy.

Another example is a project called Open ESB, which implements an enterprise service bus runtime with sample service engines and binding components. Open ESB allows easy integration of enterprise applications and web services as loosely coupled composite applications. This allows an enterprise to seamlessly compose and recompose composite applications, realizing the benefits of a true service-oriented architecture.

Today, most users of open source agree that these products have now reached a level of maturity equal to and, in some cases, better than their commercial counterparts. Open source products have forced commercial vendors to compete on price and quality of service. Because open source code is open and transparent, developers can troubleshoot problems and learn how other developers have addressed issues. Users gain the freedom to use these products across their organizations, all over the world, without worrying about tracking client licenses.

3.8   Where Open Source Software Is Used

Perhaps because of the great flexibility of open source, which facilitates the efforts of large commercial users, cloud implementors, and vendors most of all, the successful applications of open source have evolved from within consortia. These consortia employ other means, such as trademarks, to control releases, documentation, etc., and they require specific performance guarantees from their members to assure reintegration of improvements. Accordingly, consortia do not want or need potentially conflicting clauses in their licenses. Perens's open source definition has led to a proliferation of other types of licenses that claim to be open source but would not satisfy the *share alike* provision that free software and Open Content Licenses require.

An alternative, commonly used license, the Creative Commons License, requires commercial users to acquire a separate license when the product is used for profit. This contradicts open source principles, because it discriminates against a type of use or user. However, the requirement imposed by free software to reliably redistribute derived works does not violate these principles. Accordingly, free software and consortia licenses are a variant of open source, while an Open Content License is not.

Now that we understand exactly what open source is, lets look at how some open source software is used in cloud computing.

3.8.1 Web Presence

Web presence refers to the appearance of an entity on the World Wide Web. It is said that a company has web presence if it is accessible on the WWW. A common measure of web presence tends to be the number of pages or sites an entity owns. This web presence may include web sites, social network profiles, and search engine ranking, traffic, popularity, and links. Open source software commonly used to assist in web presence includes Apache, the Zend Framework, and Jetty.

Apache

The Apache project began in 1995 as a collaborative effort between a group of webmasters who wanted to build a robust and commercial-grade implementation of the HTTP protocol and make it available to everyone free of charge. Originally conceived as a series of patches to the original NCSA httpd daemon, the project ultimately took on a life of its own, with the NCSA daemon undergoing several redesigns in order to make it more extensible and modular. The term Apache Server is derived from a play on the words A PAtCHy sErver—paying homage to Apache's birth as a continual series of patches applied to the existing Linux-based daemon httpd. Today, the Apache product is powerful enough to meet the needs of nearly any enterprise, yet it is simple enough to configure that most administrators can get it up and running in a few minutes.

To illustrate the powerful effect that open source software is having on cloud architectures today, the January 2009 survey conducted by Netcraft evaluated responses from 185,497,213 sites, reflecting an uncharacteristic monthly loss of 1.23 million sites.[11] Analysis showed that Apache's market share grew by more than 1 percentage point during the month of January

---

11.   http://news.netcraft.com/archives/web_server_survey.html, retrieved 08 Feb 2009.

2009, extending its lead over second-ranked commercial product Microsoft IIS (which has fallen to less than a third of the market share at 32.91%). During this time, Apache gained 1.27 million sites and enjoyed a 52.26% market share. The Microsoft IIS product showed the largest loss for this period, after more than 2 million blogging sites running Microsoft-IIS expired from the survey. This is very impressive for a free, open source product that began life as a series of patches to a little-bitty Linux daemon.

Apache is truly a cloud-based and cloud-owned tool. Today, the Apache HTTP Server Project continues to be a collaborative software development effort boasting a commercial-grade, full-featured, freely available (with source code) implementation of an HTTP (web) server. The project is jointly managed by a group of volunteers located around the world, using the Internet and the web to communicate, plan, and develop the server and its related documentation.

Jetty

Jetty is also an open source, standards-based, full-featured web server implemented entirely in Java.[12] Java implementation means that it is capable across platforms—meaning it can run on pretty much any platform that can run Java. Jetty is released under the Apache 2.0 licence and is therefore free for commercial use and distribution. It was created in 1995 and since then has benefitted from input from a vast user community and consistent development by a strong core of open source developers. Jetty aims to be as unobtrusive as possible. Built with such a strong focus on simplicity, the Jetty mantra is "simplicity not complexity." Once it is installed, Jetty configuration is accomplished by either an API or XML configuration file. Default configuration files provided with the open source download make Jetty usable right out of the box. Jetty is also highly scalable. For example, in asynchronous Web 2.0 applications using AJAX (Asynchronous JavaScript and XML), connections to the server can stay open longer than when serving up static pages. This can cause thread and memory requirements to escalate drastically. Cloud infrastructure must be able to cope with these types of load situations gracefully or risk catastrophes such as the possibility of a slow database connection bringing down an entire site because of a lack of available resources (threads). Jetty ensures performance degrades gracefully under stress, providing a higher

---

12.   http://www.mortbay.org/jetty, retrieved 08 Feb 2009.

quality of service. Leveraging existing web specifications, Jetty can handle large user loads and long-lived sessions easily.

Zend Framework

The Zend Framework (ZF) was conceived in early 2005 and was publicly announced at the first Zend Conference.[13] ZF is an open source, object-oriented web application framework for the hyptertext preprocessor language PHP. At the time of its introduction, no other framework was widely available to the PHP community to fill the need for an industrial-strength open source web development toolset. Wanting more than a simple toolset, the designers of ZF sought to combine ease of use and rapid application development features with the simplicity and pragmatic approach to web development that is highly valued in the PHP community.

ZF is often called a component library because it has many components that can be used more or less independently. However, ZF provides an advanced Model-View-Controller (MVC) that can be used to establish basic structure for ZF applications. All components are object-oriented using PHP 5 and support "use at will," in that using these components entails only minimal interdependencies. ZF provides support for many of the major commercial and open source database systems, including MySQL, Oracle, IBM DB2, Microsoft SQL Server, PostgreSQL, SQLite, and Informix Dynamic Server. ZF also provides email composition and delivery features, and supports retrieval of email via mbox, Maildir, POP3, and IMAP4. It has a flexible caching subsystem with support for many types of back-end architectures (e.g., memory or file systems).

The ZF MVC implementation has become a *de facto* standard in the design of modern web applications because it leverages the fact that most web application code falls into one of three categories: presentation, business logic, or data access. MVC models this separation of categories quite well. This allows presentation code to be consolidated in one part of an application, business logic in another part of the application, and data access code in yet another. Many developers have found this well-defined separation indispensable for maintaining their code.

Let's take a quick look at what MVC really entails, starting with the Model. This is the part of a ZF application that defines basic functionality

---

13.   Oonagh Morgan, "Zend Announces Industry-Wide PHP Collaboration Project at Its Inaugural PHP Conference," Zend Technologies, http://www.zend.com//news/zendpr.php?ozid=109, 19 Oct 2005, retrieved 8 Feb 2009.

using a set of abstractions. Data access routines and some business logic can also be defined in the Model. The View defines exactly what is presented to the user. The Controller binds the whole thing together. Usually, controllers pass data to each view, specifying how it should be rendered. Views often are used to collect data from the user. This is where standardized HTML markup can be used in MVC applications. They manipulate models, decide which view to display based on user input and other factors, then pass along the data to each view as needed.

Sometimes, there is a need to hand off control to another controller entirely. In cloud computing, having a standardized architecture that facilitates web presence is highly desirable and explains the increased use seen with open source in data centers. Now let's move from web presence influences to the data tier[14] itself.

3.8.2   Database Tier

Whether an application resides on a desktop or is virtualized in a cloud somewhere, when data is used or stored, it often requires the use of a database. A database is a structured collection of records or data that is stored in a computer system. A database relies on software known as a database management system (DBMS) to organize, store, and retrieve data. Database management systems are categorized according to the database model that they support. The model chosen often determines the type of (often structured) query language that is used to access the database. The structure is achieved by organizing the data according to a database model. The model in most common use today is the relational database model. Other models, such as the hierarchical model and the network model, use a more explicit representation of relationships, but they are not commonly used in cloud environments.

A great deal of the internal engineering of a DBMS is done independent of the data model it supports. While data storage, access, and retrieval are important, they are most often defined by standards and implemented accordingly. A DBMS implementation is often less concerned with how the data is accessed and retrieved and more concerned with managing performance, concurrency, integrity, and recovery from hardware failures. In these areas, there are large differences between almost all products. It is these differences that separate them from one another.

---

14.   In computing usage, the word tier is synonymous with layer. As such, a tier implies something that sits on top of or between something else.

All of the products we will discuss in this section are relational database management systems (RDBMS) and implement the features of the relational model outlined above.

MySQL

MySQL is *the* preferred open source database based on usage. According to the MySQL web site,[15] it has become the world's most popular open source database. It is used by individual developers as well as by many of the world's largest companies, including Yahoo!, Alcatel-Lucent, Google, Nokia, YouTube, and Zappos.com. MySQL runs on more than 20 platforms, including Linux, Windows, OS/X, HP-UX, AIX, and Netware. Users can freely download and deploy MySQL from the official web site without cost. This product is in use in millions of small to medium-scale applications. MySQL is the preferred database in LAMP architecture (Linux/Apache/MySQL/PHP-Python-Perl). This regal position affords MySQL access to over two-thirds of the world's web database servers. MySQL is deployed with nearly every Linux distribution, and is easily installed on Windows, Mac, and Solaris platforms for both server and client use. In the cloud, MySQL is the king of the database server packages because it is proven, reliable, scalable, and free.

However, MySQL is not without some minor problems. The rapid pace of development has left some of its users faced with major upgrade tasks. Until the release of version 5.1, MySQL had to take a back seat to commercial enterprise-grade database products such as Oracle and IBM's DB2 because of a lack of clustering, partitioning, and replication features. With the 5.1 release, those hurdles were overcome. Now, spatial data, Web Services, and native XML support are what has to be overcome.

PostgreSQL

PostgreSQL is another powerful open source DBMS. According to the official web site,[16] it has more than 15 years of active development and a proven architecture that has earned it a strong reputation for reliability, data integrity, and correctness. It runs on all major operating systems and prides itself in standards compliance. PostgreSQL has a fully relational system catalog which itself supports multiple schemas per database.

---

15.   http://www.mysql.com/why-mysql, retrieved 08 Feb 2009.
16.   http://www.postgresql.org, retrieved 08 Feb 2009.

PostgreSQL is highly scalable, both in the magnitude of data it can manage and in the number of concurrent users it can accommodate. There are active PostgreSQL systems in production environments that manage in excess of 4 TB of data. For larger cloud implementations, PostgreSQL may be the DBMS of choice. Another important point to consider for any cloud implementation of a database tier is the security of the database. Accordingly, PostgreSQL is considered by many to be the most secure out-of-the-box configuration available for a database. PostgreSQL boasts many sophisticated features and is another good choice for cloud computing applications.

Data is used in many applications in the cloud. What specific applications—particularly open source applications—use this data? Let's find out.

3.8.3   Application Tier

A multitier architecture (or *n*-tier architecture) is a client-server architecture in which the presentation, application processing, and data management are logically separate processes. Most often, multitier architecture refers to a three-tier architecture—that is, presentation, application, and data tiers. The presentation tier is the topmost level of the application. The presentation tier displays information to the user, often via a web browser or windowed form. It communicates with other tiers by transferring input or data results to the other tiers in the architecture. The application tier is sometimes referred to as the business logic tier. It controls an application's functionality by performing detailed processing to satisfy specific requirements. Finally, the data tier consists of a database server or servers which are used to store and retrieve data. This tier keeps all data independent from the application or business logic tier and the presentation tier. Giving data its own tier greatly improves scalability and performance and allows applications to share data from a centralized repository.

Zope

In cloud computing, most back-end infrastructures rely an *n*-tier architecture, as shown in Figure 3.1. Zope is an open source application server for building content management systems, intranets, portals, and custom applications.

The Zope community consists of hundreds of companies and thousands of developers all over the world, working on building the platform itself and the resulting Zope applications. Zope can help developers quickly create dynamic web applications such as portal and intranet sites. Zope

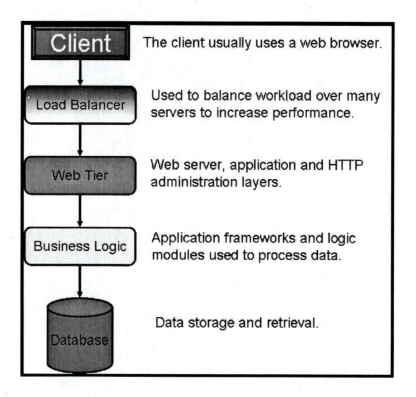

Client	The client usually uses a web browser.
Load Balancer	Used to balance workload over many servers to increase performance.
Web Tier	Web server, application and HTTP administration layers.
Business Logic	Application frameworks and logic modules used to process data.
Database	Data storage and retrieval.

Figure 3.1   The n-tier architecture used in cloud environments.

comes with everything you need, including support for membership, search, and news. Zope provides top-notch access to databases and other legacy data. Zope is written in Python, a highly productive, object-oriented scripting language.

Zope features a transactional object database which can store not only content and custom data, but also dynamic HTML templates, scripts, a search engine, and relational database connections and code. It features a strong through-the-web development model, allowing you to update your web site from anywhere in the world. To allow for this particular feature, Zope integrates a tightly integrated security model. Built around the concept of *safe delegation of control,* Zope's security architecture also allows you to turn control over parts of a web site to other organizations or individuals.

The transactional model applies not only to Zope's object database, but, through connectors, to many other relational databases as well. This helps to ensure strong data integrity. This transaction model ensures that all data is successfully stored in connected data stores by the time a response is returned to a web browser. According to the Zope web site,[17] numerous products (plug-in Zope components) are available for download to extend the basic set of site building tools. These products include new content objects; relational database and other external data source connectors; advanced content management tools; and full applications for e-commerce, content and document management, or bug and issue tracking. Zope includes its own HTTP, FTP, WebDAV, and XML-RPC serving capabilities, but it can also be used with Apache or other web servers. Zope users include major business entities such as Viacom, SGI, AARP, Verizon Wireless, Red Hat, NASA, and the U.S. Navy.

Zope Content Management Framework

On top of what Zope offers out of the box, there are a variety useful applications available for those who need something right away. The Content Management Framework (CMF) adds many tools and services to Zope to allow community- or organization-based content management. It comes with a workflow system and a powerful customization framework. The CMF Workflow system leverages Zope's built-in security architecture. A major feature of the CMF Workflow system is the ability for edit permissions to be taken away from an author once he or she has submitted a document for review and publishing. This ensures that what the reviewer sees won't change during or after review without the author intentionally taking control of the document.

Plone

Plone is built to leverage the CMF platform and is basically a very well designed interface that sits on top of the CMF. You can download Plone, run the installer, and in short order have a community or organizational web site (i.e., a *collab-net*) with content such as news, documentation, and events, which are supplied by members of the collab-net. The collab-net can be comprised of almost any grouping that shares common goals or interests. Because Plone is built on the CMF, it delivers the same powerful set of tools mentioned above while adding helpful content entry forms and validation.

AJAX

AJAX (Asynchronous JavaScript and XML) is a collection of interrelated standards-based web development techniques that are used to create highly

---

17.   http://www.zope.org/WhatIsZope, retrieved 08 Feb 2009.

interactive (rich) Internet applications. The use of AJAX has led to an increase in interactive animation on web pages. AJAX web applications can retrieve data from the server asynchronously,[18] without interfering with the display or behavior of the current page. In many cases, related pages on a web site consist of much content that is common between them. Using traditional methods, that content must be reloaded with every request. With AJAX, however, a web application can request only the content that needs to be updated, thus drastically reducing bandwidth usage and load time. AJAX can reduce connections to the server, since scripts and style sheets only have to be requested once. Users may perceive the application to be faster or more responsive, even if the application has not changed on the server side.

In current use, JavaScript and XML are no longer required and the requests don't actually need to be asynchronous. The acronym AJAX has thus changed to Ajax, which does not represent use of these specific technologies. Microsoft, of course, has its version of AJAX, called ASP.NET AJAX. This is also a free framework for quickly creating efficient and interactive web applications that work across all popular browsers. ASP.NET AJAX is built into ASP.NET 3.5.

Apache Struts

Apache Struts is another open source framework for creating Java web applications. The Apache Struts Project is the open source community that creates and maintains the Apache Struts framework. The project is called "Struts" because the framework is meant to furnish the invisible underpinnings that support professional application development. Struts provides the glue that joins the various elements of the standard Java platform into a coherent whole. The goal is to leverage existing standards by producing the missing pieces to create enterprise-grade applications that are easy to maintain over time.

The Apache Struts Project offers two major versions of the Struts framework. Struts 1 is recognized as the most popular web application framework for Java. The 1.x framework is mature, well documented, and widely supported. Struts 1 is the best choice for teams that value proven solutions to common problems. Struts 2 was originally known as WebWork

---

18.   In computer programming, an asynchronous operation is a process capable of operating independently of other processes. Conversely, a synchronous operation means that the process runs only as a result of some other process being completed or handing off the operation.

2. After working independently for several years, the WebWork and Struts communities joined forces to create Struts 2. The 2.x framework is the best choice for teams that value elegant solutions to difficult problems.

Web applications differ from conventional web sites in that web applications can create a dynamic response. Many web sites deliver only static pages. A web application can interact with databases and business logic engines to customize a response. Web applications based on JavaServer Pages sometimes commingle database code, page design code, and control flow code. In practice, unless these concerns are separated, larger applications may become difficult to maintain. One way to separate concerns in a software application is to use a Model-View-Controller architecture, as described previously. The Struts framework is designed to help developers create web applications that utilize a MVC architecture. The Struts framework provides three key components:

1. A request handler that is mapped to a standard URI.[19]

2. A response handler that transfers control to another resource to complete the response.

3. A tag library that helps developers create interactive form-based applications with server pages.

The Struts framework's architecture and tags are compliant with most common applicable standards. Struts works well with conventional REST[20] applications and with newer technologies such as SOAP (Simple Object Access Protocol) and AJAX.

3.8.4   Systems and Network Management Tier

Open source software has developed strong roots in the cloud community. Much of the cloud operates in a mission-critical space, so there is often great trepidation about whether investment in a commercial application may be a better option. However, many developers have come to realize that the "sweet spot" for open source is actually that mission-critical space. Given the high reliability and maturity of many of the better-known open

---

19.   A Uniform Resource Identifier (URI) is a string of characters used to identify or name a resource on the Internet.

20.   REpresentational State Transfer (REST) is a style of software architecture for distributed hypermedia systems such as the World Wide Web.

source solutions available, there are many reasons why implementers are starting to give open source more than a passing glance when evaluating options. Many of the commercial offerings available offer open source solutions and make their money providing enhancements to the open source, service and support, and other types of services that enhance customer adoption of their product.

Open source is not with its detractors, however. Many experts still advise caution when it comes to adopting open source solutions. They argue that users of open source software can potentially risk encountering security issues because the software internals are so widely known. Adoptors are encouraged to research into which industrial-strength software is available for their particular mission-critical environment and to compare potential open source candidates. For mission-critical environments, especially within the context of cloud computing, we see several major categories:

1. Administrative and management applications
2. Performance applications
3. Monitoring and security applications
4. Virtualization applications

In the next few paragraphs, we will discuss the salient features of each of these categories and provide examples of the types of open source and (sometimes) commercial applications used today. This will provide a good starting point for understanding what implementation of cloud infrastructure entails from the perspective of the engineering team that is tasked with putting a solution architecture together and making it work for a business.

Performance Monitoring and Management Applications

Performance monitoring is critical for businesses operating mission-critical or data-intensive IT infrastructure that provides access to users on-site, from remote office locations, and from mobile devices. Many factors can influence the performance of a network, such as the number of users accessing it, the bandwidth capacity, use of coding platforms and protocols, and attacks on its vulnerabilities. Performance monitoring tools are used by organizations to ensure that their networks and the applications delivered over them operate at the highest levels of performance achievable. Monitoring performance is a proactive approach to mitigating risk and limiting potential damage.

The purpose of administrative and management applications is to facilitate systems personnel in administering large numbers of hosts and services running simultaneously. The monitoring software watches over hosts and services, alerting administrators when conditions are detected operating outside defined parameters. Common tasks performed by this type of software include monitoring network services (SMTP, POP3, HTTP, NNTP, PING, etc.) and host resources (processor load, disk usage, etc.). Many packages support the use of plug-ins that allow users to easily develop their own service checks or add functionality from third-party developers (this is especially common in the open source development arena). The ability to define a hierarchy of network host parent–child node relationships is desirable because it allows detection of and distinction between hosts that are down and those that are unreachable.

An important feature that nearly all such products support is contact notification whenever a service or host problem is detected and/or is resolved. Such notification usually occurs using email, a pager, or Instant Messaging (IM). When a problem occurs that needs to be resolved, some packages offer the ability to define event handlers to be executed when service or host events are detected, which then initiate proactive problem resolution. Some of the many other commonly available features of administrative and management applications include automatic log file rotation and support for implementing redundant monitoring hosts. Most packages interact with administrative staff using a web interface (which generally can be accessed remotely) for viewing current network status, notification and problem history, log file, etc.

Now that we understand the types of application used for administering cloud infrastructure, let's take a look at a couple of examples.

openQRM

openQRM is a comprehensive, flexible, open source infrastructure management solution. Supporting a highly modular architecture, openQRM focuses on automatic, rapid, appliance-based deployment. It is used for monitoring high-availability cloud computing infrastructure, especially when deployment is implementing multiple virtualization technologies. openQRM is a unified management console for IT infrastructure, and it provides a well-defined API that can be used to integrate third-party tools as plug-ins. This feature provides companies with a highly scalable system that supports any size business with high-availability requirements running multiple operating systems on various platforms.

Key features of openQRM include complete separation of the physical devices and virtual machines from the software (or virtualized server-images/instances. With openQRM, hardware is seen as a computing resource that can be easily replaced without reconfiguring hardware. Support for different virtualization technologies such as VMware, Xen, KVM, and Linux-VServer vms can be managed transparently via openQRM. It can support P2V (physical to virtual), V2P (virtual to physical), and V2V (virtual to virtual) migration efforts. Because of this flexibility, not only can servers be migrated from physical to virtual environments or virtual to physical environments easily, they can be easily migrated from virtual environment A to virtual environment B.

The commercial product Nagios is one of the best available. Nagios also performs system, network, and application monitoring. openQRM supports fully automatic Nagios configuration to monitor all systems and services using a completely automatic configuration module that maps the entire network. When administrators deploy a new bank of servers, it is quite easy to configure them for Nagios using openQRM.

High-availability is another strong feature that OpenQRM supports. It follows a many-to-one fail-over model. This means that multiple high-availability servers can operate using a single standby system. It is a simple matter to bring up a virtual machine as a standby. In case of problems, the high-availability devices will fail-over from their physical environment to a virtual environment or from one virtual to another virtual environment. To facilitate this, ready-made server images are available from the image shelf plug-in. openQRM provides out-of-the-box images for Debian, Ubuntu, CentOS, and openSuse via a web interface. OpenQRM supports integrated storage management;there is a single place for backup/restore on the storage server, so its cloning/snapshot features can be reused at any time to create "hot backups" for servers without a service interruption.

Zenoss

Zenoss (also called Zenoss Core), another open source application, is a server and network management platform based on the Zope application server. It is released under the GNU General Public License (GPL) version 2. Zenoss Core provides a web interface that allows system administrators to monitor availability, inventory/configuration, performance, and events. It is the most popular IT management project on SourceForge.Net.[21] According to the Zenoss web site,[22] Zenoss software has been downloaded over 750,000 times and deployed in over 18,000 organizations in over 175 countries. Zenoss Core provides nearly all of the same capabilities mentioned above for openQRM. Additionally, Zenoss offers the Zenoss Configuration Management Database (CMDB).

The CMDB houses a unified model of the entire IT environment and provides the basis for the Zenoss "model-driven" IT monitoring approach. The first commercial open source CMDB on the market, Zenoss CMDB features include modeling the entire environment—networks, servers, software, and applications. Zenoss provides inventory management, change tracking services, and availability monitoring, so users can have a real-time of view of availability throughout the IT infrastructure. This feature provides IT staff with information they need to quickly identify problems and potential outage locations. Zenoss has the ability to map IT elements and cross-platform information into a normalized data structure and to create logical and physical groupings that relate to business systems, locations, and responsible parties. Data is populated using a combination of processes such as auto-discovery, the web services API and XML import/export, and manual input. Zenoss also allows administrators to create configuration policies that specify required configuration items.

Performance monitoring with Zenoss provides high-speed collection, historical graphing, and real-time threshold analysis for any available metric in the IT environment. Event monitoring and management provides the ability to aggregate log and event information from various sources, including availability monitoring, performance monitoring, syslog sources, SNMP trap sources, and the Windows Event log. IT staff can create event processing rules through a graphical user interface (GUI) with automatic event classification and prioritization. Alerting and reporting is also an integral part of Zenoss solutions. Customized alert messages are sent via paging or emails. Zenoss also includes basic and advanced escalation rules to avoid alarm fatigue.[23] Finally, the browser-based Zenoss Dashboard is easily customized to provide personal views based on geographies, systems, business applications, or other options to suit the needs of the end users. A web portal ensures secure web-based access using role-based permissions.

---

21.   Sourceforge.net is the largest repository for open source software.
22.   http://www.zenoss.com/product/network-monitoring, retrieved 09 Feb 2009.
23.   Like the little boy who cried wolf, too many alarms can desensitize one to the value of an alarm.

The personalized dashboard summarizes active events by business system and severity.

Load Balancing

With the explosive growth of the Internet and its increasingly important role in our lives, the traffic on the Internet is increasing dramatically, which has been growing at over 100% annualy. The workload on servers is increasing rapidly, so servers may easily be overloaded, especially serversfor a popular web site. There are two basic solutions to the problem of overloaded servers, One is a single-server solution, i.e., upgrade the server to a higher-performance server. However, the new server may also soon be overloaded, requiring another upgrade. Further, the upgrading process is complex and the cost is high. The second solution is a multiple-server solution, i.e., build a scalable network service system on a cluster of servers. When load increases, you can simply add one or more new servers to the cluster, and commodity servers have the highest performance/cost ratio. Therefore, it is more scalable and more cost-effective to build a server cluster system for network services.

A server is limited in how many users it can serve in a given period of time, and once it hits that limit, the only options are to replace it with a newer, faster machine, or to add another server and share the load between them. A load balancer can distribute connections among two or more servers, proportionally cutting the work each has to do. Load balancing can help with almost any kind of service, including HTTP, DNS, FTP, POP/IMAP, and SMTP. According to the online web encyclopedia Wikipedia, load balancing is

> a technique to spread work between two or more computers, network links, CPUs, hard drives, or other resources, in order to get optimal resource utilization, maximize throughput, and minimize response time. Using multiple components with load balancing, instead of a single component, may increase reliability through redundancy. The balancing service is usually provided by a dedicated program or hardware device (such as a multilayer switch). It is commonly used to mediate internal communications in computer clusters, especially high-availability clusters.[24]

---

24.   http://en.wikipedia.org/wiki/Load_balancing_(computing), retrieved 10 Feb 2009.

Cloud-based server farms can achieve high scalability and availability using server load balancing. This technique makes the server farm appear to clients as a single server. Load balancing distributes service requests from clients across a bank of servers and makes those servers appear as if it is only a single powerful server responding to client requests.

In most common server load balancing architectures, an incoming request is redirected to a load balancer that is transparent to the client making the request. Based on predetermined parameters, such as availability or current load, the load balancer typically uses a round-robin scheduling algorithm to determine which server should handle the request and then forwards the request on to the selected server. To make the final determination, the load balancing algorithm, the load balancer retrieves information about the candidate server's health and current workload in order to verify its ability to respond to a request.

Load balancing solutions can be divided into software-based load balancers and hardware-based load balancers. Hardware-based load balancers are specialized boxes that include Application Specific Integrated Circuits (ASICs) customized for a specific use.[25] ASICs enable high-speed forwarding of network traffic and are often used for transport-level load balancing, because hardware-based load balancers are much faster than software solutions. Software-based load balancers run on standard operating systems and standard hardware components such as desktop PCs. We will look at an open source software solution called Linux Virtual Server next.

Linux Virtual Server Load Balancer

The Linux Virtual Server is an advanced load balancing solution that can be used to build highly scalable and highly available network services such as HTTP, POP3, SMTP, FTP, media and caching, and Voice over Internet Protocol (VoIP). There are more than a few open source load balancing applications available today, but the Linux Virtual Server (LVS) continues to be one of the most popular. LVS is a simple, powerful product used for load balancing and fail-over. LVS behavior is controlled at runtime by issuing commands using a Command Line Interface (CLI). The syntax used for issuing these commands is very straightforward and simple. The LVS cluster[26] system is also known as a load balancing server cluster. It is built over a cluster of physical servers with the load balancer running on top of the

25.   Gregor Roth, "Server Load Balancing Architectures, Part 1: Transport-Level Load Balancing: High Scalability and Availability for Server Farms," JavaWorld.com, 21 Oct 2008, retrieved 10 Feb 2009.

Linux operating system. The architecture of the server cluster is fully transparent to end users, and they interact with it as if they were using a single high-performance virtual server.

The physical servers and the load balancers may be interconnected by either a -speed local-area network (LAN) or by a geographically dispersed wide-area network (WAN). The load balancers dispatch requests to the different servers and make parallel services of the cluster appear as a virtual service using a single IP address. Scalability of the system is achieved by transparently adding or removing servers (often referred to as nodes) in the cluster. High availability is provided by detecting node or daemon failures and reconfiguring the system dynamically to prevent performance degradation.

The LVS employs a common three-tier architecture that consists of the load balancer, which acts as a front end to the cluster and balances (or distributes) requests from clients across a set of servers (sometimes called a bank) so that the client's perception is that all the services come from a single IP address. The second tier, the server cluster, is a group of servers running network services, such as HTTP, POP3, SMTP, FTP, or DNS. The third tier is shared storage, which provides a shared storage space for the servers so it is easy for them to use/reuse the same contents and provide the same services for each client request.

The load balancer itself is the primary entry point of server cluster systems. It can run Internet Protocol Virtual Server (IPVS), which implements transport-layer load balancing inside the Linux kernel. In network parlance, this is known as Layer-4 switching. IPVS running on a host can direct requests for Transmission Control Protocol (TCP) and User Datagram Protocol (UDP)[27] services to the physical servers, and this redirect makes it appear as if it were a virtual service running on a single IP address. When IPVS is used, all servers must provide the same services and content. The load balancer forwards a new client request to a server based on a scheduling algorithm and the current workload for each server. Regardless of which server is selected, the client should always see the same result. The number of nodes active in a server cluster can be changed according to the load that system encounters. When all servers are operating at capacity, more servers can be added to handle a larger workload. For most Internet services,

---

26.   According to the online encyclopedia Wikipedia, "A computer cluster is a group of linked computers, working together closely so that in many respects they form a single computer." http://en.wikipedia.org/wiki/Computer_cluster, retrieved 10 Feb 2009.

27.   TCP and UDP are common transport protocols defined in Request for Comment RFC 1122.

requests are not usually interrelated and can be run in parallel on multiple servers. As the number of nodes active in a server cluster increases, the performance of the entire cluster scales linearly.

Physically, the shared storage tier can be a database system, a network file system, or a distributed file system, or any combination thereof. The data that cluster nodes must update dynamically should be stored in database systems because whenever a node performs a read or write operation in a database system, the database system can guarantee the integrity and consistency of concurrent data access. Static data is stored using a network file system so data can be shared by all cluster nodes. Because scalability using a single network file system is limited, it can only support data operations from a limited number of nodes (typically four to eight).

For large-scale cluster systems, distributed file systems[28] can be used for shared storage and scaled according to system requirements. The load balancer, server cluster, and shared storage are usually interconnected by high-speed networks, such as Gigabit Ethernet, so the network will not become a bottleneck. Common methods used to construct the clusters are Domain Name System (DNS)-based load balancing and dispatcher-based load balancing. We will take a look at both methods in the following sections.

DNS-Based Load Balancing Clusters

DNS load balancing is probably the simplest method for building a network service cluster.[29] The Domain Name System is a hierarchical naming system for computers, services, or any resource used on the Internet. DNS associates various information with domain names assigned to such Internet participants. DNS translates Internet domain names (which are meaningful to humans) into the binary identifiers associated with networking equipment in order to locate and address Internet devices globally. This process is known as name resolution and is used to distribute requests to different IP addresses of cluster servers.

When a DNS request comes to the DNS server, it provides an available IP address based on scheduling strategies such as are used in a round-robin scheduler. Subsequent requests from clients using the same local caching name server are sent to the same server if they occur within the specified time-to-live (TTL) parameter set for name resolving. The original idea of

---

28.   A Distributed File System (DFS) provides a means for administrators to create logical views of directories and files that can be used in a cluster regardless of where those files physically reside on the network.

29.   http://www.linuxvirtualserver.org/why.html, retrieved 10 Feb 2009.

TTL was that it would specify a time span in seconds that, when expired, would cause the packet to be discarded. Because every router along the path from one device to another is required to subtract at least one count from the TTL field, the count is usually used to mean the number of router hops the packet is allowed to take before it must be discarded. Each router that receives a packet subtracts one from the current count in the TTL field. When the count reaches zero, the router detecting it will discard the packet and send an Internet Control Message Protocol (ICMP) message back to the originating host, letting it know that the packet was discarded.

The caching nature of clients in a hierarchical DNS system can easily lead to a dynamic load imbalance condition across cluster nodes. This makes it difficult for a node to operate efficiently at peak load capacity. Since it is impossible for the DNS system to guess the TTL value of a domain name, adjustments are often required to "tweak" the system in order for it to operate efficiently. If the TTL value is set too small, DNS traffic increases and the DNS server itself will bottleneck. If the TTL value is set too high, the dynamic load imbalance will only get worse. Even if the TTL value is set to zero, scheduling granularity is based on each host, so different user access patterns can also lead to dynamic load imbalances. This is because some people may pull lots of pages from a site, while others may just surf a few pages and leave. Load imbalance can also occur when a server node fails and the client request that was mapped to the failing IP address responds to the client, who often exacerbates the problem by clicking the reload or refresh button in the browser, sending yet another request to a dead node. Other nodes in the cluster pick up the load of the failed node, and the workload for all nodes increases accordingly.

Dispatcher-Based Load Balancing Clusters

A dispatcher performs intelligent load balancing by using server availability, capability, workload, and other user-defined criteria to determine where to send a TCP/IP request. The dispatcher component of a load balancer can distribute HTTP requests among nodes in a cluster. The dispatcher distributes the load among servers in a cluster so the services of nodes appear as a virtual service on a single IP address; end users interact as if it were a single server, without knowing anything about the back-end infrastructure. Compared to DNS-based load balancing, dispatcher load balancing can schedule requests at a much finer granularity (such as per connection) for better load balancing among servers. Failure can be masked when one or more nodes fail. Server management is becoming easy with the new tools available today. An administrator can take put any number of nodes online or take them offline at any time without interrupting services to end users, which is exactly what is required for operating a cloud.

The Direct Routing Request Dispatching Technique

This request dispatching approach is similar to the one implemented in IBM's NetDispatcher. The virtual IP address is shared by real servers and the load balancer. The load balancer has an interface configured with the virtual IP address too, which is used to accept request packets, and it directly routes the packets to the chosen servers. All the real servers have their non-arp (address resolution protocol) alias interface configured with the virtual IP address or redirect packets destined for the virtual IP address to a local socket, so that real servers can process the packets locally. The load balancer and the real servers must have one of their interfaces physically linked by a hub or switch.

When a user accesses a virtual service provided by the server cluster, the packet destined for the virtual IP address (the IP address for the virtual server) arrives. The load balancer (Linux Director) examines the packet's destination address and port. If they are matched for a virtual service, a real server is chosen from the cluster by a scheduling algorithm, and the connection is added into the hash table which records connections. Then, the load balancer forwards the packet directly to the chosen server. When the incoming packet belongs to this connection and the chosen server can be found in the hash table, the packet is also routed directly to the server. When the server receives the forwarded packet, the server finds that the packet is for the address on its alias interface or for a local socket, so it processes the request and finally returns the result directly to the user. After a connection terminates or times out, the connection record is removed from the hash table. The load balancer simply changes the MAC address of the data frame to that of the chosen server and retransmits it on the LAN. This is why the load balancer and each server must be connected directly to one another by a single uninterrupted segment of a LAN.

Virtualization Applications

Application virtualization describes software technologies that improve portability, manageability, and compatibility of applications by encapsulating them from the underlying operating system on which they are executed.[30] A virtualized application is redirected at runtime to interface with the virtual operating system and all related resources that are managed by it rather than an actual, physical implementation of that operating system.

Full application virtualization requires a virtualization layer.[31] The virtualization layer must be installed on a machine to intercept file and registry operations performed by a virtualized application, where it can transparently redirect those operations to a virtualized destination. The application that performs file operations never knows that it is not directly accessing a physical resource. Using this approach, applications can be made portable by redirecting their I/O tasks to a single physical file, and traditionally incompatible applications can be executed side by side.

Using application virtualization allows applications to run in non-native environments. For example, Wine allows Linux users to run Microsoft Windows applications from the Linux platform. Virtualization also helps protect the operating system and isolate other applications from poorly written or buggy code. With application virtualization, physical resources can be shared so an implementation uses fewer resources than a separate virtual machine. Simplified operating system migrations are possible because administrators are able to maintain a standardized configuration in the underlying operating system and propagate that configuration across multiple servers in an organization, regardless of whatever applications may be used. In the next few sections, we will take a look at some of the more popular virtualization environments in use today.

VMWare

The VMware virtualization platform is built to virtualize hardware resources found on an x86-based computer (e.g., the CPU, RAM, hard disk, and network controller) to create a fully functional virtual machine that can run its own operating system and applications just like a standard computer. Each virtual machine is completely encapsulated in order to eliminate any potential conflicts. VMware virtualization works by inserting a thin layer of software directly on the computer hardware or on a host operating system. This layer is actually a monitor called a Hypervisor, and its task is to allocate hardware resources dynamically and transparently. Multiple operating systems can run concurrently on a single computer and share that computer's hardware. A virtual machine is completely compatible with all standard x86 operating systems, applications, and device drivers. It

---

30.   http://en.wikipedia.org/wiki/Application_virtualization, retrieved 11 Feb 2009.
31.   Amir Husain, "How to Build an Application Virtualization Framework," http://vdiworks.com/wp/?p=15, retrieved 11 Feb 2009.

is possible to run several operating systems and applications simultaneously on a single computer, and each operating system has access to the physical resources it needs on demand.

Readers interested in trying virtualization may consider using VMware ESXi (a free download from the official web site).[32] With ESXi, you can create virtual machines quickly and easily. A menu-driven startup and automatic configurations enable you to get virtual machines set up and running in minutes. You can even import a virtual appliance using the VMware Virtual Appliance Marketplace. For more information on VMware, the reader is encouraged to visit the official web site.

Xen

Xen is a unique open source technology[33] invented by a team led by Ian Pratt at the University of Cambridge. Xen was originally developed by the Systems Research Group at the University of Cambridge Computer Laboratory as part of the XenoServers project, funded by the UK-EPSRC. XenoServers aimed to provide a public infrastructure for global distributed computing. Xen plays a key part in that, allowing one to efficiently partition a single machine to enable multiple independent clients to run their operating systems and applications in an environment. This environment provides protection, resource isolation, and accounting. The project web page contains further information as well as pointers to papers and technical reports.[34]

Using Xen server virtualization, the Xen Hypervisor is installed directly on the host hardware and exists as a thin layer between the hardware and the operating system. This abstraction layer allows the host device to run one or more virtual servers. It isolates hardware from the operating system and its applications. Xen is licensed under the GNU General Public License (GPL2) and is available at no charge in both source and object format. According to the official web site, "Xen is, and always will be, open sourced, uniting the industry and the Xen ecosystem to speed the adoption of virtualization in the enterprise."

The Xen Hypervisor supports a wide range of guest operating systems including Windows, Linux, Solaris, and various versions of the BSD operating systems. The Xen Hypervisor has an exceptionally lean footprint. The Xen Hypervisor offers a smaller code base, greater security, and up to 10

---

32.   http://www.vmware.com.
33.   http://www.xen.org.
34.   http://www.cl.cam.ac.uk/xeno, retrieved 11 Feb 2009.

times less overhead than alternative virtualization approaches. That means that it has extremely low overhead and near-native performance for guests. Xen reuses existing device drivers (both closed and open source) from Linux, making device management easy. Xen is robust to device driver failure and protects both guests and the Hypervisor from faulty or malicious drivers.

Virtual device monitors (which are also known as hypervisors) are often used on mainframes and large servers seen in data center architectures. Increasingly, they are being used by Internet service providers (ISPs) to provide virtual dedicated servers to their customers. Xen support for virtual-machine live migration from one host to another allows workload balancing and avoids system downtime. Some of the main advantages of Xen server virtualization are

- Consolidation and increased utilization
- The ability to rapidly provision and start a virtual machine
- Better ability to dynamically respond to faults by rebooting a virtual machine or moving a virtual machine to a different hardware platform
- The ability to securely separate virtual operating systems on the same platform
- The ability to support legacy software as well as new operating system instances on the same computer

Xen may also be used on personal computers configured in a dual-boot configuration (e.g., those that run Linux but also have Windows installed). Traditionally, such systems provided the user the option of either running Windows or Linux, but with Xen it is possible to start Windows and allow it to run from in a separate Window on the Linux desktop, enabling the user to run applications from both systems simultaneously.

For operating system development tasks, virtualization has a significant additional benefit—running the new system as a guest avoids any need to reboot the computer whenever a bug is encountered. This protected or insulated environment is known as a "sandbox," and such sandboxed guest systems are useful in computer security research and development. In order to study the effects of malware, viruses, and worms without compromising the host system, developers often prefer to use a sandbox. Hardware appliance vendors increasingly have begun to ship their products preconfigured with several guest systems. This allows them to deliver complex solutions that are able to execute various software applications running on different operating systems.

Xen touts a para-virtualization technology that is widely acknowledged as the fastest and most secure virtualization software in the industry. Para-virtualization takes full advantage of the latest Intel and AMD hardware virtualization advancements and has fundamentally altered the way virtualization technology is built. Virtual servers and the Hypervisor cooperate to achieve very high performance for I/O, CPU, and memory virtualization.

According to the Xen User Manual,[35] the Xen system has multiple layers, the lowest and most privileged of which is Xen itself. Xen can host multiple guest operating systems. Each operating system is run within a secure virtual machine environment known as a domain. In order to make effective use of the available physical CPUs, such domains are scheduled by Xen. Each guest operating system is responsible for managing its own applications. This management includes scheduling each application within the time allotted by Xen to the virtual machine. The primary domain, domain 0, is created automatically when the system boots, and it has special management privileges. Domain 0 builds other domains and manages their virtual devices. Domain 0 also performs administrative tasks such as suspending, resuming, and migrating other virtual machines. Within domain 0, a process called *xend* is responsible for managing virtual machines and providing access to their consoles.

3.9   Chapter Summary

In this chapter we discussed what it takes to build a cloud network, evolution from the managed service provider model to cloud computing and SaaS and from single-purpose architectures to multipurpose architectures, the concept and design of data center virtualization, the role and importance of collaboration, service-oriented architectures as an intermediary step and the basic approach to data center-based SOAs, and the role of open source software in data centers and where and how it is used in cloud architecture. Cloud computing provides an end-to-end, unified solution that maximizes the ability to address the performance, scalability, virtualization, and collaboration requirements being driven by today's global business challenges and opportunities. It should be clear that a properly designed and

35.   http://tx.downloads.xensource.com/downloads/docs/user/user.html, retrieved 11 Feb 2009.

implemented cloud infrastructure provides the benefit of substantially lowering the total cost of ownership over the traditional hosting environment though the use of virtualization and the use of open source software. Cloud infrastructure maximizes the potential for creating value through collaboration. In future chapters we will discuss the ability of cloud computing to provide a solution to current challenges in presence and identity while enhancing security and privacy. First, however, we will give you a chance to see for yourself the value and process in implementing and using cloud computing. In the next chapter, we will give guide you through a practicum on the how you can build a virtualized computing infrastructure using open source software.

Chapter 4

Virtualization Practicum

4.1 Chapter Overview

In this chapter, we are going to download and install the Sun VirtualBox product. Then, we will show you how to install and configure it. Next, we will add a virtual operating environment on top of your existing operating system. The beauty of virtualization solutions is that you can run multiple operating systems simultaneously on a single computer. To really understand how powerful an ability that is, you need to see it for yourself. The following illustration shows a draft version of this chapter being written on an Open-Solaris virtual guest operating system running on Windows XP host.

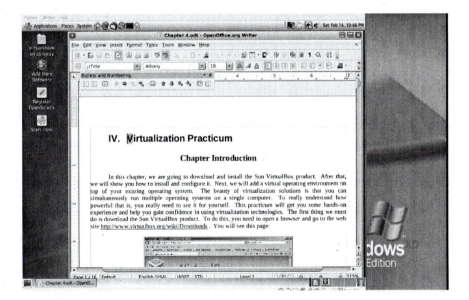

4.2   Downloading Sun xVM VirtualBox

This practicum will provide you with some guided hands-on experience and help you gain confidence in using virtualization technologies. To begin, the first thing to do is to **download the Sun VirtualBox product.** To do this, you need to open a browser and go to the web site

```
http://www.virtualbox.org/wiki/Downloads
```

where you will see this page:

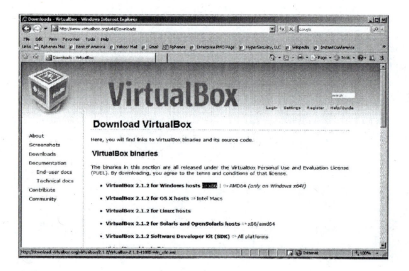

Choose the type of download file that is most suitable to the operating system you are using and download the product. Save the file—in Microsoft Windows, you will be prompted to save the file from the **File Download – Security Warning** dialog:

Choose **Save** and you will be shown a **Save As** file selection dialog to choose where you wish to save the downloaded file. The dialog box should look like this:

Select a location for the file to be saved to and click the **Save** button to continue. The download status dialog will appear:

4.3   Installing Sun xVM VirtualBox

Once the download has completed, you must locate the file wherever you saved it and execute the installer. If you are not using a Microsoft operating system, the procedure for executing the installer will be slightly different than what is shown here. Regardless of which non-Microsoft operating system you may be using, launch the installer according to your specific operating system's instructions. The VirtualBox installation can be started from a Windows environment by double-clicking on its Microsoft Installer archive (MSI file) or by entering this command from the prompt of a command-line interface:

```
msiexec /i VirtualBox.msi
```

The figure below shows the highlighted selection of the Sun VirtualBox (Windows version) installer from the root of the D: drive.

Using just the standard settings, VirtualBox will be installed for all users on the local system. If this is not what you want, it is necessary to invoke the installer from a command-line prompt as follows:

```
msiexec /i VirtualBox.msi ALLUSERS=2
```

Executing the installer in this fashion will install VirtualBox for the current user only.

Once the installer begins executing, the first thing you will see is the installation welcome dialog, which looks like this:

Click **Next >** to continue on to the **End-User License Agreement** (EULA), as shown below. In order to proceed, you must accept this agreement to use the product. Click the **Next >** button to continue.

Once the EULA is accepted, the **Custom Setup** screen will appear, as shown below.

Here you can change the default settings, choosing where and how VirtualBox will be installed. Usually, the defaults are satisfactory for installation. If you choose this option, all features will be installed.

In addition to the VirtualBox application, the components for USB support and networking are available. These packages contains special drivers for your Windows host that VirtualBox requires to fully support networking and USB devices in your virtual machine (VM). The networking package contains extra networking drivers for your Windows host that VirtualBox needs to support Host Interface Networking (to make your VM's virtual network cards accessible from other machines on your physical network).

Depending on your Windows configuration, you may see warnings about "unsigned drivers" or similar messages. Select **Continue** on these warnings, because otherwise VirtualBox may not function correctly after installation. Click **Next >** to continue to the **Ready to Install** dialog box, shown below.

To start the installation process, just click **Install.** It may take a minute or so for the installer to complete, depending on your system's processor and memory resources. You will see an installation progress dialog, similar to this one:

On Microsoft Windows operating systems, you may see the **Software Installation** dialog box shown below, warning you that the product you are installing has not passed Windows Logo testing to verify its compatibility with Windows XP. Click the **Continue Anyway** button to proceed.

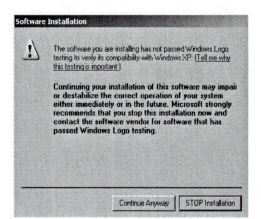

You will be notified when the installation has completed, and given the opportunity to launch the application automatically. Be sure the box in the following dialog is checked:

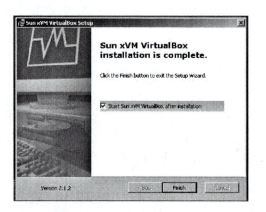

Click **Finish** to complete the installation process and continue. The **VirtualBox Registration Dialog** will appear:

Registration is very simple, and it is recommended that you register your product. Just fill in your name and an email address. Once the registration form has been completed, a **Confirm** button will appear. You can choose to allow Sun to contact you or not by checking or unchecking the box above the **Confirm** button. Once you have clicked **Confirm,** instant kudos appear:

Click **OK** and you are rewarded with the initial display of the Sun xVM VirtualBox product. For Microsoft Windows-based systems, the installer will create a **VirtualBox** group in the Programs folder of the Start menu, which will allow you to launch the application and access its documentation. If you choose later to uninstall this product, VirtualBox can be safely uninstalled at any time by choosing the program entry in the **Add/ Remove Programs** applet in the Windows **Control Panel.** For non-Windows operating systems, you must uninstall according to your system's recommended procedures. However, let's not do that yet! The following picture shows you what the opening screen looks like after you have installed and filled out the product registration form:

4.4   Adding a Guest Operating System to VirtualBox

VirtualBox allows you to run *guest operating systems* using its own virtual computer system, which is why it is called a "virtual machine." The guest system will run in its VM environment just as if it were installed on a real computer. It operates according to the VM settings you have specified (we will talk about settings a bit more later in this chapter). All software that you choose to run on the guest system will operate just as it would on a physical computer.

With the options available, you have quite a bit of latitude in deciding what virtual hardware will be provided to the guest. The virtual hardware you specify can be used to communicate with the host system or even with other guests. For instance, if you provide VirtualBox with the image of a CD-ROM in the form of an ISO file, VirtualBox can make this image available to a guest system just as if it were a physical CD-ROM. You can also give a guest system access to the real network (and network shares) via its virtual network card. It is even possible to give the host system, other guests, or computers on the Internet access to the guest system.

4.5   Downloading FreeDOS as a Guest OS

For our first guest, we will be adding an open source operating system called FreeDOS to the host machine. In order to do this, we must first go to the

Internet and download FreeDOS. Minimize the VirtualBox application for now and open a web browser. Go to

```
http://virtualbox.wordpress.com/images
```

When your browser has brought up the site, it should look similar to the figure below. You will see a list of virtual operating systems, with the sponsoring web site for each one in parentheses.

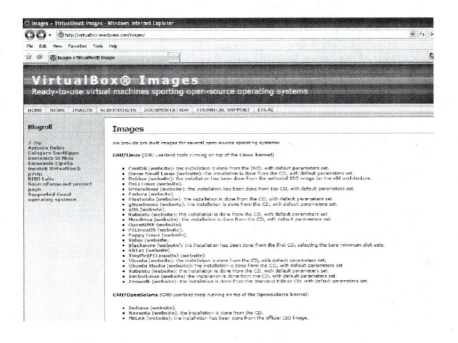

Towards the bottom of the page, you will find the FreeDOS entry. The reader is encouraged to go to the web site of each operating system and check it out before downloading a file. Click on the FreeDOS entry to start the download process. When you click on any of the operating system links, you will be taken to that system's download page. There, you are given the choice of which architecture (i.e., 32-bit or 64-bit) you want to install. What is important for almost every operating system displayed on this page is that you must *write down the passwords for the root user and default user*. An example similar to what you will see is shown below:

FreeDOSThere are several FreeDOS images available.

FreeDOS 1.0

Size (compressed/<u>uncompressed</u>): 82.3 MBytes / <u>394 MBytes</u>

Link: http://downloads.sourceforge.net/virtualboximage/freedos

Of course, FreeDOS is the exception to the rule above, since it does not require a root or user password. Click the link to download the image and save it to a location you will remember—later in this practicum, you will need to unzip this file and extract the images. We recommend that you choose to save the files on a drive with plenty of space available.

4.6   Downloading the 7-Zip Archive Tool

Next, you will need to download an open source product called 7-zip (it works on both Linux and Windows platforms), which can be accessed from

```
http://www.7-zip.org/download.html
```

Once the download is complete, perform the following steps *in sequence:*

1.   Pick a drive with plenty of spare room on it and create a folder named **VirtualGuests.**

2.   Download the **7-zip file** to the VirtualGuests folder and install it using the standard options.

3.   Once you have installed 7-zip, find the FreeDOS file you downloaded previously.

4.   Highlight the file and right-click on it—choose the **7-zip extraction** option to extract files.

5.   Extract the files to your VirtualGuests folder.

6.   Your VirtualGuests folder will now contain two folders, **Machines** and **VDI.** The virtualBox image for FreeDOS will be in the VDI folder.

4.7   Adding a Guest OS to Sun xVM VirtualBox

Now you will add the FreeDOS guest operating system to your virtualBox host. Start by clicking on the **New** button. The **New Virtual Machine Wizard** dialog box will appear:

The wizard is an easy-to-follow guided setup for installation of your guest operating system. Click **Next >** to continue and you will be presented with the **Virtual Machine Name and OS Type** dialog box:

Type **FreeDOS** in the **Name** field. Select **Other** for the **Operating System,** and for the **Version** we will choose **DOS.** Click **Next >** to continue on to the dialog for memory configuration. In this part of the wizard, you have the option of increasing or decreasing the amount of memory that will be used for the guest operating system. For those of us old enough to remember DOS, 32 MB of memory is plenty.

Just accept the default settings for now (you can always change them later) and click **Next >** to proceed to the next section of the wizard, the **Virtual Hard Disk** dialog box:

This dialog box allows you to select the virtual device image file (.vdi file) that was previously downloaded and saved to the VirtualGuests folder you created. What you see displayed in the dialog box is the name of the last image added. In this case, it was an image of Damn Small Linux (dsl). If no images have been installed on the host, the default selection will be similar to the one shown below:

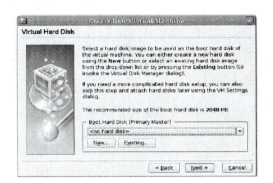

If you had previously created any virtual hard disks which have not been attached to other virtual machines, you could select from among those using the drop-down list in the Wizard window. Since we have downloaded and extracted a new image of FreeDos, it won't be in the list. Click the **Existing...** button to continue on to the **Virtual Media Manager.** In the figure below, FreeDOS is listed as an available selection. If it is not listed, then you need to add it by clicking on the **Add** button at the top of the dialog box.

VirtualBox's Virtual Media Manager keeps an internal registry of all available hard disk, CD/DVD-ROM, and floppy disk images. This registry can be viewed and changed in the Virtual Disk Manager, which you can access from the **File** menu in the VirtualBox main window. The **Disk Image Manager** shows you all images that are registered with VirtualBox, grouped in three tabs for the three supported formats. These are hard disk images, either in VirtualBox's own Virtual Disk Image (VDI) format or the widely supported **Virtual Machine DisK** (VMDK) format. CD and DVD images in standard ISO format are supported. There is support for floppy images in standard RAW format. As you can see in the figure below, for each image, the Virtual Disk Manager shows you the full path of the image file and other information, such as the virtual machine the image is currently attached to, if any.

Clicking the **Add** button will bring you to the **Select a hard disk image file** dialog box, as shown below:

Using this file dialog, you must navigate to your VirtualGuests folder. In your VirtualGuests folder, open the **VDI** folder and highlight the **Free-DOS** .vdi file. Once you have it highlighted, simply click on the **Open** button. You are returned to the **Virtual Hard Disk** dialog box, where you earlier clicked the **Existing...** button:

Click **Next >** to complete the addition of the FreeDOS virtual image. A summary screen, as shown below, will appear:

Here, simply click the **Finish** button and you will be returned to the Sun xVM VirtualBox main display. FreeDOS should be displayed in the left panel (it should be the only entry on your system) similar to the list shown in the following image:

Before we explore the FreeDOS environment, it is a good idea to check the settings to ensure that the guest system will work the way you want. The **Settings** button (in the figure above, it looks like a gear) in the toolbar at the top of the VirtualBox main window brings up a detailed window where you can configure many of the properties of the VM that is currently selected:

Click your desired settings—but be careful. Even though it is possible to change all VM settings after installing a guest operating system, certain changes after installation may prevent a guest operating system from functioning correctly.

Since you have just created an empty VM, you will probably be most interested in the settings in the **CD/DVD-ROM** section if you want to make a CD-ROM or a DVD-ROM available the first time you start Free-DOS, so that you can use it with your guest operating system. This will allow your VM to access the media in your host drive, and you can proceed to install from there. Check the box in the CD/DVD section if you want to use an optical device.

For now, that is all you need to do in Settings to prepare to run your virtual image. The next part of our practicum will take you inside the virtual guest system to use and and see for yourself that it is a real, functioning environment. We will show you how to set up a graphical user interface within the DOS environment using an open source product called Open-GEM. OpenGEM was modeled after GEM, one of the earliest GUI environments widely available on the DOS platform.

To start FreeDOS, highlight **FreeDOS** in the selections panel and click
the green **Start** arrow as shown below.

When you first start FreeDOS, you are presented with a "Load" menu,
as shown below. Usually, the default selection best for your system is highlighted automatically. Choose the default option and press **Enter** (or just let
the 5-second timer expire).

Since the operating system in the virtual machine does not "know" that it is not running on a real computer, it expects to have exclusive control over your keyboard and mouse. This is not so, however, since, unless you are running the VM in full-screen mode, your VM needs to share the keyboard and mouse with other applications and possibly other VMs on your host. This becomes evident when you look at the figure below, showing FreeDOS running on a Windows XP installation.

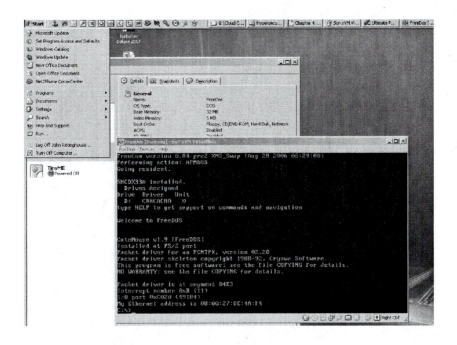

Only one of the two—either the VM or the host—can "own" the keyboard and the mouse at any one time. You will see a second mouse pointer, which will always be confined to the limits of the VM window. Basically, you activate the VM by clicking inside it. To return ownership of the keyboard and mouse to your host operating system, VirtualBox reserves a special key on your keyboard, called the **Host key,** for itself. *By default, this is the Control (CTRL) key on the right lower part of your keyboard.* You can change this default in the VirtualBox Global Settings if you wish. In any case, the current setting for the Host key is always displayed at the bottom right of your VM window in case you may have forgotten which key to use. If needed, click the mouse in the virtualized window to gain focus in the guest system. Press the Host key to give focus back to the host.

FreeDOS comes with a graphical user interface (GUI) called Open-GEM that is ready to install. We are going to install OpenGEM in the Free-DOS environment to show you that it is a fully functioning virtualized platform. At the **c:\>** command prompt, type

```
FDOS\OPENGEM\INSTALL
```

and press **Enter.** The following screen appears when the GEM installer starts:

Choose option **1** from the menu and press **Enter.** The next screen to appear is the OpenGEM license agreement. Here, you must accept the license agreement by once again choosing option **1** (Accept and Install OpenGEM) and pressing **Enter** to continue the install process.

The installation will proceed and when it is completed, you will see the screen below:

Press any key as instructed. You will then be shown an information screen and acknowledgment of your installation. Some basic information telling you how to start OpenGEM is displayed. Press any key again to continue.

From the DOS command prompt c:\>, type **GEM** and press **Enter.** The GEM environment starts up and you should see something similar to the screen below.

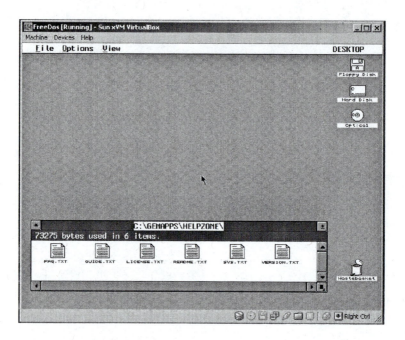

Play around with the environment and (for some of us) reminisce about the "good" old days. Once you are satisfied that everything works, you can exit GEM by using the **File |> Quit** option on the menu bar at the top. GEM will exit and show the following screen, where you are given the option to restart OpenGEM, return to DOS, reboot, or shut down.

Choose option **4** and press **Enter.** You will be returned to the Sun xVM program. Note that FreeDOS is shown in a powered-off state.

4.8 Chapter Summary

At this point, you have learned the basics of using the Sun xVM VirtualBox product and should have a pretty good idea of what virtualization is and how it can be used. The evolution to cloud computing has advanced rapidly over the last few years through such technological developments as service-oriented architectures, collaboration software, and virtualization, which you just experienced through this practicum. This advancement is creating a new corporate "edge" that has to consider the complex relationships and risks that exist on shared infrastructures. As a result of this loss of traditional perimeter boundaries, businesses are no longer operating from within the confines of a traditional corporate boundary, but rather as part of a global ecosystem of supply chains, strategic alliances, and partnerships. Increasingly ubiquitous connectivity, coupled with advances in mobile device capabilities and strategies, as well as new and exciting collaboration and remote service delivery paradigms, have all begun to erode traditional corporate perimeters and thinking that is fundamentally altering how we think about work, let alone how it is accomplished. This paradigm shift is forcing businesses to think beyond their over-reliance on Layer 2 and 3 perimeters and begin to strengthen traditionally weak spaces revolving around identity, entitlement, and policy enforcement. Businesses must think about tiered perimeters without abandoning core infrastructure. This has also resulted in new security challenges that organizations did not have to face when critical resources and transactions were behind their firewalls or controlled partner networks. The glue that will make this work in the cloud computing environment is federated identity, presence, and privacy controls—all of which will be discussed in the next chapter. Their role will also be critical in providing a baseline for some of the security solutions required for cloud computing, to be discussed in Chapter 6.

Chapter 5

Federation, Presence, Identity, and Privacy in the Cloud

5.1 Chapter Overview

Building a seamless federated communications capability in a cloud environment, one that is capable of supporting people, devices, information feeds, documents, application interfaces, and other entities, is affected by the architecture that is implemented. The solution chosen must be able to find such entities, determine their purpose, and request presence data so that others can interact with them in real time. This process is known as discovery. Providing discovery information about the availability of various entities enables organizations to deploy real-time services and achieve significant revenue opportunities and productivity improvements.

The advent of on-demand cloud services is changing the landscape for identity management because most current identity management solutions are focused on the enterprise and/or create a very restrictive, controlled, and static environment. We are now moving into a new world, where cloud services are offered on demand and they continuously evolve to meet user needs. Previous models are being challenged by such innovations. For example, in terms of trust assumptions, privacy implications, and operational aspects of authentication and authorization, solutions that seemed to work before are now considered old, outdated, and clunky fixes to identity management. The fluid and omnipresent aspects of federation, presence, and identity in the cloud create new opportunities for meeting the challenges that businesses face in managing security and privacy in the cloud.

5.2 Federation in the Cloud

One challenge in creating and managing a globally decentralized cloud computing environment is maintaining consistent connectivity between untrusted components while remaining fault-tolerant. A key opportunity for the emerging cloud industry will be in defining a federated cloud ecosystem by connecting multiple cloud computing providers using a common standard.

A notable research project being conducted by Microsoft, called the Geneva Framework, focuses on issues involved in cloud federation. Geneva has been described as a claims-based access platform and is said to help simplify access to applications and other systems. The concept allows for multiple providers to interact seamlessly with others, and it enables developers to incorporate various authentication models that will work with any corporate identity system, including Active Directory, LDAPv3-based directories, application-specific databases, and new user-centric identity models such as LiveID, OpenID, and InfoCard systems. It also supports Microsoft's CardSpace and Novell's Digital Me.

The remainder of this section focuses on federation in the cloud through use of the Internet Engineering Task Force (IETF) standard Extensible Messaging and Presence Protocol (XMPP) and interdomain federation using the Jabber Extensible Communications Platform (Jabber XCP),[1] because this protocol is currently used by a wide range of existing services offered by providers as diverse as Google Talk, Live Journal, Earthlink, Facebook, ooVoo, Meebo, Twitter, the U.S. Marines Corps, the Defense Information Systems Agency (DISA), the U.S. Joint Forces Command (USJFCOM), and the National Weather Service. We also look at federation with non-XMPP technologies such as the Session Initiation Protocol (SIP), which is the foundation of popular enterprise messaging systems such as IBM's Lotus Sametime and Microsoft's Live Communications Server (LCS) and Office Communications Server (OCS).

Jabber XCP is a highly scalable, extensible, available, and device-agnostic presence solution built on XMPP and supports multiple protocols such as Session Initiation Protocol for Instant Messaging and Presence Leveraging Extensions (SIMPLE) and Instant Messaging and Presence Service (IMPS). Jabber XCP is a highly programmable platform, which makes it ideal for adding presence and messaging to existing applications or services and for building next-generation, presence-based solutions.

Over the last few years there has been a controversy brewing in web services architectures. Cloud services are being talked up as a fundamental shift in web architecture that promises to move us from interconnected silos to a

---

1.   Jabber was acquired by Cisco Systems in November 2008.

collaborative network of services whose sum is greater than its parts. The problem is that the protocols powering current cloud services, SOAP (Simple Object Access Protocol) and a few other assorted HTTP-based protocols, are all one-way information exchanges. Therefore cloud services aren't real-time, won't scale, and often can't clear the firewall. Many believe that those barriers can be overcome by XMPP (also called Jabber) as the protocol that will fuel the Software-as-a-Service (SaaS) models of tomorrow. Google, Apple, AOL, IBM, Livejournal, and Jive have all incorporated this protocol into their cloud-based solutions in the last few years.

Since the beginning of the Internet era, if you wanted to synchronize services between two servers, the most common solution was to have the client "ping" the host at regular intervals, which is known as polling. Polling is how most of us check our email. We ping our email server every few minutes to see if we have new mail. It's also how nearly all web services application programming interfaces (APIs) work.

XMPP's profile has been steadily gaining since its inception as the protocol behind the open source instant messenger (IM) server jabberd in 1998. XMPP's advantages include:

- It is decentralized, meaning anyone may set up an XMPP server.
- It is based on open standards.
- It is mature—multiple implementations of clients and servers exist.
- Robust security is supported via Simple Authentication and Security Layer (SASL) and Transport Layer Security (TLS).
- It is flexible and designed to be extended.

XMPP is a good fit for cloud computing because it allows for easy two-way communication; it eliminates the need for polling; it has rich publish-subscribe (pub-sub) functionality built in; it is XML-based and easily extensible, perfect for both new IM features and custom cloud services; it is efficient and has been proven to scale to millions of concurrent users on a single service (such as Google's GTalk); and it also has a built-in worldwide federation model.

Of course, XMPP is not the only pub-sub enabler getting a lot of interest from web application developers. An Amazon EC2-backed server can run Jetty and Cometd from Dojo. Unlike XMPP, Comet is based on HTTP, and in conjunction with the Bayeux Protocol, uses JSON to exchange data. Given the current market penetration and extensive use of XMPP and XCP for federation in the cloud and that it is the dominant open protocol in that space, we will focus on its use in our discussion of federation.

The ability to exchange data used for presence, messages, voice, video, files, notifications, etc., with people, devices, and applications gain more power when they can be shared across organizations and with other service providers. Federation differs from peering, which requires a prior agreement between parties before a server-to-server (S2S) link can be established. In the past, peering was more common among traditional telecommunications providers (because of the high cost of transferring voice traffic). In the brave new Internet world, federation has become a *de facto* standard for most email systems because they are federated dynamically through Domain Name System (DNS) settings and server configurations.

5.2.1   Four Levels of Federation

Technically speaking, federation is the ability for two XMPP servers in different domains to exchange XML stanzas. According to the XEP-0238: XMPP Protocol Flows for Inter-Domain Federation, there are at least four basic types of federation[2]:

1.   **Permissive federation**. Permissive federation occurs when a server accepts a connection from a peer network server without verifying its identity using DNS lookups or certificate checking. The lack of verification or authentication may lead to domain spoofing (the unauthorized use of a third-party domain name in an email message in order to pretend to be someone else), which opens the door to widespread spam and other abuses. With the release of the open source jabberd 1.2 server in October 2000, which included support for the Server Dialback protocol (fully supported in Jabber XCP), permissive federation met its demise on the XMPP network.

2.   **Verified federation.** This type of federation occurs when a server accepts a connection from a peer after the identity of the peer has been verified. It uses information obtained via DNS and by

---

2.   Peter Saint-Andre, "XEP-0238: XMPP Protocol Flows for Inter-Domain Federation," http://xmpp.org/extensions/xep-0238.html, retrieved 1 Mar 2009.

means of domain-specific keys exchanged beforehand. The connection is not encrypted, and the use of identity verification effectively prevents domain spoofing. To make this work, federation requires proper DNS setup, and that is still subject to DNS poisoning attacks. Verified federation has been the default service policy on the open XMPP since the release of the open-source jabberd 1.2 server.

3.   **Encrypted federation.** In this mode, a server accepts a connection from a peer if and only if the peer supports Transport Layer Security (TLS) as defined for XMPP in Request for Comments (RFC) 3920. The peer must present a digital certificate. The certificate may be self-signed, but this prevents using mutual authentication. If this is the case, both parties proceed to weakly verify identity using Server Dialback. XEP-0220 defines the Server Dialback protocol,[3] which is used between XMPP servers to provide identity verification. Server Dialback uses the DNS as the basis for verifying identity; the basic approach is that when a receiving server receives a server-to-server connection request from an originating server, it does not accept the request until it has verified a key with an authoritative server for the domain asserted by the originating server. Although Server Dialback does not provide strong authentication or trusted federation, and although it is subject to DNS poisoning attacks, it has effectively prevented most instances of address spoofing on the XMPP network since its release in 2000.[4] This results in an encrypted connection with weak identity verification.

4.   **Trusted federation.** Here, a server accepts a connection from a peer only under the stipulation that the peer supports TLS and the peer can present a digital certificate issued by a root certification authority (CA) that is trusted by the authenticating server. The list of trusted root CAs may be determined by one or more factors, such as the operating system, XMPP server software, or local service policy. In trusted federation, the use of digital certificates results not only in a channel encryption but also in strong authentication. The use of trusted domain certificates effectively prevents DNS poisoning attacks but makes federation

---

3.   http://xmpp.org/extensions/xep-0220.html, retrieved 28 Feb 2009.
4.   http://xmpp.org/extensions/xep-0220.html, retrieved 28 Feb 2009.

more difficult, since such certificates have traditionally not been easy to obtain.

5.2.2   How Encrypted Federation Differs from Trusted Federation

Verified federation serves as a foundation for encrypted federation, which builds on it concepts by requiring use of TLS for channel encryption. The Secure Sockets Layer (SSL) technology, originally developed for secure communications over HTTP, has evolved into TLS. XMPP uses a TLS profile that enables two entities to upgrade a connection from unencrypted to encrypted. This is different from SSL in that it does not require that a separate port be used to establish secure communications. Since XMPP S2S communication uses two connections (bi-directionally connected), encrypted federation requires each entity to present a digital certificate to the reciprocating party.

Not all certificates are created equal, and trust is in the eye of the beholder. For example, I might not trust your digital certificates if your certificate is "self-signed" (i.e., issued by you rather than a recognized CA), or your certificate is issued by a CA but I don't know or trust the CA. In either case, if Joe's server connects to Ann's server, Ann's server will accept the untrusted certificate from Joe's server solely for the purpose of bootstrapping channel encryption, not for domain verification. This is due to the fact that Ann's server has no way of following the certificate chain back to a trusted root. Therefore both servers complete the TLS negotiation, but Ann's server then require's Joe's server to complete server Dialback.

In the trusted federation scenario, Dialback can be avoided if, after using TLS for channel encryption, the server verifying identity proceeds to use the SASL protocol for authentication based on the credentials presented in the certificates. In this case, the servers dispense with server Dialback, because SASL (in particular the EXTERNAL mechanism) provides strong authentication.

5.2.3   Federated Services and Applications

S2S federation is a good start toward building a real-time communications cloud. Clouds typically consist of all the users, devices, services, and applications connected to the network. In order to fully leverage the capabilities of this cloud structure, a participant needs the ability to find other entities of interest. Such entities might be end users, multiuser chat rooms, real-time content feeds, user directories, data relays, messaging gateways, etc. Finding these entities is a process called discovery.

XMPP uses service discovery (as defined in XEP-0030) to find the aforementioned entities. The discovery protocol enables any network participant to query another entity regarding its identity, capabilities, and associated entities. When a participant connects to the network, it queries the authoritative server for its particular domain about the entities associated with that authoritative server.

In response to a service discovery query, the authoritative server informs the inquirer about services hosted there and may also detail services that are available but hosted elsewhere. XMPP includes a method for maintaining personal lists of other entities, known as roster technology, which enables end users to keep track of various types of entities. Usually, these lists are comprised of other entities the users are interested in or interact with regularly. Most XMPP deployments include custom directories so that internal users of those services can easily find what they are looking for.

5.2.4   Protecting and Controlling Federated Communication

Some organizations are wary of federation because they fear that real-time communication networks will introduce the same types of problems that are endemic to email networks, such as spam and viruses. While these concerns are not unfounded, they tend to be exaggerated for several reasons:

- Designers of technologies like XMPP learned from past problems with email systems and incorporated these lessons to prevent address spoofing, unlimited binary attachments, inline scripts, and other attack tactics in XMPP.

- The use of point-to-point federation will avoid problem that occur with multihop federation. This includes injection attacks, data loss, and unencrypted intermediate links.

- Using certificates issued by trusted root CAs ensures encrypted connections and strong authentication, both of which are currently feasible with an email network.

- Employing intelligent servers that have the ability to blacklist (explicitly block) and whitelist (explicitly permit) foreign services, either at the host level or the IP address level, is a significant mitigating factor.

5.2.5   The Future of Federation

The implementation of federated communications is a precursor to building a seamless cloud that can interact with people, devices, information feeds, documents, application interfaces, and other entities. The power of a federated, presence-enabled communications infrastructure is that it enables software developers and service providers to build and deploy such applications without asking permission from a large, centralized communications operator. The process of server-to-server federation for the purpose of interdomain communication has played a large role in the success of XMPP, which relies on a small set of simple but powerful mechanisms for domain checking and security to generate verified, encrypted, and trusted connections between any two deployed servers. These mechanisms have provided a stable, secure foundation for growth of the XMPP network and similar real-time technologies.

5.3   Presence in the Cloud

Understanding the power of presence is crucial to unlocking the real potential of the Internet. Presence data enables organizations to deploy innovative real-time services and achieve significant revenue opportunities and productivity improvements. At the most fundamental level, understanding presence is simple: It provides true-or-false answers to queries about the network availability of a person, device, or application. Presence is a core component of an entity's *real-time* identity. Presence serves as a catalyst for communication. Its purpose is to signal availability for interaction over a network. It is being used to determine availability for phones, conference rooms, applications, web-based services, routers, firewalls, servers, appliances, buildings, devices, and other applications. The management of presence is being extended to capture even more information about availability, *or even the attributes associated with such availability,* such as a person's current activity, mood, location (e.g., GPS coordinates), or preferred communication method (phone, email, IM, etc.). While these presence extensions are innovative and important, they serve mainly to supplement the basic information about an entity's network connectivity, which remains the core purpose of presence.

Presence is an enabling technology for peer-to-peer interaction. It first emerged as an aspect of communication systems, especially IM systems such as ICQ, which allowed users to see the availability of their friends. The huge role that IM has had in establishing presence is evident with the protocols available today, such as Instant Messaging and Presence Service (IMPS), Session Initiation Protocol (SIP) for Instant Messaging and Presence Leveraging Extensions (SIMPLE), the Extensible Messaging and Presence Protocol (XMPP), first developed in the Jabber open source community and subsequently ratified as an Internet standard by the IETF.

Implementation of presence follows the software design pattern known as publish-and-subscribe (pub-sub). This means that a user or application publishes information about its network availability to a centralized location and that information is broadcast to all entities that are authorized to receive it. The authorization usually takes the form of a subscription. In IM implementations, contacts or buddies are the authorized entities. The popularity of these services among millions of people validated the value of the concept of presence.

For enterprise solutions, the limits of consumer-based IM services quickly became clear when enterprises tried to integrate presence into business-critical systems and services. Because business organizations require a great deal more control and flexibility over the technologies they deploy, they needed a presence solution that could provide separation between the presence service and the communication mechanisms (e.g., IM or VoIP) that presence enables. Any solution had to be scalable, extensible, and support a distributed architecture with its own presence domain. It should not overload the network and should support strong security management, system authentication, and granular subscription authorization. Also, any device or application should be able to publish and subscribe to presence information. Enterprise solutions should have the ability to federate numerous cross-protocol presence sources and integrate presence information from multiple sources. Any solution should be able to access presence data via multiple methods. The ability to integrate presence information with existing organizational infrastructure such as active directory is very important. Being able to publish content and allow other people and/or applications to subscribe to that information ensures that updates and changes are done in real time based on the presence/availability of those people/applications.

5.3.1 Presence Protocols

Proprietary, consumer-oriented messaging services do not enable enterprises or institutions to leverage the power of presence. A smarter approach is to use one of the standard presence protocols, SIMPLE or XMPP. is an instant messaging and presence protocol suite based on SIP and managed by the Internet Engineering Task Force (IETF). XMPP is the IETF's formalization of the core XML messaging and presence protocols originally developed by the open source Jabber community in 1999. These protocols have been in wide use on the Internet for over five years. Both of these protocols will be explained in greater detail in Chapter 7.

The modern, reliable method to determine another entity's capabilities is called *service discovery,* wherein applications and devices exchange information about their capabilities directly, without human involvement. Even though no framework for service discovery has been produced by a standards development organization such as the IETF, a capabilities extension for SIP/SIMPLE and a robust, stable service discovery extension for XMPP does exist.

The SIMPLE Working Group is developing the technology to embed capabilities information within broadcasted presence information. A capability already exists in a widely-deployed XMPP extension. Together, service discovery and capabilities broadcasts enable users and applications to gain knowledge about the capabilities of other entities on the network, providing a real-time mechanism for additional use of presence-enabled systems.

5.3.2   Leveraging Presence

The real challenge today is to figure out how to leverage the power of presence within an organization or service offering. This requires having the ability to publish presence information from a wide range of data sources, the ability to receive or embed presence information in just about any platform or application, and having a robust presence engine to tie ubiquitous publishers and subscribers together.

It is safe to assume that any network-capable entity can establish presence. The requirements for functioning as a presence publisher are fairly minimal. As a result, SIP software stacks are available for a wide range of programming languages and it is relatively easy to add native presence publishing capabilities to most applications and devices. Enabling devices and applications to publish presence information is only half of the solution, however; delivering the right presence information to the right subscribers at the right time is just as important.

5.3.3   Presence Enabled

What does it mean to be "presence-enabled"? The basic concept is to show availability of an entity in an appropriate venue. Some modern applications aggregate presence information about all of a person's various connections. For communication devices such as phones and applications such as IM, presence information is often built into the device itself. For less communication-centric applications, such as a document or web page, presence may be gathered by means of a web services API or channeled through a presence daemon. Providing presence data through as many avenues as possible is in large measure the responsibility of a presence engine, as described below.

The presence engine acts as a broker for presence publishers and subscribers. A presence broker provides aggregation of information from many sources, abstraction of that information into open and flexible formats, and distribution of that information to a wide variety of interested parties. In the realm of presence, the qualities of aggregation, abstraction, and distribution imply that the ideal presence broker is trustworthy, open, and intelligent. As presence becomes more prevalent in Internet communications, presence engines need to provide strong authentication, channel encryption, explicit authorization and access control policies, high reliability, and the consistent application of aggregation rules. Being able to operate using multiple protocols such as IMPS, SIMPLE, and XMPP is a basic requirement in order to distribute presence information as widely as possible. Aggregating information from a wide variety of sources requires presence rules that enable subscribers to get the right information at the right time.

5.3.4   The Future of Presence

It will remain to be seen if XMPP is the future of cloud services, but for now it is the dominant protocol for presence in the space. Fixing the polling and scaling problems with XMPP (which we will discuss in Chapter 8, has been challenging but has been accomplished by providers such as Tivo, and the built-in presence functionality offers further fascinating possibilities. Presence includes basic availability information, but it is extensible and can also include abilities such as geo-location. Imagine cloud services taking different actions based on *where* the client initiated a connection.

5.3.5 The Interrelation of Identity, Presence, and Location in the Cloud

Digital identity refers to the traits, attributes, and preferences on which one may receive personalized services. Identity traits might include government-issued IDs, corporate user accounts, and biometric information. Two user attributes which may be associated with identity are presence and location. Over the last few years, there has been an aggressive move toward the convergence of identity, location, and presence. This is important because a standard framework tying identity to presence and location creates the ability to develop standards-based services for identity management that incorporate presence and location. Identity, presence, and location are three characteristics that lie at the core of some of the most critical emerging technologies in the market today: real-time communications (including VoIP, IM, and mobile communications), cloud computing, collaboration, and identity-based security.

Presence is most often associated with real-time communications systems such as IM and describes the state of a user's interaction with a system, such as which computer they are accessing, whether they are idle or working, and perhaps also which task they are currently performing (reading a document, composing email etc.). Location refers to the user's physical location and typically includes latitude, longitude, and (sometimes) altitude. Authentication and authorization mechanisms generally focus on determining the "who" of identity, location defines the "where," and presence defines the "what"—all critical components of the identity-based emerging technologies listed above, including cloud computing.

5.3.6 Federated Identity Management

Network identity is a set of attributes which describes an individual in the digital space. Identity management is the business processes and technologies of managing the life cycle of an identity and its relationship to business applications and services. Federated identity management (IdM) refers to standards-based approaches for handling authentication, single sign-on (SSO, a property of access control for multiple related but independent software systems), role-based access control, and session management across diverse organizations, security domains, and application platforms. It is a system that allows individuals to use the same user name, password, or other personal identification to sign on to the networks of more than one entity in order to conduct transactions. Federation is enabled through the use of open industry standards and/or openly published specifications, such that multiple parties can achieve interoperability for common use cases. Typical use cases involve things such as cross-domain, web-based single sign-on, cross-domain user account provisioning, cross-domain entitlement management, and cross-domain user attribute exchange.

Single sign-on enables a user to log in once and gain access to the resources of multiple software systems without being prompted to log in again. Because different applications and resources support different authentication mechanisms, single sign-on has to internally translate to and store different credentials compared to what is used for initial authentication. The most widely implemented federated IdM/SSO protocol standards are Liberty Alliance Identity Federation Framework (ID-FF), OASIS Security Assertion Markup Language (SAML), and WS-Federation.

Within a typical cross-carrier internetworking environment, federated IdM may be implemented in layers. For converged IP services, federated IdM may involve separate authentications at the application layer and the network layer. Increasingly, the application-layer authentications rely on any or all of the federated IdM standards mentioned above.

5.3.7   Cloud and SaaS Identity Management

As SaaS vendors and their customers sort through the security implications of the hybrid on-demand/on-premises model for cloud applications, they face a number of very interesting identity management challenges. The typical large enterprise IT shop has relatively mature production implementations for standard identity management functionalities such as user authentication, single sign-on, user management, provisioning/deprovisioning, and audit. Because these implementations were designed and deployed to support users accessing applications running inside the enterprise, they often do not transition well to a model that calls for users to access applications (such as Salesforce.com and GoogleApps) which are hosted outside the corporate firewall.

With the advent of cloud computing and the identity requirements that corporate IT departments are putting on SaaS providers, the line between on-demand applications and on-premises applications is blurring, and a hybrid model is emerging in which the goal is closer integration of SaaS applications and functionality within enterprise IT infrastructure. The result is that sometimes corporate IT may have deployed an effective common model for identity management within the enterprise, but that common model breaks down when requirements call for integration with on-demand applications. This breakdown comes in the form of proliferating on-demand user name and password accounts for users, manual processes for provisioning and deprovisioning users to on-demand applications, limited audit visibility across on-demand applications, and constraints on data integration between external and internal applications.

With the success of single sign-on inside the enterprise, users are calling for interoperability outside the enterprise's security domain to outsourced services, including business process outsourcing (BPO) and SaaS providers, and trading partners, as well as within the enterprise to affiliates and subsidiaries.

As a result of business demands that employees be able to traverse the Internet with highly sensitive data, using secure connections that protect the user, the enterprise, and the service provider, Internet-based SSO has seen a substantial increase over the last few years. There are many options to consider for delivering a SSO that works over the Internet. Choosing the right technology is crucial to successfully implementing federated identity management and mitigating long deployment times. The typical options for SSO are either a proprietary SSO (web agents) or standards-based SSO (identity federation). The idea of SSO has been around for years; it was the reason why enterprise portal software was invented in the late 1990s, and why many companies built proprietary SSO solutions. However, proprietary solutions that had to be rolled out by IT departments proved to have serious time, cost, complexity, and security implications.

In June 2008, Salesforce.com disclosed that it was using Security Assertion Markup Language (SAML), an open identity federation standard from OASIS, to implement SSO. The key benefit of using SAML instead of a proprietary SSO is that with SAML the same solution a customer uses for SSO to Salesforce.com can be used with GoogleApps or any of the other hundreds of companies that now support the SAML standard. This eliminated the need for multiple one-offs for SSO. The fact that the leading on-demand application made the move to SAML is a signal that the SaaS/on-demand community is on the path to adopting common models for identity management and security. SAML is the dominant web services standard for federated identity management today. It defines a set of XML formats for representing identity and attribute information, as well as protocols for requests and responses for access control information.

The key principle behind SAML is an *assertion,* a statement made by a trusted party about another. For example, a federated identity management server produces assertions about the identity and rights of users. An individual application does not need to have direct access to the user repository or trust a user—it only needs to know and trust the assertions source. Assertions can be encoded in browser requests or included in web services transactions, enabling log-ins for both person-to-machine and machine-to-machine communications. This was another first, the ability to use the same standards protocol for both back-end transactions and web portal access control.

5.3.8   Federating Identity

Identity federation standards describe two operational roles in an Internet SSO transaction: the identity provider (IdP) and the service provider (SP). An IdP, for example, might be an enterprise that manages accounts for a large number of users who may need secure Internet access to the web-based applications or services of customers, suppliers, and business partners. An SP might be a SaaS or a business-process outsourcing (BPO) vendor wanting to simplify client access to its services. Identity federation allows both types of organizations to define a trust relationship whereby the SP provides access to users from the IdP. There are four common methods to achieve identity federation: Use proprietary solutions, use open source solutions, contract a vendor to do it, or implement a standards-based federated solution.

Many attempt to write their own solution, only to find out there is a huge learning curve and a very high risk that the solution will be incompatible with the external applications and partners they want to connect to. Proprietary solutions rarely scale to connect with multiple partners. Open source libraries are often missing key abilities such as partner enablement and integration, rarely support the SAML 2.0 communication standard, and require significant continuous effort to adapt and maintain. If you choose to contract an identity management stack vendor, the federation component of the stack vendor's suite is usually the newest, least mature component, and its connection capabilities may be very limited in scope.

The most successful way to achieve identity federation is to choose a standalone federation vendor, whose sole focus is to provide secure Internet SSO through identity federation to numerous applications and partners. These vendors provide best-of-breed functionality, and they will work with the identity management system you already have in place. Theses vendors should proactively go beyond the standards to address loopholes associated with underlying technologies such as XML digital signatures and provide centralizing management and monitoring of security credentials and identity traffic. Without a standards-based identity federation server, implementing SSO that works over the Internet can take 6 to 9 months. A properly configured standards-based identity federation server as provided by current SaaS cloud providers should facilitate an implementation in less than 30 to 45 days.

5.3.9 Claims-Based Solutions

Traditional means of authentication and authorization will eventually give way to an identity system where users will present claims that answer who they are or what they can do in order to access systems and content or complete transactions. Microsoft has developed a flexible claims architecture[5] based on standard protocols such as WS-Federation, WS-Trust, and the Security Assertion Markup Language (SAML), which should replace today's more rigid systems based on a single point of truth, typically a directory of user information. The claims model can grow out of the infrastructure users have today, including Public Key Infrastructure (PKI), directory services, and provisioning systems. This approach supports the shared industry vision of an identity metasystem that creates a single-user access model for any application or service and enables security-enhanced collaboration. Microsoft Geneva,mentioned at the beginning of the chapter, allows developers to use prebuilt identity logic and enables seamless interoperability between claims-based and non-claims-based systems.

5.3.10 Identity-as-a-Service (IaaS)

Identity-as-a-Service essentially leverages the SaaS model to solve the identity problem and provides for single sign-on for web applications, strong authentication, federation across boundaries, integration with internal identities and identity monitoring, compliance and management tools and services as appropriate. The more services you use in the cloud, the more you need IaaS, which should also includes elements of governance, risk management, and compliance (GRC) as part of the service. GRC is an increasingly recognized term that reflects a new way in which organizations can adopt an integrated approach to these three areas. However, this term

---

5.   http://msdn.microsoft.com/en-us/security/aa570351.aspx.

is often positioned as a single business activity, when in fact it includes multiple overlapping and related activities, e.g., internal audit, compliance programs such as Sarbanes-Oxley, enterprise risk management, operational risk, and incident management.

IaaS is a prerequisite for most other aspects of cloud computing because you cannot become compliant if you cannot manage your identities and their access rights consistently in the cloud. That goes well beyond authentication. Approaches for consistent policy management across different cloud services will again require new standards, going beyond what federation standards such as SAML, authorization standards such as eXtensible Access Control Markup Language (XACML), and other standards such as the Identity Governance Framework (IGF) provide today. Some of the current IaaS vendors include Ping Identity, Symplified, TriCipher and Arcot Systems.

The biggest threat in cloud computing is manageability. The biggest threat to business by far is managing identities, authentication, authorization, and all of the regulatory auditing requirements. Within any cloud environment, an identity access strategy is a vital component and a prerequisite. GRC services are moving to the cloud as well, and these are the topic of the next section.

5.3.11   Compliance-as-a-Service (CaaS)[6]

Managed services providers historically have faced contractual difficulties with their customers in negotiating information assurance requirements, particularly regarding regulatory compliance verification. This problem becomes even more complex in a cloud computing environment, where physical resources can be geographically diverse, the regulatory landscape is vast and international in nature, and no single one-to-one relationship can determine the outcome of anything in the cloud.

Although this complexity may seem untenable at first glance, cloud computing potentially furnishes an exciting and cost-effective layer of opportunity in the creation of a "Compliance-as-a-Service" (CaaS) offering. CaaS could solve a number of problems that have been viewed as difficult or impossible, both by service providers and by their customers:

---

6.   This section is based on email exchanges and input from Eddie Schwartz, CSO of Netwitness (www.netwitness.com), 12 Mar 2009.

- **Cost-effective multiregulation compliance verification:** A dominant percentage of all security and privacy regulations utilize a common base of security controls and best practices. These regulations, which have developed over many years, have been built on an identical, common body of knowledge augmented by a small percentage of nuance associated with industry-specific requirements. In a CaaS environment, next-generation network security monitoring technology could be deployed in the cloud to perform automated, rules-based data mining of cloud traffic flows. Compliance-oriented security services could be created to support verification of specific regulatory controls, from the network to the application layers, with commensurate alerting and reporting mechanisms.

- **Continuous audit:** A CaaS offering could provide continuous audit of security controls associated with the compliance domains within its scope. This approach would provide a higher level of information assurance than daily scans, quarterly spot audits, or statistical sampling methodologies. Additionally, the classic problem of third-party assurance and verification of a service provider's security would be resolved because of the transparency thatCaaS would provide into the service provider's security controls.

- **Threat intelligence:** Any CaaS offering would benefit from the aggregate threat intelligence and distributed security analytics associated with multiple cloud customers. This situational visibility would be invaluable in understanding and defending against current and emerging threats to the cloud computer environment.

5.3.12 The Future of Identity in the Cloud

As more business applications are delivered as cloud-based services, more identities are being created for use in the cloud. The challenges of managing identity in the cloud are far-reaching and include ensuring that multiple identities are kept secure. There must be coordination of identity information among various cloud services and among enterprise identity data stores and other cloud services. A flexible, user-centric identity management system is needed. It needs to support all of the identity mechanisms and protocols that exist and those that are emerging. It should be capable of operating on various platforms, applications, and service-oriented architectural patterns. Users must be empowered to execute effective controls over their personal information. In the future, they will have control over who has their personal data and how it is used, minimizing the risk of identity theft and fraud. Their identity and reputation will be transferable. If they establish a good reputation on one site, they will be able to use that fact on other sites as well.

5.4   Privacy and Its Relation to Cloud-Based Information Systems

Information privacy[7] or data privacy is the relationship between collection and dissemination of data, technology, the public expectation of privacy, and the legal issues surrounding them. The challenge in data privacy is to share data while protecting personally identifiable information. The fields of data security and information security design and utilize software, hardware, and human resources to address this issue. The ability to control what information one reveals about oneself over the Internet, and who can access that information, has become a growing concern. These concerns include whether email can be stored or read by third parties without consent, or whether third parties can track the web sites someone has visited. Another concern is whether web sites which are visited collect, store, and possibly share personally identifiable information about users. *Personally identifiable information* (PII), as used in information security, refers to information that can be used to uniquely identify, contact, or locate a single person or can be used with other sources to uniquely identify a single individual.[8]

Privacy is an important business issue focused on ensuring that personal data is protected from unauthorized and inappropriate collection, use, and disclosure, ultimately preventing the loss of customer trust and inappropriate fraudulent activity such as identity theft, email spamming, and phishing. According to the results of the Ponemon Institute and TRUSTe's 2008 Most Trusted Companies for Privacy Survey, privacy is a key market differentiator in today's cyberworld. "Consumer perceptions are not superficial, but are in fact the result of diligent and successful execution of thoughtful privacy strategies," said Dr. Larry Ponemon, chairman and founder of the Ponemon Institute. "Consumers want to do business with brands they believe they can trust."[9]

---

7.   http://en.wikipedia.org/wiki/Information_privacy, retrieved 28 Feb 2009.
8.   http://en.wikipedia.org/wiki/Personally_identifiable_information, retrieved 28 Feb 2009.
9.   http://www.truste.org/about/press_release/12_15_08.php, retrieved 28 Feb 2009.

Adhering to privacy best practices is simply good business but is typically ensured by legal requirements. Many countries have enacted laws to protect individuals' right to have their privacy respected, such as Canada's Personal Information Protection and Electronic Documents Act (PIPEDA), the European Commission's directive on data privacy, the Swiss Federal Data Protection Act (DPA), and the Swiss Federal Data Protection Ordinance. In the United States, individuals' right to privacy is also protected by business-sector regulatory requirements such as the Health Insurance Portability and Accountability Act (HIPAA), The Gramm-Leach-Bliley Act (GLBA), and the FCC Customer Proprietary Network Information (CPNI) rules.

Customer information may be "user data" and/or "personal data." User data is information collected from a customer, including:

- Any data that is collected directly from a customer (e.g., entered by the customer via an application's user interface)
- Any data about a customer that is gathered indirectly (e.g., meta-data in documents)
- Any data about a customer's usage behavior (e.g., logs or history)
- Any data relating to a customer's system (e.g., system configuration, IP address)

Personal data (sometimes also called personally identifiable information) is any piece of data which can potentially be used to uniquely identify, contact, or locate a single person or can be used with other sources to uniquely identify a single individual. Not all customer/user data collected by a company is personal data. Examples of personal data include:

- Contact information (name, email address, phone, postal address)
- Forms of identification (Social Security number, driver's license, passport, fingerprints)
- Demographic information (age, gender, ethnicity, religious affiliation, sexual orientation, criminal record)
- Occupational information (job title, company name, industry)
- Health care information (plans, providers, history, insurance, genetic information)

- Financial information (bank and credit/debit card account numbers, purchase history, credit records)
- Online activity (IP address, cookies, flash cookies, log-in credentials)

A subset of personal data is defined as sensitive and requires a greater level of controlled collection, use, disclosure, and protection. Sensitive data includes some forms of identification such as Social Security number, some demographic information, and information that can be used to gain access to financial accounts, such as credit or debit card numbers and account numbers in combination with any required security code, access code, or password. Finally, it is important to understand that user data may also be personal dasta.

5.4.1   Privacy Risks and the Cloud

Cloud computing has significant implications for the privacy of personal information as well as for the confidentiality of business and governmental information. Any information stored locally on a computer can be stored in a cloud, including email, word processing documents, spreadsheets, videos, health records, photographs, tax or other financial information, business plans, PowerPoint presentations, accounting information, advertising campaigns, sales numbers, appointment calendars, address books, and more. The entire contents of a user's storage device may be stored with a single cloud provider or with many cloud providers. Whenever an individual, a business, a government agency, or other entity shares information in the cloud, privacy or confidentiality questions may arise.

A user's privacy and confidentiality risks vary significantly with the terms of service and privacy policy established by the cloud provider. For some types of information and some categories of cloud computing users, privacy and confidentiality rights, obligations, and status may change when a user discloses information to a cloud provider. Disclosure and remote storage may have adverse consequences for the legal status of or protections for personal or business information. The location of information in the cloud may have significant effects on the privacy and confidentiality protections of information and on the privacy obligations of those who process or store the information. Information in the cloud may have more than one legal location at the same time, with differing legal consequences. Laws could oblige a cloud provider to examine user records for evidence of criminal activity and other matters. Legal uncertainties make it difficult to assess the status of information in the cloud as well as the privacy and confidentiality protections available to users.

5.4.2   Protecting Privacy Information

The Federal Trade Commission is educating consumers and businesses about the importance of personal information privacy, including the security of personal information. Under the FTC Act, the Commission guards against unfairness and deception by enforcing companies' privacy promises about how they collect, use, and secure consumers' personal information. The FTC publishes a guide that is a great educational tool for consumers and businesses alike, titled "Protecting Personal Information: A Guide for Business."[10] In general, the basics for protecting data privacy are as follows, whether in a virtualized environment, the cloud, or on a static machine:

- **Collection:** You should have a valid business purpose for developing applications and implementing systems that collect, use or transmit personal data.
- **Notice:** There should be a clear statement to the data owner of a company's/providers intended collection, use, retention, disclosure, transfer, and protection of personal data.
- **Choice and consent:** The data owner must provide clear and unambiguous consent to the collection, use, retention, disclosure, and protection of personal data.
- **Use:** Once it is collected, personal data must only be used (including transfers to third parties) in accordance with the valid business purpose and as stated in the Notice.
- **Security:** Appropriate security measures must be in place (e.g., encryption) to ensure the confidentiality, integrity, and authentication of personal data during transfer, storage, and use.
- **Access:** Personal data must be available to the owner for review and update. Access to personal data must be restricted to relevant and authorized personnel.
- **Retention:** A process must be in place to ensure that personal data is only retained for the period necessary to accomplish the intended business purpose or that which is required by law.

---

10.   http://www.ftc.gov/bcp/edu/pubs/business/idtheft/bus69.pdf, retrieved 27 Feb 2009.

- **Disposal:** The personal data must be disposed of in a secure and appropriate manner (i.e., using encryption disk erasure or paper shredders).

Particular attention to the privacy of personal information should be taken in an a SaaS and managed services environment when (1) transferring personally identifiable information to and from a customer's system, (2) storing personal information on the customer's system, (3) transferring anonymous data from the customer's system, (4) installing software on a customer's system, (5) storing and processing user data at the company, and (6) deploying servers. There should be an emphasis on notice and consent, data security and integrity, and enterprise control for each of the events above as appropriate.[11]

5.4.3 The Future of Privacy in the Cloud

There has been a good deal of public discussion of the technical architecture of cloud computing and the business models that could support it; however, the debate about the legal and policy issues regarding privacy and confidentiality raised by cloud computing has not kept pace. A report titled "Privacy in the Clouds: Risks to Privacy and Confidentiality from Cloud Computing," prepared by Robert Gellman for the World Privacy Forum, provides the following observations on the future of policy and confidentiality in the cloud computing environment:

- Responses to the privacy and confidentiality risks of cloud computing include better policies and practices by cloud providers, more vigilance by users, and changes to laws.

- The cloud computing industry could establish standards that would help users to analyze the difference between cloud providers and to assess the risks that users face.

- Users should pay more attention to the consequences of using a cloud provider and, especially, to the provider's terms of service.

- For those risks not addressable solely through policies and practices, changes in laws may be needed.

---

11. Further details on privacy guidelines for developing software products and services can be found at http://www.microsoft.com/downloads/details.aspx?FamilyID=c48cf80f-6e87-48f5-83ec-a18d1ad2fc1f&displaylang=en.

- Users of cloud providers would benefit from greater transparency about the risks and consequences of cloud computing, from fairer and more standard terms, and from better legal protections. The cloud computing industry would also benefit.[12]

5.5   Chapter Summary

In this chapter, we covered the importance and relevance of federation, presence, identity, and privacy in cloud computing. We covered the latest challenges, solutions, and potential future for each area. Combined with the standards for cloud computing, the concepts of this chapter are the glue for the architectural elements that make the cloud a highly distributed, reliable, flexible, and cost-efficient functional medium in which to conduct business. The number-one concern and challenge concerning cloud computing and services is security It is a critical element of cloud computing and is associated with the other areas discussed in this chapter. In the next chapter, we will discuss the latest security vulnerabilities, challenges, and best practices for security in the cloud.

---

12.   http://www.worldprivacyforum.org/pdf/WPF_Cloud_Privacy_Report.pdf, 23 Feb 2009, retrieved 28 Feb 2009.

Chapter 6

Security in the Cloud

6.1 Chapter Overview

As discussed at the beginning of this book, cloud service providers are leveraging virtualization technologies combined with self-service capabilities for computing resources via the Internet. In these service provider environments, virtual machines from multiple organizations have to be co-located on the same physical server in order to maximize the efficiencies of virtualization. Cloud service providers must learn from the managed service provider (MSP) model and ensure that their customers' applications and data are secure if they hope to retain their customer base and competitiveness. Today, enterprises are looking toward cloud computing horizons to expand their on-premises infrastructure, but most cannot afford the risk of compromising the security of their applications and data. For example, IDC recently conducted a survey[1] (see Figure 6.1) of 244 IT executives/CIOs and their line-of-business (LOB) colleagues to gauge their opinions and understand their companies' use of IT cloud services. Security ranked first as the greatest challenge or issue of cloud computing.

This chapter identifies current security concerns about cloud computing environments and describes the methodology for ensuring application and data security and compliance integrity for those resources that are moving from on-premises to public cloud environments. More important, this discussion focuses on why and how these resources should be protected in the Software-as-a-Service (SaaS), Platform-as-a-Service (PaaS), and Infrastructure-as-a-Service (IaaS) environments and offers security "best practices" for service providers and enterprises that are in or are contemplating

---

1.   http://cloudsecurity.org/2008/10/14/biggest-cloud-challenge-security, retrieved 21 Feb 2009.

153

Figure 6.1   Results of IDC survey ranking security challenges.

moving into the cloud computing space. First, let's review the concepts of the three major cloud computing service provider models.

Software-as-a-Service is a model of software deployment in which an application is licensed for use as a service provided to customers on demand. On-demand licensing and use relieves the customer of the burden of equipping a device with every application to be used.[2] Gartner predicts that 30% of new software will be delivered via the SaaS model by 2010.

Platform-as-a-Service is an outgrowth of the SaaS application delivery model. With the PaaS model, all of the facilities required to support the complete life cycle of building and delivering web applications and services are available to developers, IT managers, and end users entirely from the Internet, without software downloads or installation. PaaS is also sometimes known as "cloudware." PaaS offerings include workflow facilities for application design, application development, testing, deployment, and hosting, as well as application services such as team collaboration, web service integration and marshalling, database integration, security, scalability, storage, persistence, state management, application versioning, application

2.   http://en.wikipedia.org/wiki/Software_as_a_service.

instrumentation, and developer community facilitation. These services are provisioned as an integrated solution over the web.[3]

Infrastructure-as-a-Service is the delivery of computer infrastructure (typically a platform virtualization environment) as a service. These "virtual infrastructure stacks"[4] are an example of the everything-as-a-service trend and share many of the common characteristics. Rather than purchasing servers, software, data center space, or network equipment, clients buy these resources as a fully outsourced service. The service is typically billed on a utility computing basis, and the quantity of resources consumed (and therefore the cost) typically reflects the level of activity. It is an evolution of web hosting and virtual private server offerings.[5]

Inspired by the IT industry's move toward SaaS, in which software is not purchased but rented as a service from providers, **IT-as-a-Service (ITaaS)** is being proposed to take this concept further, to bring the service model right to your IT infrastructure. The modern IT organization must run itself as a separate operation and become more strategic in operational decisions. Many organizations are in the process of transforming their IT departments into self-sustaining cost-center operations, treating internal users as if they were customers.

This transformation is not trivial and usually involves elements of project portfolio management, workflow reengineering, and process improvement. The transformation can take several years to be completed. Many large IT organizations have adopted the Information Technology Infrastructure Library (ITIL) framework to help with this transformation. Organizations can harness their help desks, avoid downtime resulting from unauthorized changes, and deliver better service to their internal customers simply by adopting best practices for managing service requests, changes, and IT assets. The adoption of IT-as-a-Service can help enterprise IT functions focus on strategic alignment with business goals. However, if efforts in this direction are poorly implemented, organizations risk further alienating their technical support staff from the rest of the organization—turning them into order takers for the enterprise rather than business advisers. When it is done properly, a customer-centric IT

---

3.   http://blogs.zdnet.com/Hinchcliffe/?p=166&tag=btxcsim; http://en.wikipedia.org/wiki/PaaS.
4.   http://www.cbronline.com/article_feature.asp?guid=E66B8BF0-43BB-4AB1-9475-5884D82C897F.
5.   http://en.wikipedia.org/wiki/IaaS.

department increases productivity, drives up project success rates, and creates a higher profile for technology within the organization.

While enterprises cope with defining the details of cloud computing, the single, unifying theme is *service*. Cloud computing, on-demand applications, and managed security are now perceived as part of an emerging ITaaS paradigm. Current industry buzz seems to reinforce the message that significant investments of capital, time, and intellectual resources are indeed being directed toward offering next-generation information and communication technology (ICT) infrastructure, which may allow enterprises to outsource IT completely and confidently. Only time will tell if ITaaS is really on the edge of enterprise adoption. Many in the industry believe that the advent of developer platforms designed for the cloud will hasten this transition and, as a result, fewer enterprises will need to deploy middleware to manage patchwork-implemented business applications, legacy or otherwise. Infrastructure vendors are also jumping on this bandwagon. Amazon has been a pioneer, with the release of Amazon S3 (Storage-as-a-Service). With the maturation of virtualization technologies, the adoption of virtual infrastructure and storage-on-demand services will accelerate along with the SaaS model.

There are some key financial benefits in moving to an ITaaS model, such has not having to incur capital costs; having a transparent, monthly pricing plan; scalability; and reasonable costs of expansion. Operational benefits of ITaaS include increased reliability because of a centralized infrastructure, which can ensure that critical services and applications are monitored continually; software flexibility, with centrally maintained products that allow for quick rollout of new functionalities and updates; and data security, since company data can be stored on owner-managed premises and backed up using encryption to a secure off-site data center.

Another service that is being discussed as we are writing this book is the concept of **Anything-as-a-Service (XaaS),** which is also a subset of cloud computing. XaaS broadly encompasses a process of activating reusable software components over the network. The most common and successful example is Software-as-a-Service. The growth of "as-a-service" offerings has been facilitated by extremely low barriers to entry (they are often accessible for free or available as recurring charges on a personal credit card). As a result, such offerings have been adopted by consumers and small businesses well before pushing into the enterprise space. All "as-a-service" offerings share a number of common attributes, including little or no capital expenditure since the required infrastructure is owned by the service provider, massive scalability, multitenancy, and device and location independence allowing consumers remote access to systems using nearly any current available technology.

On the surface, it appears that XaaS is a potentially game-changing technology that could reshape IT. However, most CIOs still depend on internal infrastructures because they are not convinced that cloud computing is ready for prime time. Many contend that if you want real reliability, you must write more reliable applications. Regardless of one's view on the readiness of cloud computing to meet corporate IT requirements, it cannot be ignored. The concept of pay-as-you-go applications, development platforms, processing power, storage, or any other cloud-enabled services has emerged and can be expected to reshape IT over the next decade.

Other concerns plague IT executives. They fear their data won't be safe in the hands of cloud providers and that they won't be able to manage cloud resources effectively. They may also worry that the new technology will threaten their own data centers and staff. Collectively, these fears tend to hold back the cloud computing market that some perceive growing to nearly $100 billion in the next decade.

Although there is a significant benefit to leveraging cloud computing, security concerns have led organizations to hesitate to move critical resources to the cloud. Corporations and individuals are often concerned about how security and compliance integrity can be maintained in this new environment. Even more worrying, however, may be those corporations that are jumping into cloud computing that may be oblivious to the implications of putting critical applications and data in the cloud. This chapter will answer the security concerns of the former and educate the latter.

Moving critical applications and sensitive data to public and shared cloud environments is of great concern for those corporations that are moving beyond their data center's network perimeter defense. To alleviate these concerns, a cloud solution provider must ensure that customers will continue to have the same security and privacy controls over their applications and services, provide evidence to customers that their organization and customers are secure and they can meet their service-level agreements, and that they can prove compliance to auditors.

6.2   Cloud Security Challenges

Although virtualization and cloud computing can help companies accomplish more by breaking the physical bonds between an IT infrastructure and its users, heightened security threats must be overcome in order to benefit fully from this new computing paradigm. This is particularly true for the SaaS provider. Some security concerns are worth more discussion. For example, in the cloud, you lose control over assets in some respects, so your security model must be reassessed. Enterprise security is only as good as the least reliable partner, department, or vendor. Can you trust your data to your service provider? In the following paragraphs, we discuss some issues you should consider before answering that question.

With the cloud model, you lose control over physical security. In a public cloud, you are sharing computing resources with other companies. In a shared pool outside the enterprise, you don't have any knowledge or control of where the resources run. Exposing your data in an environment shared with other companies could give the government "reasonable cause" to seize your assets because another company has violated the law. Simply because you share the environment in the cloud, may put your data at risk of seizure.

Storage services provided by one cloud vendor may be incompatible with another vendor's services should you decide to move from one to the other. Vendors are known for creating what the hosting world calls "sticky services"—services that an end user may have difficulty transporting from one cloud vendor to another (e.g., Amazon's "Simple Storage Service" [S3] is incompatible with IBM's Blue Cloud, or Google, or Dell).

If information is encrypted while passing through the cloud, who controls the encryption/decryption keys? Is it the customer or the cloud vendor? Most customers probably want their data encrypted both ways across the Internet using SSL (Secure Sockets Layer protocol). They also most likely want their data encrypted while it is at rest in the cloud vendor's storage pool. Be sure that you, the customer, control the encryption/decryption keys, just as if the data were still resident on your own servers.

Data integrity means ensuring that data is identically maintained during any operation (such as transfer, storage, or retrieval). Put simply, data integrity is assurance that the data is consistent and correct. Ensuring the integrity of the data really means that it changes only in response to authorized transactions. This sounds good, but you must remember that a common standard to ensure data integrity does not yet exist.

Using SaaS offerings in the cloud means that there is much less need for software development. For example, using a web-based customer relationship management (CRM) offering eliminates the necessity to write code and "customize" a vendor's application. If you plan to use internally developed code in the cloud, it is even more important to have a formal secure software development life cycle (SDLC). The immature use of mashup technology (combinations of web services), which is fundamental to cloud applications, is inevitably going to cause unwitting security vulnerabilities in those applications. Your development tool of choice should have a security model embedded in it to guide developers during the development phase and restrict users only to their authorized data when the system is deployed into production.

As more and more mission-critical processes are moved to the cloud, SaaS suppliers will have to provide log data in a real-time, straightforward manner, probably for their administrators as well as their customers' personnel. Someone has to be responsible for monitoring for security and compliance, and unless the application and data are under the control of end users, they will not be able to. Will customers trust the cloud provider enough to push their mission-critical applications out to the cloud? Since the SaaS provider's logs are internal and not necessarily accessible externally or by clients or investigators, monitoring is difficult. Since access to logs is required for Payment Card Industry Data Security Standard (PCI DSS) compliance and may be requested by auditors and regulators, security managers need to make sure to negotiate access to the provider's logs as part of any service agreement.

Cloud applications undergo constant feature additions, and users must keep up to date with application improvements to be sure they are protected. The speed at which applications will change in the cloud will affect both the SDLC and security. For example, Microsoft's SDLC assumes that mission-critical software will have a three- to five-year period in which it will not change substantially, but the cloud may require a change in the application every few weeks. Even worse, a secure SLDC will not be able to provide a security cycle that keeps up with changes that occur so quickly. This means that users must constantly upgrade, because an older version may not function, or protect the data.

Having proper fail-over technology is a component of securing the cloud that is often overlooked. The company can survive if a non-mission-critical application goes offline, but this may not be true for mission-critical applications. Core business practices provide competitive differentiation. Security needs to move to the data level, so that enterprises can be sure their data is protected wherever it goes. Sensitive data is the domain of the enterprise, not the cloud computing provider. One of the key challenges in cloud computing is data-level security.

Most compliance standards do not envision compliance in a world of cloud computing. There is a huge body of standards that apply for IT security and compliance, governing most business interactions that will, over time, have to be translated to the cloud. SaaS makes the process of compliance more complicated, since it may be difficult for a customer to discern where its data resides on a network controlled by its SaaS provider, or a partner of that provider, which raises all sorts of compliance issues of data privacy, segregation, and security. Many compliance regulations require that data not be intermixed with other data, such as on shared servers or databases. Some countries have strict limits on what data about its citizens can be stored and for how long, and some banking regulators require that customers' financial data remain in their home country.

Compliance with government regulations such as the Sarbanes-Oxley Act (SOX), the Gramm-Leach-Bliley Act (GLBA), and the Health Insurance Portability and Accountability Act (HIPAA), and industry standards such as the PCI DSS, will be much more challenging in the SaaS environment. There is a perception that cloud computing removes data compliance responsibility; however, it should be emphasized that the data owner is still fully responsible for compliance. Those who adopt cloud computing must remember that it is the responsibility of the data owner, not the service provider, to secure valuable data.

Government policy will need to change in response to both the opportunity and the threats that cloud computing brings. This will likely focus on the off-shoring of personal data and protection of privacy, whether it is data being controlled by a third party or off-shored to another country. There will be a corresponding drop in security as the traditional controls such as VLANs (virtual local-area networks) and firewalls prove less effective during the transition to a virtualized environment. Security managers will need to pay particular attention to systems that contain critical data such as corporate financial information or source code during the transition to server virtualization in production environments.

Outsourcing means losing significant control over data, and while this isn't a good idea from a security perspective, the business ease and financial savings will continue to increase the usage of these services. Security managers will need to work with their company's legal staff to ensure that appropriate contract terms are in place to protect corporate data and provide for acceptable service-level agreements.

Cloud-based services will result in many mobile IT users accessing business data and services without traversing the corporate network. This will increase the need for enterprises to place security controls between mobile users and cloud-based services. Placing large amounts of sensitive data in a globally accessible cloud leaves organizations open to large distributed threats—attackers no longer have to come onto the premises to steal data, and they can find it all in the one "virtual" location.

Virtualization efficiencies in the cloud require virtual machines from multiple organizations to be co-located on the same physical resources. Although traditional data center security still applies in the cloud environment, physical segregation and hardware-based security cannot protect against attacks between virtual machines on the same server. Administrative access is through the Internet rather than the controlled and restricted direct or on-premises connection that is adhered to in the traditional data center model. This increases risk and exposure and will require stringent monitoring for changes in system control and access control restriction.

The dynamic and fluid nature of virtual machines will make it difficult to maintain the consistency of security and ensure the auditability of records. The ease of cloning and distribution between physical servers could result in the propagation of configuration errors and other vulnerabilities. Proving the security state of a system and identifying the location of an insecure virtual machine will be challenging. Regardless of the location of the virtual machine within the virtual environment, the intrusion detection and prevention systems will need to be able to detect malicious activity at virtual machine level. The co-location of multiple virtual machines increases the attack surface and risk of virtual machine-to-virtual machine compromise.

Localized virtual machines and physical servers use the same operating systems as well as enterprise and web applications in a cloud server environment, increasing the threat of an attacker or malware exploiting vulnerabilities in these systems and applications remotely. Virtual machines are vulnerable as they move between the private cloud and the public cloud. A fully or partially shared cloud environment is expected to have a greater attack surface and therefore can be considered to be at greater risk than a dedicated resources environment.

Operating system and application files are on a shared physical infrastructure in a virtualized cloud environment and require system, file, and activity monitoring to provide confidence and auditable proof to enterprise customers that their resources have not been compromised or tampered with. In the cloud computing environment, the enterprise subscribes to cloud computing resources, and the responsibility for patching is the subscriber's rather than the cloud computing vendor's. The need for patch maintenance vigilance is imperative. Lack of due diligence in this regard could rapidly make the task unmanageable or impossible, leaving you with "virtual patching" as the only alternative.

Enterprises are often required to prove that their security compliance is in accord with regulations, standards, and auditing practices, regardless of the location of the systems at which the data resides. Data is fluid in cloud computing and may reside in on-premises physical servers, on-premises virtual machines, or off-premises virtual machines running on cloud computing resources, and this will require some rethinking on the part of auditors and practitioners alike.

In the rush to take advantage of the benefits of cloud computing, not least of which is significant cost savings, many corporations are likely rushing into cloud computing without a serious consideration of the security implications. To establish zones of trust in the cloud, the virtual machines must be self-defending, effectively moving the perimeter to the virtual machine itself. Enterprise perimeter security (i.e., firewalls, demilitarized zones [DMZs], network segmentation, intrusion detection and prevention systems [IDS/IPS], monitoring tools, and the associated security policies) only controls the data that resides and transits behind the perimeter. In the cloud computing world, the cloud computing provider is in charge of customer data security and privacy.

6.3 Software-as-a-Service Security

Cloud computing models of the future will likely combine the use of SaaS (and other XaaS's as appropriate), utility computing, and Web 2.0 collaboration technologies to leverage the Internet to satisfy their customers' needs. New business models being developed as a result of the move to

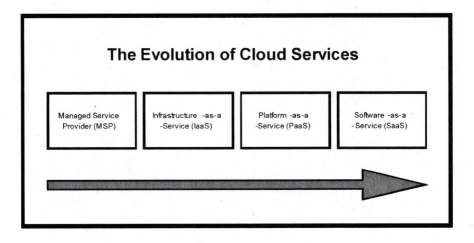

Figure 6.2   The evolution of cloud services.

cloud computing are creating not only new technologies and business operational processes but also new security requirements and challenges as described previously. As the most recent evolutionary step in the cloud service model (see Figure 6.2), SaaS will likely remain the dominant cloud service model for the foreseeable future and the area where the most critical need for security practices and oversight will reside.

Just as with an managed service provider, corporations or end users will need to research vendors' policies on data security before using vendor services to avoid losing or not being able to access their data. The technology analyst and consulting firm Gartner lists seven security issues which one should discuss with a cloud-computing vendor:

1. **Privileged user access**—Inquire about who has specialized access to data, and about the hiring and management of such administrators.

2. **Regulatory compliance**—Make sure that the vendor is willing to undergo external audits and/or security certifications.

3. **Data location**—Does the provider allow for any control over the location of data?

4. **Data segregation**—Make sure that encryption is available at all stages, and that these encryption schemes were designed and tested by experienced professionals.

5. **Recovery**—Find out what will happen to data in the case of a disaster. Do they offer complete restoration? If so, how long would that take?

6. **Investigative support**—Does the vendor have the ability to investigate any inappropriate or illegal activity?

7. **Long-term viability**—What will happen to data if the company goes out of business? How will data be returned, and in what format?[6]

Determining data security is harder today, so data security functions have become more critical than they have been in the past. A tactic not covered by Gartner is to encrypt the data yourself. If you encrypt the data using a trusted algorithm, then regardless of the service provider's security and encryption policies, the data will only be accessible with the decryption keys. Of course, this leads to a follow-on problem: How do you manage private keys in a pay-on-demand computing infrastructure?[7]

To address the security issues listed above along with others mentioned earlier in the chapter, SaaS providers will need to incorporate and enhance security practices used by the managed service providers and develop new ones as the cloud computing environment evolves. The baseline security practices for the SaaS environment as currently formulated are discussed in the following sections.

6.3.1   Security Management (People)

One of the most important actions for a security team is to develop a formal charter for the security organization and program. This will foster a shared vision among the team of what security leadership is driving toward and expects, and will also foster "ownership" in the success of the collective team. The charter should be aligned with the strategic plan of the organization or company the security team works for. Lack of clearly defined roles and responsibilities, and agreement on expectations, can result in a general feeling of loss and confusion among the security team about what is expected of them, how their skills and experienced can be leveraged, and

---

6.   http://www.infoworld.com/article/08/07/02/
      Gartner_Seven_cloudcomputing_security_risks_1.html, retrieved 20 Feb 2009.
7.   http://en.wikipedia.org/wiki/Cloud_service#Cloud_storage, retrieved 15 Feb 2009.

meeting their performance goals. Morale among the team and pride in the team is lowered, and security suffers as a result.

6.3.2   Security Governance

A security steering committee should be developed whose objective is to focus on providing guidance about security initiatives and alignment with business and IT strategies. A charter for the security team is typically one of the first deliverables from the steering committee. This charter must clearly define the roles and responsibilities of the security team and other groups involved in performing information security functions. Lack of a formalized strategy can lead to an unsustainable operating model and security level as it evolves. In addition, lack of attention to security governance can result in key needs of the business not being met, including but not limited to, risk management, security monitoring, application security, and sales support. Lack of proper governance and management of duties can also result in potential security risks being left unaddressed and opportunities to improve the business being missed because the security team is not focused on the key security functions and activities that are critical to the business.

6.3.3   Risk Management

Effective risk management entails identification of technology assets; identification of data and its links to business processes, applications, and data stores; and assignment of ownership and custodial responsibilities. Actions should also include maintaining a repository of information assets. Owners have authority and accountability for information assets including protection requirements, and custodians implement confidentiality, integrity, availability, and privacy controls. A formal risk assessment process should be created that allocates security resources linked to business continuity.

6.3.4   Risk Assessment

Security risk assessment is critical to helping the information security organization make informed decisions when balancing the dueling priorities of business utility and protection of assets. Lack of attention to completing formalized risk assessments can contribute to an increase in information security audit findings, can jeopardize certification goals, and can lead to inefficient and ineffective selection of security controls that may not adequately mitigate information security risks to an acceptable level. A formal information security risk management process should proactively assess information security risks as well as plan and manage them on a periodic or as-needed basis. More detailed and technical security risk assessments in the form of threat modeling should also be applied to applications and infrastructure. Doing so can help the product management and engineering groups to be more proactive in designing and testing the security of applications and systems and to collaborate more closely with the internal security team. Threat modeling requires both IT and business process knowledge, as well as technical knowledge of how the applications or systems under review work.

6.3.5 Security Portfolio Management

Given the fast pace and collaborative nature of cloud computing, security portfolio management is a fundamental component of ensuring efficient and effective operation of any information security program and organization. Lack of portfolio and project management discipline can lead to projects never being completed or never realizing their expected return; unsustainable and unrealistic workloads and expectations because projects are not prioritized according to strategy, goals, and resource capacity; and degradation of the system or processes due to the lack of supporting maintenance and sustaining organization planning. For every new project that a security team undertakes, the team should ensure that a project plan and project manager with appropriate training and experience is in place so that the project can be seen through to completion. Portfolio and project management capabilities can be enhanced by developing methodology, tools, and processes to support the expected complexity of projects that include both traditional business practices and cloud computing practices.

6.3.6 Security Awareness

People will remain the weakest link for security. Knowledge and culture are among the few effective tools to manage risks related to people. Not providing proper awareness and training to the people who may need them can expose the company to a variety of security risks for which people, rather than system or application vulnerabilities, are the threats and points of entry. Social engineering attacks, lower reporting of and slower responses to potential security incidents, and inadvertent customer data leaks are all possible and probable risks that may be triggered by lack of an effective security awareness program. The one-size-fits-all approach to security awareness is not necessarily the right approach for SaaS organizations; it is more important to have an information security awareness and training program that tailors the information and training according the individual's role in the organization. For example, security awareness can be provided to development engineers in the form of secure code and testing training, while customer service representatives can be provided data privacy and security certification awareness training. Ideally, both a generic approach and an individual-role approach should be used.

6.3.7   Education and Training

Programs should be developed that provide a baseline for providing fundamental security and risk management skills and knowledge to the security team and their internal partners. This entails a formal process to assess and align skill sets to the needs of the security team and to provide adequate training and mentorship—providing a broad base of fundamental security, inclusive of data privacy, and risk management knowledge. As the cloud computing business model and its associated services change, the security challenges facing an organization will also change. Without adequate, current training and mentorship programs in place, the security team may not be prepared to address the needs of the business.

6.3.8   Policies, Standards, and Guidelines

Many resources and templates are available to aid in the development of information security policies, standards, and guidelines. A cloud computing security team should first identify the information security and business requirements unique to cloud computing, SaaS, and collaborative software application security. Policies should be developed, documented, and implemented, along with documentation for supporting standards and guidelines. To maintain relevancy, these policies, standards, and guidelines should be reviewed at regular intervals (at least annually) or when significant changes occur in the business or IT environment. Outdated policies, standards, and guidelines can result in inadvertent disclosure of information as a cloud computing organizational business model changes. It is important to maintain the accuracy and relevance of information security policies, standards, and guidelines as business initiatives, the business environment, and the risk landscape change. Such policies, standards, and guidelines also provide the building blocks with which an organization can ensure consistency of performance and maintain continuity of knowledge during times of resource turnover.

6.3.9   Secure Software Development Life Cycle (SecSDLC)

The SecSDLC involves identifying specific threats and the risks they represent, followed by design and implementation of specific controls to counter those threats and assist in managing the risks they pose to the organization and/or its customers. The SecSDLC must provide consistency, repeatability, and conformance. The SDLC consists of six phases, and there are steps unique to the SecSLDC in each of phases:

- **Phase 1.Investigation:** Define project processes and goals, and document them in the program security policy.
- **Phase 2.Analysis:** Analyze existing security policies and programs, analyze current threats and controls, examine legal issues, and perform risk analysis.
- **Phase 3.Logical design:** Develop a security blueprint, plan incident response actions, plan business responses to disaster, and determine the feasibility of continuing and/or outsourcing the project.
- **Phase 4.Physical design:** Select technologies to support the security blueprint, develop a definition of a successful solution, design physical security measures to support technological solutions, and review and approve plans.
- **Phase 5.Implementation:** Buy or develop security solutions. At the end of this phase, present a tested package to management for approval.
- **Phase 6.Maintenance:** Constantly monitor, test, modify, update, and repair to respond to changing threats.[8]

In the SecSDLC, application code is written in a consistent manner that can easily be audited and enhanced; core application services are provided in a common, structured, and repeatable manner; and framework modules are thoroughly tested for security issues before implementation and continuously retested for conformance through the software regression test cycle. Additional security processes are developed to support application development projects such as external and internal penetration testing and

---

8.   Michael E. Whitman and Herbert J. Mattord, Management of Information Security, Thomson Course Technology, 2004, p. 57.

standard security requirements based on data classification. Formal training and communications should also be developed to raise awareness of process enhancements.

6.3.10   Security Monitoring and Incident Response

Centralized security information management systems should be used to provide notification of security vulnerabilities and to monitor systems continuously through automated technologies to identify potential issues. They should be integrated with network and other systems monitoring processes (e.g., security information management, security event management, security information and event management, and security operations centers that use these systems for dedicated 24/7/365 monitoring). Management of periodic, independent third-party security testing should also be included.

Many of the security threats and issues in SaaS center around application and data layers, so the types and sophistication of threats and attacks for a SaaS organization require a different approach to security monitoring than traditional infrastructure and perimeter monitoring. The organization may thus need to expand its security monitoring capabilities to include application- and data-level activities. This may also require subject-matter experts in applications security and the unique aspects of maintaining privacy in the cloud. Without this capability and expertise, a company may be unable to detect and prevent security threats and attacks to its customer data and service stability.

6.3.11   Third-Party Risk Management

As SaaS moves into cloud computing for the storage and processing of customer data, there is a higher expectation that the SaaS will effectively manage the security risks with third parties. Lack of a third-party risk management program may result in damage to the provider's reputation, revenue losses, and legal actions should the provider be found not to have performed due diligence on its third-party vendors.

6.3.12   Requests for Information and Sales Support

If you don't think that requests for information and sales support are part of a security team's responsibility, think again. They are part of the business, and particularly with SaaS, the integrity of the provider's security business model, regulatory and certification compliance, and your company's reputation, competitiveness, and marketability all depend on the security team's ability to provide honest, clear, and concise answers to a customer request for information (RFI) or request for proposal (RFP). A structured process and a knowledge base of frequently requested information will result in considerable efficiency and the avoidance of ad-hoc, inefficient, or inconsistent support of the customer RFI/RFP process. Members of the security team should be not only internal security evangelists but also security evangelists to customers in support of the sales and marketing teams. As discussed earlier, security is top-of-mind and a primary concern for cloud computing customers, and lack of information security representatives who can provide support to the sales team in addressing customer questions and concerns could result in the potential loss of a sales opportunity.

6.3.13   Business Continuity Plan

The purpose of business continuity (BC)/disaster recovery (DR) planning is to minimize the impact of an adverse event on business processes. Business continuity and resiliency services help ensure uninterrupted operations across all layers of the business, as well as helping businesses avoid, prepare for, and recover from a disruption. SaaS services that enable uninterrupted communications not only can help the business recover from an outage, they can reduce the overall complexity, costs, and risks of day-to-day management of your most critical applications. The cloud also offers some dramatic opportunities for cost-effective BC/DR solutions.

Some of the advantages that SaaS can provide over traditional BC/DR are eliminating email downtime, ensuring that email messages are never lost, and making system outages virtually invisible to end users no matter what happens to your staff or infrastructure; maintaining continuous telephone communication during a telecommunication outage so your organization can stay open and in contact with employees, customers, and partners at virtually any location, over any network, over any talking device; and providing wireless continuity for WiFi-enabled "smart" phones that ensures users will always be able to send and receive corporate email from their WiFi-enabled devices, even if your corporate mail system, data center, network, and staff are unavailable.[9]

6.3.14   Forensics

Computer forensics is used to retrieve and analyze data. The practice of computer forensics means responding to an event by gathering and preserving data, analyzing data to reconstruct events, and assessing the state of an

---

9.   http://www.eseminarslive.com/c/a/Cloud-Computing/Dell030509, retrieved 15 Feb 2009.

event. Network forensics includes recording and analyzing network events to determine the nature and source of information abuse, security attacks, and other such incidents on your network. This is typically achieved by recording or capturing packets long-term from a key point or points in your infrastructure (such as the core or firewall) and then data mining for analysis and re-creating content.[10]

Cloud computing can provide many advantages to both individual forensics investigators and their whole team. A dedicated forensic server can be built in the same cloud as the company cloud and can be placed offline but available for use when needed. This provides a cost-effective readiness factor because the company itself then does not face the logistical challenges involved. For example, a copy of a virtual machine can be given to multiple incident responders to distribute the forensic workload based on the job at hand or as new sources of evidence arise and need analysis. If a server in the cloud is compromised, it is possible to clone that server at the click of a mouse and make the cloned disks instantly available to the cloud forensics server, thus reducing evidence-acquisition time. In some cases, dealing with operations and trying to abstract the hardware from a data center may become a barrier to or at least slow down the process of doing forensics, especially if the system has to be taken down for a significant period of time while you search for the data and then hope you have the right physical acquisition toolkit and supports for the forensic software you are using.

Cloud computing provides the ability to avoid or eliminate disruption of operations and possible service downtime. Some cloud storage implementations expose a cryptographic checksum or hash (such as the Amazon S3 generation of an MD5 hash) when you store an object. This makes it possible to avoid the need to generate MD5 checksums using external tools—the checksums are already there, thus eliminating the need for forensic image verification time. In today's world, forensic examiners typically have to spend a lot of time consuming expensive provisioning of physical devices. Bit-by-bit copies are made more quickly by replicated, distributed file systems that cloud providers can engineer for their customers, so customers have to pay for storage only for as long as they need the. You can now test a wider range of candidate passwords in less time to speed investigations by accessing documents more quickly because of the significant increase in CPU power provided by cloud computing.[11]

---

10.   http://www.bitcricket.com/downloads/Network%20Forensics.pdf, retrieved 15 Feb 2009.

6.3.15   Security Architecture Design

A security architecture framework should be established with consideration of processes (enterprise authentication and authorization, access control, confidentiality, integrity, nonrepudiation, security management, etc.), operational procedures, technology specifications, people and organizational management, and security program compliance and reporting. A security architecture document should be developed that defines security and privacy principles to meet business objectives. Documentation is required for management controls and metrics specific to asset classification and control, physical security, system access controls, network and computer management, application development and maintenance, business continuity, and compliance. A design and implementation program should also be integrated with the formal system development life cycle to include a business case, requirements definition, design, and implementation plans. Technology and design methods should be included, as well as the security processes necessary to provide the following services across all technology layers:

1.   Authentication

2.   Authorization

3.   Availability

4.   Confidentiality

5.   Integrity

6.   Accountability

7.   Privacy

The creation of a secure architecture provides the engineers, data center operations personnel, and network operations personnel a common blueprint to design, build, and test the security of the applications and systems. Design reviews of new changes can be better assessed against this architecture to assure that they conform to the principles described in the architecture, allowing for more consistent and effective design reviews.

---

11.   http://cloudsecurity.org/2008/07/21/assessing-the-security-benefits-of-cloud-computing, retrieved 15 Feb 2009.

6.3.16   Vulnerability Assessment

Vulnerability assessment classifies network assets to more efficiently prioritize vulnerability-mitigation programs, such as patching and system upgrading. It measures the effectiveness of risk mitigation by setting goals of reduced vulnerability exposure and faster mitigation. Vulnerability management should be integrated with discovery, patch management, and upgrade management processes to close vulnerabilities before they can be exploited.

6.3.17   Password Assurance Testing

If the SaaS security team or its customers want to periodically test password strength by running password "crackers," they can use cloud computing to decrease crack time and pay only for what they use. Instead of using a distributed password cracker to spread the load across nonproduction machines, you can now put those agents in dedicated compute instances to alleviate mixing sensitive credentials with other workloads.[12]

6.3.18   Logging for Compliance and Security Investigations

When your logs are in the cloud, you can leverage cloud computing to index those logs in real-time and get the benefit of instant search results. A true real-time view can be achieved, since the compute instances can be examined and scaled as needed based on the logging load. Due to concerns about performance degradation and log size, the use of extended logging through an operating system C2 audit trail is rarely enabled. If you are willing to pay for enhanced logging, cloud computing provides the option.

6.3.19   Security Images

With cloud computing, you don't have to do physical operating system installs that frequently require additional third-party tools, are time-consuming to clone, and can add another agent to each endpoint. Virtualization-based cloud computing provides the ability to create "Gold image" VM secure builds and to clone multiple copies.[13] Gold image VMs also provide the ability to keep security up to date and reduce exposure by patching offline. Offline VMs can be patched off-network, providing an easier, more cost-effective, and less production-threatening way to test the impact of security changes. This is a great way to duplicate a copy of your production environment, implement a security change, and test the impact at low cost,

---

12.   http://cloudsecurity.org/2008/07/21/assessing-the-security-benefits-of-cloud-computing, retrieved 15 Feb 2009.

with minimal start-up time, and it removes a major barrier to doing security in a production environment.[14]

6.3.20 Data Privacy

A risk assessment and gap analysis of controls and procedures must be conducted. Based on this data, formal privacy processes and initiatives must be defined, managed, and sustained. As with security, privacy controls and protection must an element of the secure architecture design. Depending on the size of the organization and the scale of operations, either an individual or a team should be assigned and given responsibility for maintaining privacy.

A member of the security team who is responsible for privacy or a corporate security compliance team should collaborate with the company legal team to address data privacy issues and concerns. As with security, a privacy steering committee should also be created to help make decisions related to data privacy. Typically, the security compliance team, if one even exists, will not have formalized training on data privacy, which will limit the ability of the organization to address adequately the data privacy issues they currently face and will be continually challenged on in the future. The answer is to hire a consultant in this area, hire a privacy expert, or have one of your existing team members trained properly. This will ensure that your organization is prepared to meet the data privacy demands of its customers and regulators.

---

13.   When companies create a pool of virtualized servers for production use, they also change their deployment and operational practices. Given the ability to standardize server images (since there are no hardware dependencies), companies consolidate their server configurations into as few as possible "gold images" which are used as templates for creating common server configurations. Typical images include baseline operating system images, web server images, application server images, etc. This standardization introduces an additional risk factor: monoculture. All the standardized images will share the same weaknesses. Whereas in a traditional data center there are firewalls and intrusion-prevention devices between servers, in a virtual environment there are no physical firewalls separating the virtual machines. What used to be a multitier architecture with firewalls separating the tiers becomes a pool of servers. A single exposed server can lead to a rapidly propagating threat that can jump from server to server. Standardization of images is like dry tinder to a fire: A single piece of malware can become a firestorm that engulfs the entire pool of servers. The potential for loss and vulnerability increases with the size of the pool—in proportion to the number of virtual guests, each of which brings its own vulnerabilities, creating a higher risk than in a single-instance virtual server. Moreover, the risk of the sum is greater than the sum of the risk of the parts, because the vulnerability of each system is itself subject to a "network effect." Each additional server in the pool multiplies the vulnerability of other servers in the pool. See http://www.nemertes.com/issue_papers/virtualatization_risk_analysis.

14.   http://cloudsecurity.org/2008/07/21/assessing-the-security-benefits-of-cloud-computing, retrieved 15 Feb 2009.

For example, customer contractual requirements/agreements for data privacy must be adhered to, accurate inventories of customer data, where it is stored, who can access it, and how it is used must be known, and, though often overlooked, RFI/RFP questions regarding privacy must answered accurately. This requires special skills, training, and experience that do not typically exist within a security team.

As companies move away from a service model under which they do not store customer data to one under which they do store customer data, the data privacy concerns of customers increase exponentially. This new service model pushes companies into the cloud computing space, where many companies do not have sufficient experience in dealing with customer privacy concerns, permanence of customer data throughout its globally distributed systems, cross-border data sharing, and compliance with regulatory or lawful intercept requirements.

6.3.21   Data Governance

A formal data governance framework that defines a system of decision rights and accountability for information-related processes should be developed. This framework should describe who can take what actions with what information, and when, under what circumstances, and using what methods. The data governance framework should include:

- Data inventory
- Data classification
- Data analysis (business intelligence)
- Data protection
- Data privacy
- Data retention/recovery/discovery
- Data destruction

6.3.22   Data Security

The ultimate challenge in cloud computing is data-level security, and sensitive data is the domain of the enterprise, not the cloud computing provider. Security will need to move to the data level so that enterprises can be sure their data is protected wherever it goes. For example, with data-level security, the enterprise can specify that this data is not allowed to go outside of the United States. It can also force encryption of certain types of data, and permit only specified users to access the data. It can provide compliance with the Payment Card Industry Data Security Standard (PCI DSS). True unified end-to-end security in the cloud will likely requires an ecosystem of partners.

6.3.23 Application Security

Application security is one of the critical success factors for a world-class SaaS company. This is where the security features and requirements are defined and application security test results are reviewed. Application security processes, secure coding guidelines, training, and testing scripts and tools are typically a collaborative effort between the security and the development teams. Although product engineering will likely focus on the application layer, the security design of the application itself, and the infrastructure layers interacting with the application, the security team should provide the security requirements for the product development engineers to implement. This should be a collaborative effort between the security and product development team. External penetration testers are used for application source code reviews, and attack and penetration tests provide an objective review of the security of the application as well as assurance to customers that attack and penetration tests are performed regularly. Fragmented and undefined collaboration on application security can result in lower-quality design, coding efforts, and testing results.

Since many connections between companies and their SaaS providers are through the web, providers should secure their web applications by following Open Web Application Security Project (OWASP)[15] guidelines for secure application development (mirroring Requirement 6.5 of the PCI DSS, which mandates compliance with OWASP coding practices) and locking down ports and unnecessary commands on Linux, Apache, MySQL, and PHP (LAMP) stacks in the cloud, just as you would on-premises. LAMP is an open-source web development platform, also called a web stack, that uses Linux as the operating system, Apache as the web server, MySQL as the relational database management system RDBMS, and PHP as the object-oriented scripting language. Perl or Python is often substituted for PHP.[16]

---

15. http://www.owasp.org/index.php/Main_Page, retrieved 15 Feb 2009.
16. http://www.webopedia.com/TERM/L/LAMP.html, retrieved 15 Feb 2009.

6.3.24   Virtual Machine Security

In the cloud environment, physical servers are consolidated to multiple virtual machine instances on virtualized servers. Not only can data center security teams replicate typical security controls for the data center at large to secure the virtual machines, they can also advise their customers on how to prepare these machines for migration to a cloud environment when appropriate.

Firewalls, intrusion detection and prevention, integrity monitoring, and log inspection can all be deployed as software on virtual machines to increase protection and maintain compliance integrity of servers and applications as virtual resources move from on-premises to public cloud environments. By deploying this traditional line of defense to the virtual machine itself, you can enable critical applications and data to be moved to the cloud securely. To facilitate the centralized management of a server firewall policy, the security software loaded onto a virtual machine should include a bi-directional stateful firewall that enables virtual machine isolation and location awareness, thereby enabling a tightened policy and the flexibility to move the virtual machine from on-premises to cloud resources. Integrity monitoring and log inspection software must be applied at the virtual machine level.

This approach to virtual machine security, which connects the machine back to the mother ship, has some advantages in that the security software can be put into a single software agent that provides for consistent control and management throughout the cloud while integrating seamlessly back into existing security infrastructure investments, providing economies of scale, deployment, and cost savings for both the service provider and the enterprise.

6.3.25   Identity Access Management (IAM)

As discussed in Chapter 5, identity and access management is a critical function for every organization, and a fundamental expectation of SaaS customers is that the principle of least privilege is granted to their data. The principle of least privilege states that only the minimum access necessary to perform an operation should be granted, and that access should be granted only for the minimum amount of time necessary.[17] However, business and IT groups will need and expect access to systems and applica-

---

17.   http://web.mit.edu/Saltzer/www/publications/protection/Basic.html, retrieved 15 Feb 2009.

tions. The advent of cloud services and services on demand is changing the identity management landscape. Most of the current identity management solutions are focused on the enterprise and typically are architected to work in a very controlled, static environment. User-centric identity management solutions such as federated identity management, as mentioned in Chapter 5, also make some assumptions about the parties involved and their related services.

In the cloud environment, where services are offered on demand and they can continuously evolve, aspects of current models such as trust assumptions, privacy implications, and operational aspects of authentication and authorization, will be challenged. Meeting these challenges will require a balancing act for SaaS providers as they evaluate new models and management processes for IAM to provide end-to-end trust and identity throughout the cloud and the enterprise. Another issue will be finding the right balance between usability and security. If a good balance is not achieved, both business and IT groups may be affected by barriers to completing their support and maintenance activities efficiently.

6.3.26   Change Management

Although it is not directly a security issue, approving production change requests that do not meet security requirements or that introduce a security vulnerability to the production environment may result in service disruptions or loss of customer data. A successful security team typically collaborates with the operations team to review production changes as they are being developed and tested. The security team may also create security guidelines for standards and minor changes, to provide self-service capabilities for these changes and to prioritize the security team's time and resources on more complex and important changes to production.

6.3.27   Physical Security

Customers essentially lose control over physical security when they move to the cloud, since the actual servers can be anywhere the provider decides to put them. Since you lose some control over your assets, your security model may need to be reevaluated. The concept of the cloud can be misleading at times, and people forget that everything is somewhere actually tied to a physical location. The massive investment required to build the level of security required for physical data centers is the prime reason that companies don't build their own data centers, and one of several reasons why they are moving to cloud services in the first place.

For the SaaS provider, physical security is very important, since it is the first layer in any security model. Data centers must deliver multilevel physical security because mission-critical Internet operations require the highest level of security. The elements of physical security are also a key element in ensuring that data center operations and delivery teams can provide continuous and authenticated uptime of greater than 99.9999%. The key components of data center physical security are the following:

- Physical access control and monitoring, including 24/7/365 on-site security, biometric hand geometry readers inside "man traps," bullet-resistant walls, concrete bollards, closed-circuit TV (CCTV) integrated video, and silent alarms. Security personnel should request government-issued identification from visitors, and should record each visit. Security cameras should monitor activity throughout the facility, including equipment areas, corridors, and mechanical, shipping, and receiving areas. Motion detectors and alarms should be located throughout the facilities, and silent alarms should automatically notify security and law enforcement personnel in the event of a security breach.

- Environmental controls and backup power: Heat, temperature, air flow, and humidity should all be kept within optimum ranges for the computer equipment housed on-site. Everything should be protected by fire-suppression systems, activated by a dual-alarm matrix of smoke, fire, and heat sensors located throughout the entire facility. Redundant power links to two different local utilities should also be created where possible and fed through additional batteries and UPS power sources to regulate the flow and prevent spikes, surges, and brownouts. Multiple diesel generators should be in place and ready to provide clean transfer of power in the event that both utilities fail.

- Policies, processes, and procedures: As with information security, policies, processes, and procedures are critical elements of successful physical security that can protect the equipment and data housed in the hosting center.

6.3.28 Business Continuity and Disaster Recovery

In the SaaS environment, customers rely heavily on 24/7 access to their services, and any interruption in access can be catastrophic. The availability of your software applications is the definition of your company's service and the life blood of your organization. Given the virtualization of the SaaS environment, the same technology will increasingly be used to support business continuity and disaster recovery, because virtualization software effectively "decouples" application stacks from the underlying hardware, and a virtual server can be copied, backed up, and moved just like a file. A growing number of virtualization software vendors have incorporated the ability to support live migrations. This, plus the decoupling capability, provides a low-cost means of quickly reallocating computing resources without any downtime. Another benefit of virtualization in business continuity and disaster recovery is its ability to deliver on service-level agreements and provide high-quality service.

Code escrow is another possibility, but object code is equivalent to source code when it comes to a SaaS provider, and the transfer and storage of that data must be tightly controlled. For the same reason that developer will not automatically provide source code outside their control when they license their software, it will be a challenge for SaaS escrow account providers to obtain a copy of the object code from a SaaS provider. Of course, the data center and its associated physical infrastructure will fall under standard business continuity and disaster recovery practices.

6.3.29   The Business Continuity Plan

A business continuity plan should include planning for non-IT-related aspects such as key personnel, facilities, crisis communication, and reputation protection, and it should refer to the disaster recovery plan for IT-related infrastructure recovery/continuity. The BC plan manual typically has five main phases: analysis, solution design, implementation, testing, and organization acceptance and maintenance. Disaster recovery planning is a subset of a larger process known as business continuity planning and should include planning for resumption of applications, data, hardware, communications (such as networking), and other IT infrastructure. Disaster recovery is the process, policies, and procedures related to preparing for recovery or continuation of technology infrastructure critical to an organization after a natural or human-induced disaster.[18,19]

---

18.   http://en.wikipedia.org/wiki/Business_continuity_planning, retrieved 21 Feb 2009.
19.   http://en.wikipedia.org/wiki/Disaster_recovery, retrieved 21 Feb 2009.

6.4   Is Security-as-a-Service the New MSSP?

Managed security service providers (MSSPs) were the key providers of security in the cloud that was created by Exodus Communications, Global Crossing, Digital Island, and others that dominated the outsourced hosting environments that were the norm for corporations from the mid-1990s to the early 2000's. The cloud is essentially the next evolution of that environment, and many of the security challenges and management requirements will be similar. An MSSP is essentially an Internet service provider (ISP) that provides an organization with some network security management and monitoring (e.g., security information management, security event management, and security information and event management, which may include virus blocking, spam blocking, intrusion detection, firewalls, and virtual private network [VPN] management and may also handle system changes, modifications, and upgrades. As a result of the .dot.com bust and the subsequent Chapter 11 bankruptcies of many of the dominant hosting service providers, some MSSPs pulled the plug on their customers with short or no notice. With the increasing reluctance of organizations to give up complete control over the security of their systems, the MSSP market has dwindled over the last few years. The evolution to cloud computing has changed all this, and managed service providers that have survived are reinventing themselves along with a new concept of MSSP, which is now called Security-as-a-Service (SaaS)—not to be confused with Software-as-a-Service (SaaS), although it can be a component of the latter as well as other cloud services such as PaaS, IaaS, and MaaS.

Unlike MSSP, Security-as-a-Service does not require customers to give up complete control over their security posture. Customer system or security administrators have control over their security policies, system upgrades, device status and history, current and past patch levels, and outstanding support issues, on demand, through a web-based interface. Certain aspects of security are uniquely designed to be optimized for delivery as a web-based service, including:

- Offerings that require constant updating to combat new threats, such as antivirus and anti-spyware software for consumers
- Offerings that require a high level of expertise, often not found in-house, and that can be conducted remotely. These include ongoing

maintenance, scanning, patch management, and troubleshooting of security devices.

■ Offerings that manage time- and resource-intensive tasks, which may be cheaper to outsource and offshore, delivering results and findings via a web-based solution. These include tasks such as log management, asset management, and authentication management.[20]

6.5   Chapter Summary

Virtualization is being used in data centers to facilitate cost savings and create a smaller, "green" footprint. As a result, multitenant uses of servers are being created on what used to be single-tenant or single-purpose physical servers. The extension of virtualization and virtual machines into the cloud is affecting enterprise security as a result of the evaporating enterprise network perimeter—the de-perimeterization of the enterprise, if you will. In this chapter, we discussed the importance of security in the cloud computing environment, particularly with regard to the SaaS environment and the security challenges and best practices associated with it.

In the next chapter, we will discuss the standards associated with cloud computing. Regardless of how the cloud evolves, it needs some form of standardization so that the market can evolve and thrive. Standards also allow clouds to interoperate and communicate with each other.

20.   "Security as a Service," http://en.wikipedia.org/wiki/Security_as_a_service, retrieved 20 Feb 2009.

Chapter 7

Common Standards in Cloud Computing

7.1 Chapter Overview

In Internet circles, everything eventually gets driven by a working group of one sort or another. A working group is an assembled, cooperative collaboration of researchers working on new research activities that would be difficult for any one member to develop alone. A working group can can exist for anywhere between a few months and many years. Working groups generally strive to create an informational document a standard, or find some resolution for problems related to a system or network. Most often, the working group attempts to assemble experts on a topic. Together, they will work intensively toward their goal. Working groups are sometimes also referred to as task groups or technical advisory groups. In this chapter, we will discuss the Open Cloud Consortium (OCC) and the Distributed Management Task Force (DMTF) as examples of cloud-related working groups. We will also discuss the most common standards currently used in cloud environments.

7.2 The Open Cloud Consortium

The purpose of the Open Cloud Consortium is to support the development of standards for cloud computing and to develop a framework for interoperability among various clouds. The OCC supports the development of benchmarks for cloud computing and is a strong proponent of open source software to be used for cloud computing. OCC manages a testing platform and a test-bed for cloud computing called the Open Cloud Test-bed. The group also sponsors workshops and other events related to cloud computing.

The OCC is organized into several different working groups. For example, the Working Group on Standards and Interoperability for Clouds

That Provide On-Demand Computing Capacity focuses on developing standards for interoperating clouds that provide on-demand computing capacity. One architecture for clouds that was popularized by a series of Google technical reports describes a *storage cloud* providing a distributed file system, a *compute cloud* supporting MapReduce, and a *data cloud* supporting table services. The open source Hadoop system follows this architecture. These types of cloud architectures support the concept of on-demand computing capacity.

There is also a Working Group on Wide Area Clouds and the Impact of Network Protocols on Clouds. The focus of this working group is on developing technology for wide area clouds, including creation of methodologies and benchmarks to be used for evaluating wide area clouds. This working group is tasked to study the applicability of variants of TCP (Transmission Control Protocol) and the use of other network protocols for clouds.

The Open Cloud Test-bed uses Cisco C-Wave and the UIC Teraflow Network for its network connections. C-Wave makes network resources available to researchers to conduct networking and applications research. It is provided at no cost to researchers and allows them access to 10G Waves (Layer-1 p2p) on a per-project allocation. It provides links to a 10GE (gigabit Ethernet) switched network backbone. The Teraflow Test-bed (TFT) is an international application network for exploring, integrating, analyzing, and detecting changes in massive and distributed data over wide-area high-performance networks. The Teraflow Test-bed analyzes streaming data with the goal of developing innovative technology for data streams at very high speeds. It is hoped that prototype technology can be deployed over the next decade to analyze 100-gigabit-per-second (Gbps) and 1,000-Gbps streams.

Both of these products use wavelengths provided by the National Lambda Rail (NLR). The NLR can support many distinct networks for the U.S. research community using the same core infrastructure. Experimental and productions networks exist side by side but are physically and operationally separate. Production networks support cutting-edge applications by providing users guaranteed levels of reliability, availability, and performance. At the same time, experimental networks enable the deployment and testing of new networking technologies, providing researchers national-scale test-beds without the limitations typically associated with production networks.

The Working Group on Information Sharing, Security, and Clouds has a primary focus on standards and standards-based architectures for sharing information between clouds. This is especially true for clouds belonging to different organizations and subject to possibly different authorities and policies. This group is also concerned with security architectures for clouds. An example is exchanging information between two clouds, each of which is HIPAA-compliant, but when each cloud is administered by a different organization.

Finally, there is an Open Cloud Test-bed Working Group that manages and operates the Open Cloud Test-bed. Currently, membership in this working group is limited to those who contribute computing, networking, or other resources to the Open Cloud Test-bed. For more information on the Open Cloud Consortium, the reader is encouraged to visit the OCC website.[1]

7.3   The Distributed Management Task Force

According to their web site, the Distributed Management Task Force

> . . . enables more effective management of millions of IT systems worldwide by bringing the IT industry together to collaborate on the development, validation and promotion of systems management standards. The group spans the industry with 160 member companies and organizations, and more than 4,000 active participants crossing 43 countries. The DMTF board of directors is led by 16 innovative, industry-leading technology companies. They include Advanced Micro Devices (AMD); Broadcom Corporation; CA, Inc.; Dell; EMC; Fujitsu; HP; Hitachi, Ltd.; IBM; Intel Corporation; Microsoft Corporation; Novell; Oracle; Sun Microsystems, Inc.; Symantec Corporation and VMware, Inc. With this deep and broad reach, DMTF creates standards that enable interoperable IT management. DMTF management standards are critical to enabling management interoperability among multi-vendor systems, tools and solutions within the enterprise.[2]

The DMTF started the Virtualization Management Initiative (VMAN). The VMAN unleashes the power of virtualization by delivering broadly supported interoperability and portability standards to virtual computing environments. VMAN enables IT managers to deploy preinstalled,

---

1.   http://www.opencloudconsortium.org/working-groups.html.
2.   http://www.dmtf.org/about, retrieved 21 Feb 2009.

preconfigured solutions across heterogeneous computing networks and to manage those applications through their entire life cycle. Management software vendors offer a broad selection of tools that support the industry standard specifications that are now a part of VMAN. This helps in lowering support and training costs for IT managers. Virtualization has enhanced the IT industry by optimizing use of existing physical resources and helping reduce the number of systems deployed and managed. This consolidation reduces hardware costs and mitigates power and cooling needs. However, even with the efficiencies gained by virtualization, this new approach does add some IT cost due to increased system management complexity.

Since the DMTF builds on existing standards for server hardware, management tool vendors can easily provide holistic management capabilities to enable IT managers to manage their virtual environments in the context of the underlying hardware. This lowers the IT learning curve, and also lowers complexity for vendors implementing this support in their solutions. With the technologies available to IT managers through the VMAN Initiative, companies now have a standardized approach to

1.   Deploy virtual computer systems

2.   Discover and take inventory of virtual computer systems

3.   Manage the life cycle of virtual computer systems

4.   Add/change/delete virtual resources

5.   Monitor virtual systems for health and performance

7.3.1   Open Virtualization Format

The Open Virtualization Format (OVF) is a fairly new standard that has emerged within the VMAN Initiative. The OVF simplifies interoperability, security, and virtual machine life-cycle management by describing an open, secure, portable, efficient, and extensible format for the packaging and distribution of one or more virtual appliances. The OVF specifies procedures and technologies to permit integrity checking of the virtual machines (VM) to ensure that they have not been modified since the package was produced. This enhances security of the format and will help to alleviate security concerns of users who adopt virtual appliances produced by third parties. The OVF also provides mechanisms that support license checking for the enclosed VMs, addressing a key concern of both independent software vendors and customers. Finally, the OVF allows an installed VM to acquire information about its host virtualization platform and runtime environment, which allows the VM to localize the applications it contains and optimize its performance for the particular virtualization environment.

One key feature of the OVF is virtual machine packaging portability. Since OVF is, by design, virtualization platform-neutral, it provides the benefit of enabling platform-specific enhancements to be captured. It also supports many open virtual hard disk formats. Virtual machine properties are captured concisely using OVF metadata. OVF is optimized for secure distribution. It supports content verification and integrity checking based on industry-standard public key infrastructure and provides a basic scheme for management of software licensing.

Another benefit of the OVG is a simplified installation and deployment process. The OVF streamlines the entire installation process using metadata to validate the entire package and automatically determine whether a virtual appliance can be installed. It also supports both single-VM and multiple-VM configurations and packages containing complex, multitier services consisting of multiple interdependent VMs. Since it is vendor- and platform-independent, the OVF does not rely on the use of a specific host platform, virtualization platform, or guest operating system.

The OVF is designed to be extended as the industry moves forward with virtual appliance technology. It also supports and permits the encoding of vendor-specific metadata to support specific vertical markets. It is localizable—it supports user-visible descriptions in multiple locales, and localization of interactive processes during installation of a virtual appliance. This allows a single packaged virtual appliance to serve multiple markets.

7.4   Standards for Application Developers

The purpose of application development standards is to ensure uniform, consistent, high-quality software solutions. Programming standards are important to programmers for a variety of reasons. Some researchers have stated that, as a general rule, 80% of the lifetime cost of a piece of software goes to maintenance. Furthermore, hardly any software is maintained by the original author for its complete life cycle. Programming standards help to improve the readability of the software, allowing developers to understand new code more quickly and thoroughly. If you ship source code as a product, it is important to ensure that it is as well packaged and meets industry standards comparable to the products you compete with. For the standards to work, everyone developing solutions must conform to them. In the following sections, we discuss application standards that are commonly used across the Internet in browsers, for transferring data, sending messages, and securing data.

7.4.1 Browsers (Ajax)

Ajax, or its predecessor AJAX (Asynchronous JavaScript and XML), is a group of interrelated web development techniques used to create interactive web applications or rich Internet applications. Using Ajax, web applications can retrieve data from the server asynchronously, without interfering with the display and behavior of the browser page currently being displayed to the user. The use of Ajax has led to an increase in interactive animation on web pages. Despite its name, JavaScript and XML are not actually *required* for Ajax. Moreover, requests do not even need to be asynchronous. The original acronym AJAX has changed to the name Ajax to reflect the fact that these specific technologies are no longer required.

In many cases, related pages that coexist on a web site share much common content. Using traditional methods, such content must be reloaded every time a request is made. Using Ajax, a web application can request only the content that needs to be updated. This greatly reduces networking bandwidth usage and page load times. Using asynchronous requests allows a client browser to appear more interactive and to respond to input more quickly. Sections of pages can be reloaded individually. Users generally perceive the application to be faster and more responsive. Ajax can reduce connections to the server, since scripts and style sheets need only be requested once.

An Ajax framework helps developers create web applications that use Ajax. The framework helps them to build dynamic web pages on the client side. Data is sent to or from the server using requests, usually written in JavaScript. On the server, some processing may be required to handle these requests, for example, when finding and storing data. This is accomplished more easily with the use of a framework dedicated to process Ajax requests. One such framework, ICEfaces, is an open source Java product maintained by http://icefaces.org.

ICEfaces Ajax Application Framework

ICEfaces is an integrated Ajax application framework that enables Java EE application developers to easily create and deploy thin-client rich Internet applications in pure Java. ICEfaces is a fully featured product that enterprise developers can use to develop new or existing Java EE applications at no cost. ICEfaces is the most successful enterprise Ajax framework available under open source. The ICEfaces developer community is extremely vibrant, already exceeding 32,000 developers in 36 countries. To run ICEfaces applications, users need to download and install the following products:

- Java 2 Platform, Standard Edition
- Ant
- Tomcat
- ICEfaces
- Web browser (if you don't already have one installed)

ICEfaces leverages the entire standards-based Java EE set of tools and environments. Rich enterprise application features are developed in pure Java in a thin-client model. No Applets or proprietary browser plug-ins are required. ICEfaces applications are JavaServer Faces (JSF) applications, so Java EE application development skills apply directly and Java developers don't have to do any JavaScript-related development.

Because ICEfaces is a pure Java enterprise solution, developers can continue to work the way they normally do. They are able to leverage their existing Java integrated development environments (IDEs) and test tools for development. ICEfaces supports an array of Java Application Servers, IDEs, third-party components, and JavaScript effect libraries. ICEfaces pioneered a technique called Ajax Push. This technique enables server/application-initiated content rendering to be sent to the browser. Also, ICEfaces is the one of the most secure Ajax solutions available. Compatible with SSL (Secure Sockets Layer) protocol, it prevents cross-site scripting, malicious code injection, and unauthorized data mining. ICEfaces does not expose application logic or user data, and it is effective in preventing fake form submits and SQL (Structured Query Language) injection attacks. ICEfaces also supports third-party application server Asynchronous Request Processing (ARP) APIs provided by Sun Glassfish (Grizzly), Jetty, Apache Tomcat, and others.

7.4.2   Data (XML, JSON)

Extensible Markup Language (XML) is a specification for creating custom markup languages. It is classified as an extensible language because it allows the user to define markup elements. Its purpose is to enable sharing of structured data. XML is often used to describe structured data and to serialize objects. Various XML-based protocols exist to represent data structures for data interchange purposes. Using XML is arguably more complex than using JSON (described below), which represents data structures in simple text formatted specifically for data interchange in an uncompressed form. Both XML and JSON lack mechanisms for representing large binary data types such as images.

XML, in combination with other standards, makes it possible to define the content of a document separately from its formatting. The benefit here is the ability to reuse that content in other applications or for other presentation environments. Most important, XML provides a basic syntax that can be used to share information among different kinds of computers, different applications, and different organizations without needing to be converted from one to another.

An XML document has two correctness levels, *well formed* and *valid*. A well-formed document conforms to the XML syntax rules. A document that is not well formed is not in XML format, and a conforming parser will not process it. A valid document is well formed and additionally conforms to semantic rules which can be user-defined or exist in an XML schema. An XML schema is a description of a type of XML document, typically expressed in terms of constraints on the structure and content of documents of that type, above and beyond the basic constraints imposed by XML itself. A number of standard and proprietary XML schema languages have emerged for the purpose of formally expressing such schemas, and some of these languages are themselves XML-based.

XML documents must conform to a variety of rules and naming conventions. By carefully choosing the names of XML elements, it is possible to convey the meaning of the data in the markup itself. This increases human readability while retaining the syntactic structure needed for parsing. However, this can lead to verbosity, which complicates authoring and increases file size. When creating XML, the designers decided that by leaving the names, allowable hierarchy, and meanings of the elements and attributes open and definable by a customized schema, XML could provide a syntactic foundation for the creation of purpose-specific, XML-based markup languages. The general syntax of such languages is very rigid. Documents must adhere to the general rules of XML, ensuring that all XML-aware software can at least read and understand the arrangement of information within them. The schema merely supplements the syntax rules with a predefined set of constraints.

Before the advent of generalized data description languages such as XML, software designers had to define special file formats or small languages to share data between programs. This required writing detailed specifications and special-purpose parsers and writers. XML's regular structure and strict parsing rules allow software designers to leave the task of parsing to standard tools, since XML provides a general, data model-oriented framework for the development of application-specific languages. This allows software designers to concentrate on the development of rules for their data at relatively high levels of abstraction.

JavaScript Object Notation (JSON)

JSON is a lightweight computer data interchange format. It is a text-based, human-readable format for representing simple data structures and associative arrays (called objects). The JSON format is specified in Internet Engineering Task Force Request for Comment (RFC) 4627. The JSON format is often used for transmitting structured data over a network connection in a process called serialization. Its main application is in Ajax web application programming, where it serves as an alternative to the XML format. JSON is based on a subset of the JavaScript programming language. It is considered to be a language-independent data format. Code for parsing and generating JSON data is readily available for a large variety of programming languages. The json.org website provides a comprehensive listing of existing JSON bindings, organized by language.

Even though JSON was intended as a data serialization format, its design as a subset of the JavaScript language poses security concerns. The use of a JavaScript interpreter to dynamically execute JSON text as JavaScript can expose a program to bad or even malicious script. JSON is also subject to cross-site request forgery attacks. This can allow JSON-encoded data to be evaluated in the context of a malicious page, possibly divulging passwords or other sensitive data. This is only a problem if the server depends on the browser's Same Origin Policy to block the delivery of the data in the case of an improper request. When the server determines the propriety of the request, there is no problem because it will only output data if the request is valid. Cookies are not adequate for determining whether a request is authorized and valid. The use of cookies is subject to cross-site request forgery and should be avoided with JSON. As you can see, JSON was built for simple tasks and can be useful, but there is some risk involved in using it—especially given the alternative solutions available today.

7.4.3   Solution Stacks (LAMP and LAPP)

LAMP

LAMP is a popular open source solution commonly used to run dynamic web sites and servers. The acronym derives from the fact that it includes **L**inux, **A**pache, **M**ySQL, and **P**HP (or Perl or Python) and is considered by many to be the platform of choice for development and deployment of high-performance web applications which require a solid and reliable foundation. The combination of these technologies is used primarily to define a web server infrastructure or for creating a programming environment for developing software. While the creators of these open source products did not intend for them all to work with each other, the LAMP combination has become popular because of its open source nature, low cost, and the wide distribution of its components (most of which come bundled with nearly all of the current Linux distributions). When used in combination, they represent a solution stack of technologies that support application servers.

Linux, Apache, PostgreSQL, and PHP(or Perl or Python)

The LAPP stack is an open source web platform that can be used to run dynamic web sites and servers. It is considered by many to be a more powerful alternative to the more popular LAMP stack. These advanced and mature components provide a rock-solid foundation for the development and deployment of high-performance web applications. LAPP offers SSL, PHP, Python, and Perl support for Apache2 and PostgreSQL. There is an administration front-end for PostgreSQL as well as web-based administration modules for configuring Apache2 and PHP. PostgreSQL password encryption is enabled by default. The PostgreSQL user is trusted when connecting over local Unix sockets. Many consider the LAPP stack a more secure out-of-the-box solution than the LAMP stack. The choice of which stack to use is made by developers based on the purpose of their application and the risks they may have to contend with when users begin working with the product.

7.5   Standards for Messaging

You probably think you know what a messaging standard is. Unfortunately, the term *messaging* means different things to different people. So does the word *standard*. People may assume you are talking about networking when you begin discussing messaging standards. The term *messaging,* however, covers a lot of ground, and not all of it is specific to networking. For our purposes here, a *message* is a unit of information that is moved from one place to another. The term *standard* also is not always clearly defined. Different entities have differing interpretations of what a standard is, and we know there are open international standards, *de facto* standards, and proprietary standards. A true standard is usually characterized by certain traits, such as being managed by an international standards body or an industry consortium, and the standard is created jointly by a community of interested parties. The Internet Engineering Task Force (IETF) is perhaps the most open standards body on the planet, because it is open to everyone. Participants can contribute, and their work is available online for free. In the following sections, we discuss the most common messaging standards used in the cloud—some of which have been used so much so that they are considered *de facto* standards.

7.5.1   Simple Message Transfer Protocol (SMTP)

Simple Message Transfer Protocol is arguably the most important protocol in use today for basic messaging. Before SMTP was created, email messages were sent using File Transfer Protocol (FTP). A sender would compose a message and transmit it to the recipient as if it were a file. While this process worked, it had its shortcomings. The FTP protocol was designed to transmit files, not messages, so it did not provide any means for recipients to identify the sender or for the sender to designate an intended recipient. If a message showed up on an FTP server, it was up to the administrator to open or print it (and sometimes even deliver it) before anyone even knew who it was supposed to be receiving it.

SMTP was designed so that sender and recipient information could be transmitted with the message. The design process didn't happen overnight, though. SMTP was initially defined in 1973 by IETF RFC 561. It has evolved over the years and has been modified by RFCs 680, 724 and 733. The current RFCs applying to SMTP are RFC 821 and RFC 822. SMTP is a two-way protocol that usually operates using TCP (Transmission Control Protocol) port 25. Though many people don't realize it, SMTP can be used to both send and receive messages. Typically, though, workstations use POP (Post Office Protocol) rather than SMTP to receive messages. SMTP is usually used for either sending a message from a workstation to a mail server or for communications between mail servers.

7.5.2   Post Office Protocol (POP)

SMTP can be used both to send and receive messages, but using SMTP for this purpose is often impractical or impossible because a client must have a constant connection to the host to receive SMTP messages. The Post Office Protocol (POP) was introduced to circumvent this situation. POP is a lightweight protocol whose single purpose is to download messages from a server. This allows a server to store messages until a client connects and requests them. Once the client connects, POP servers begin to download the messages and subsequently delete them from the server (a default setting) in order to make room for more messages. Users respond to a message that was downloaded using SMTP. The POP protocol is defined by RFC 1939 and usually functions on TCP port 110.

7.5.3   Internet Messaging Access Protocol (IMAP)

Once mail messages are downloaded with POP, they are automatically deleted from the server when the download process has finished. Thus POP users have to save their messages locally, which can present backup challenges when it is important to store or save messages. Many businesses have compulsory compliance guidelines that require saving messages. It also becomes a problem if users move from computer to computer or use mobile networking, since their messages do not automatically move where they go. To get around these problems, a standard called Internet Messaging Access Protocol was created. IMAP allows messages to be kept on the server but viewed and manipulated (usually via a browser) as though they were stored locally. IMAP is a part of the RFC 2060 specification, and functions over TCP port 143.

7.5.4   Syndication (Atom, Atom Publishing Protocol, and RSS)

Content syndication provides citizens convenient access to new content and headlines from government via RSS (Really Simple Syndication) and other online syndication standards. Governments are providing access to more and more information online. As web sites become more complex and difficult to sift through, new or timely content is often buried. Dynamically presenting "what's new" an the top of the web site is only the first step. Sharing headlines and content through syndication standards such as RSS (the little orange [XML] button, ATOM, and others) essentially allows a government to control a small window of content across web sites that choose to display the government's headlines. Headlines may also be aggregated and displayed through "newsreaders" by citizens through standalone applications or as part of their personal web page.

Portals can automatically aggregate and combine headlines and/or lengthier content from across multiple agency web sites. This allows the value of distributed effort to be shared, which is more sustainable. Press releases may be aggregated automatically from different systems, as long as they all are required to offer an RSS feed with content tagged with similar metadata. Broader use of government information online, particularly time-sensitive democratic information, justifies the effort of production and the accountability of those tasked to make it available.

- **Benefits:** Ability to scan headlines from many sources, all in one place, through a newsreader. Time-saving awareness of new content from government, if the RSS feed or feeds are designed properly. Ability to monitor new content from across the council, as well as display feeds on their own web site. Awareness of new content position councilors as guides to government for citizens. Ability to aggregate new content or headlines from across multiple office locations and agencies. This allows a display of "joined-up" government despite structural realities. Journalists and other locally focused web sites will be among the primary feed users.

- **Limitations:** Dissemination via syndication is a new concept to governments just getting used to the idea of remote online public access to information. Governments need to accept that while they control the content of the feed, the actual display of the headlines and content will vary. Popular RSS feeds can use significant amounts of bandwidth. Details on how often or when a feed is usually updated should be offered to those grabbing the code behind the orange [XML] button, so they "ping" it once a day instead of every hour. Automated syndication requires use of a content management system. Most viable content management systems have integrated RSS functions, but the sophistication, ease of use, and documentation of these tools vary. There are three variants of RSS, as well as the emerging ATOM standard. It is recommended that a site pick the standard most applicable to their content rather than confuse users with different feeds providing the same content.

RSS

RSS is a family of web feed formats used to publish frequently updated works—such as blog entries, news headlines, audio, and video—in a standardized format. An RSS document includes full or summarized text, plus metadata such as publishing dates and authorship. Web feeds benefit publishers by letting them syndicate content automatically. They benefit readers who want to subscribe to timely updates from favored web sites or to aggregate feeds from many sites into one place. RSS feeds can be read using software called a reader that can be web-based, desktop-based, a mobile device, or any computerized Internet-connected device. A standardized XML file format allows the information to be published once and viewed by many different programs. The user subscribes to a feed by entering the feed's URI (often referred to informally as a URL, although technically, those two terms are not exactly synonymous) into the reader or by clicking an RSS icon in a browser that initiates the subscription process. The RSS reader checks the user's subscribed feeds regularly for new work, downloads any updates that it finds, and provides a user interface to monitor and read the feeds.

Atom and Atom Publishing Protocol (APP)

The name Atom applies to a pair of related standards. The Atom Syndication Format is an XML language used for web feeds, while the Atom Publishing Protocol (AtomPub or APP) is a simple HTTP-based protocol (HTTP is described later in this chapter) for creating and updating web resources, sometimes known as web feeds. Web feeds allow software programs to check for updates published on a web site. To provide a web feed, a site owner may use specialized software (such as a content management system) that publishes a list (or "feed") of recent articles or content in a standardized, machine-readable format. The feed can then be downloaded by web sites that syndicate content from the feed, or by feed reader programs that allow Internet users to subscribe to feeds and view their content. A feed contains entries, which may be headlines, full-text articles, excerpts, summaries, and/or links to content on a web site, along with various metadata.

The Atom format was developed as an alternative to RSS. Ben Trott, an advocate of the new format that became Atom, believed that RSS had limitations and flaws—such as lack of ongoing innovation and its necessity to remain backward compatible—and that there were advantages to a fresh design. Proponents of the new format formed the IETF Atom Publishing Format and Protocol Workgroup. The Atom syndication format was published as an IETF "proposed standard" in RFC 4287, and the Atom Publishing Protocol was published as RFC 5023.

Web feeds are used by the weblog community to share the latest entries' headlines or their full text, and even attached multimedia files. These providers allow other web sites to incorporate the weblog's "syndicated" headline or headline-and-short-summary feeds under various usage agreements. Atom and other web syndication formats are now used for many purposes, including journalism, marketing, "bug" reports, or any other activity involving periodic updates or publications. Atom also provides a standardized way to export an entire blog, or parts of it, for backup or for importing into other blogging systems.

A program known as a feed reader or aggregator can check web pages on behalf of a user and display any updated articles that it finds. It is common to find web feeds on major web sites, as well as on many smaller ones. Some web sites let people choose between RSS- or Atom-formatted web feeds; others offer only RSS or only Atom. In particular, many blog and wiki sites offer their web feeds in the Atom format.

Client-side readers and aggregators may be designed as standalone programs or as extensions to existing programs such as web browsers. Browsers are moving toward integrated feed reader functions. Such programs are available for various operating systems. Web-based feed readers and news aggregators require no software installation and make the user's feeds available on any computer with web access. Some aggregators syndicate web feeds into new feeds, e.g., taking all football-related items from several sports feeds and providing a new football feed. There are several search engines which provide search functionality over content published via these web feeds.

Web Services (REST)

REpresentational State Transfer (REST) is a style of software architecture for distributed hypermedia systems such as the World Wide Web. As such, it is not strictly a method for building "web services." The terms "representational state transfer" and "REST" were introduced in 2000 in the doctoral dissertation of Roy Fielding,[3] one of the principal authors of the Hypertext Transfer Protocol (HTTP) specification.

REST refers to a collection of network architecture principles which outline how resources are defined and addressed. The term is often used in a looser sense to describe any simple interface which transmits domain-specific data over HTTP without an additional messaging layer such as SOAP or session tracking via HTTP cookies. These two meanings can conflict as well as overlap. It is possible to design a software system in accordance with Fielding's REST architectural style without using HTTP and without interacting with the World Wide Web.[4] It is also possible to design simple XML+HTTP interfaces which do not conform to REST principles, but instead follow a model of remote procedure call. Systems which follow Fielding's REST principles are often referred to as "RESTful."

Proponents of REST argue that the web's scalability and growth are a direct result of a few key design principles. Application state and functionality are abstracted into resources. Every resource is uniquely addressable using a universal syntax for use in hypermedia links, and all resources share a uniform interface for the transfer of state between client and resource. This transfer state consists of a constrained set of well-defined operations and a constrained set of content types, optionally supporting code on demand. State transfer uses a protocol which is client-server based, stateless and cacheable, and layered. Fielding describes REST's effect on scalability thus:

> REST's client-server separation of concerns simplifies component implementation, reduces the complexity of connector semantics, improves the effectiveness of performance tuning, and increases the scalability of pure server components. Layered system constraints allow intermediaries—proxies, gateways, and firewalls—to be introduced at various points in the communication without changing the interfaces between components, thus allowing them to assist in communication translation or improve performance via large-scale, shared caching. REST enables intermediate processing by constraining messages to be self-descriptive: interaction is stateless between requests, standard methods and media types are used to indicate

3.   Roy T. Fielding, "Architectural Styles and the Design of Network-Based Software Architectures," dissertation, University of California, Irvine, 2000, http://www.ics.uci.edu/~fielding/pubs/dissertation/rest_arch_style.htm.

4.   Ibid.

semantics and exchange information, and responses explicitly indi-
cate cacheability.[5]

An important concept in REST is the existence of resources, each of
which is referenced with a global identifier (e.g., a URI in HTTP). In order
to manipulate these resources, components of the network (user agents and
origin servers) communicate via a standardized interface (e.g., HTTP) and
exchange representations of these resources (the actual documents convey-
ing the information). For example, a resource which is a circle may accept
and return a representation which specifies a center point and radius, formatted in SVG (Scalable Vector Graphics), but may also accept and return a
representation which specifies any three distinct points along the curve as a
comma-separated list.

Any number of connectors (clients, servers, caches, tunnels, etc.) can
mediate the request, but each does so without "seeing past" its own request
(referred to as "layering," another constraint of REST and a common principle in many other parts of information and networking architecture).
Thus an application can interact with a resource by knowing two things: the
identifier of the resource, and the action required—it does not need to
know whether there are caches, proxies, gateways, firewalls, tunnels, or anything else between it and the server actually holding the information. The
application does, however, need to understand the format of the information (representation) returned, which is typically an HTML, XML, or
JSON document of some kind, although it may be an image, plain text, or
any other content.

REST provides improved response time and reduced server load due
to its support for the caching of representations. REST improves server
scalability by reducing the need to maintain session state. This means that
different servers can be used to handle different requests in a session.
REST requires less client-side software to be written than other
approaches, because a single browser can access any application and any
resource. REST depends less on vendor software and mechanisms which
layer additional messaging frameworks on top of HTTP. It provides
equivalent functionality when compared to alternative approaches to
communication, and it does not require a separate resource discovery
mechanism, because of the use of hyperlinks in representations. REST

5.   Ibid.

also provides better long-term compatibility because of the capability of document types such as HTML to evolve without breaking backwards or forwards compatibility and the ability of resources to add support for new content types as they are defined without dropping or reducing support for older content types.

One benefit that should be obvious with regard to web-based applications is that a RESTful implementation allows a user to bookmark specific "queries" (or requests) and allows those to be conveyed to others across email, instant messages, or to be injected into wikis, etc. Thus this "representation" of a path or entry point into an application state becomes highly portable. A RESTFul web service is a simple web service implemented using HTTP and the principles of REST. Such a web service can be thought of as a collection of resources comprising three aspects:

1. The URI for the web service

2. The MIME type of the data supported by the web service (often JSON, XML, or YAML, but can be anything)

3. The set of operations supported by the web service using HTTP methods, including but not limited to POST, GET, PUT, and DELETE

Members of the collection are addressed by ID using URIs of the form <baseURI>/<ID>. The ID can be any unique identifier. For example, a RESTFul web service representing a collection of cars for sale might have the URI:

```
http://example.com/resources/cars
```

If the service uses the car registration number as the ID, then a particular car might be present in the collection as

```
http://example.com/resources/cars/yxz123
```

SOAP

SOAP, originally defined as Simple Object Access Protocol, is a protocol specification for exchanging structured information in the implementation of Web Services in computer networks. It relies on XML as its message format and usually relies on other application-layer protocols, most notably Remote Procedure Call (RPC) and HTTP for message negotiation and transmission. SOAP can form the foundation layer of a web services protocol stack, providing a basic messaging framework on which web services can be built.

As a simple example of how SOAP procedures can be used, a SOAP message can be sent to a web service-enabled web site—for example, a house price database—with the parameters needed for a search. The site returns an XML-formatted document with the resulting data (prices, location, features, etc). Because the data is returned in a standardized machine-parseable format, it may be integrated directly into a third-party site.

The SOAP architecture consists of several layers of specifications for message format, message exchange patterns (MEPs), underlying transport protocol bindings, message processing models, and protocol extensibility. SOAP is the successor of XML-RPC. SOAP makes use of an Internet application-layer protocol as a transport protocol. Critics have argued that this is an abuse of such protocols, as it is not their intended purpose and therefore not a role they fulfill well. Proponents of SOAP have drawn analogies to successful uses of protocols at various levels for tunneling other protocols.

Both SMTP and HTTP are valid application-layer protocols used as transport for SOAP, but HTTP has gained wider acceptance because it works well with today's Internet infrastructure; specifically, HTTP works well with network firewalls. SOAP may also be used over HTTPS (which is the same protocol as HTTP at the application level, but uses an encrypted transport protocol underneath) with either simple or mutual authentication; this is the advocated WS-I method to provide web service security as stated in the WS-I Basic Profile 1.1. This is a major advantage over other distributed protocols such as GIOP/IIOP or DCOM, which are normally filtered by firewalls. XML was chosen as the standard message format because of its widespread use by major corporations and open source development efforts. Additionally, a wide variety of freely available tools significantly eases the transition to a SOAP-based implementation.

Advantages of using SOAP over HTTP are that SOAP allows for easier communication through proxies and firewalls than previous remote execution technology. SOAP is versatile enough to allow for the use of different transport protocols. The standard stacks use HTTP as a transport protocol, but other protocols are also usable (e.g., SMTP). SOAP is platform-independent, language-independent, and it is simple and extensible.

Because of the verbose XML format, SOAP can be considerably slower than competing middleware technologies such as CORBA (Common Object Request Broker Architecture). This may not be an issue when only small messages are sent. To improve performance for the special case of XML with embedded binary objects, Message Transmission Optimization Mechanism was introduced. When relying on HTTP as a transport protocol and not using WS-Addressing or an ESB, the roles of the interacting parties are fixed. Only one party (the client) can use the services of the other. Developers must use polling instead of notification in these common cases.

Most uses of HTTP as a transport protocol are made in ignorance of how the operation is accomplished. As a result, there is no way to know whether the method used is appropriate to the operation. The REST architecture has become a web service alternative that makes appropriate use of HTTP's defined methods.

7.5.5   Communications (HTTP, SIMPLE, and XMPP)

HTTP is a request/response communications standard based on a client/server model. A client is the end user, the server is the web site. The client making a HTTP request via a web browser or other tool sends the request to the server. The responding server is called the origin server. HTTP is not constrained to use TCP/IP and its supporting layers, although this is its most popular application on the Internet. SIMPLE, the Session Initiation Protocol for Instant Messaging and Presence Leveraging Extensions, is an instant messaging (IM) and presence protocol suite based on Session Initiation Protocol, and it is managed by the IETF. Like XMPP, SIMPLE is an open standard. Extensible Messaging and Presence Protocol (XMPP) is also an open, XML-based protocol originally aimed at near-real-time, extensible instant messaging and presence information (e.g., buddy lists) but now expanded into the broader realm of message-oriented middleware. All of these protocols are discussed in detail in the following paragraphs.

Hypertext Transfer Protocol (HTTP)

HTTP is an application-level protocol for distributed, collaborative, hypermedia information systems. Its use for retrieving linked resources led to the establishment of the World Wide Web. HTTP development was coordinated by the World Wide Web Consortium and the Internet Engineering Task Force, culminating in the publication of a series of Requests for Comments, most notably RFC 2616 (June 1999), which defines HTTP/1.1, the version of HTTP in common use today.

HTTP is a request/response standard between a client and a server. A client is the end-user, the server is the web site. The client making a HTTP request—using a web browser, spider, or other end-user tool—is referred to as the user agent. The responding server—which stores or creates resources such as HTML files and images—is called the origin server. In between the user agent and origin server may be several intermediaries, such as proxies, gateways, and tunnels. HTTP is not constrained to using TCP/IP and its supporting layers, although this is its most popular application on the Internet. In fact, HTTP can be implemented on top of any other protocol; all it requires is reliable transport, so any protocol, on the Internet or any other network, that provides reliable transport can be used.

Typically, an HTTP client initiates a request. It establishes a TCP connection to a particular port on a host (port 80 by default). An HTTP server listening on that port waits for the client to send a request message. Upon receiving the request, the server sends back a status line such as "HTTP/1.1 200 OK" and a message of its own, the body of which is perhaps the requested resource, an error message, or some other information. Resources to be accessed by HTTP are identified using Uniform Resource Identifiers (URIs or, more specifically, Uniform Resource Locators, URLs) using the http: or https URI schemes.

SIMPLE

Session Initiation Protocol for Instant Messaging and Presence Leveraging Extensions (SIMPLE) is an instant messaging (IM) and presence protocol suite based on the Session Initiation Protocol (SIP). Like XMPP, SIMPLE is an open standard. SIMPLE makes use of SIP for registering for presence information and receiving notifications when presence-related events occur. It is also used for sending short messages and managing a session of real-time messages between two or more participants. Implementations of the SIMPLE-based protocols can be found in SIP softphones and also hardphones.[6] The SIMPLE presence specifications can be broken up into core

---

6.   In computing, a softphone is a software program for making telephone calls over the Internet using a general-purpose computer; a hardphone is a conventional telephone set.

protocol methods, presence information, and the handling of privacy, policy. and provisioning.

The core protocol methods provide SIP extensions for subscriptions, notifications, and publications. The methods used, **subscribe** and **notify,** are defined in RFC 3265. **Subscribe** allows a user to subscribe to an event on a server. **Notify** is the method used whenever the event arises and the server responds back to the subscriber. Another standard, RFC 3856, defines precisely how to use these methods to establish and maintain presence. Presence documents contain information encoded using XML. These documents are transported in the bodies of SIP messages.[7] Privacy, policy, and provisioning information is needed by user agents to determine who may subscribe to presence information. A framework for authorization policies controlling access to application-specific data is defined in RFC 4745 and RFC 5025. SIP defines two modes of instant messaging, the Page mode and the Session mode. Page mode makes use of the SIP method MESSAGE, as defined in RFC 3428. This mode establishes no sessions, while the Session mode based on the Message Session Relay Protocol (RFC 4975, RFC 4976) defines text-based protocol for exchanging arbitrarily sized content of any time between users.

XMPP

Extensible Messaging and Presence Protocol (XMPP) is an XML-based protocol used for near-real-time, extensible instant messaging and presence information. XMPP remains the core protocol of the Jabber Instant Messaging and Presence technology. Jabber provides a carrier-grade, best-in-class presence and messaging platform. According to a press release following its acquisition by Cisco Systems in November 2008, "Jabber's technology leverages open standards to provide a highly scalable architecture that supports the aggregation of presence information across different devices, users and applications. The technology also enables collaboration across many different presence systems such as Microsoft Office Communications Server, IBM Sametime, AOL AIM, Google and Yahoo!"

Built to be extensible, the XMPP protocol has grown to support features such as voice-over-IP and file transfer signaling. Unlike other instant messaging protocols, XMPP is an open standard. Like email, anyone who has a domain name and an Internet connection can run the Jabber server

---

7.   RFC 3863 and RFC 4479 describe this procedure.

and chat with others. The Jabber project is open source software, available from Google at http://code.google.com/p/jabber-net.

XMPP-based software is deployed on thousands of servers across the Internet. The Internet Engineering Task Force has formalized XMPP as an approved instant messaging and presence technology under the name XMPP, and the XMPP specifications have been published as RFC 3920 and RFC 3921. Custom functionality can be built on top of XMPP, and common extensions are managed by the XMPP Software Foundation.

XMPP servers can be isolated from the public Jabber network, and robust security (via SASL and TLS) is built into the core XMPP specifications. Because the client uses HTTP, most firewalls allow users to fetch and post messages without hindrance. Thus, if the TCP port used by XMPP is blocked, a server can listen on the normal HTTP port and the traffic should pass without problems. Some web sites allow users to sign in to Jabber via their browser. Furthermore, there are open public servers, such as www.jabber80.com, which listen on standard http (port 80) and https (port 443) ports and allow connections from behind most firewalls.

7.6   Standards for Security

Security standards define the processes, procedures, and practices necessary for implementing a security program. These standards also apply to cloud-related IT activities and include specific steps that should be taken to ensure a secure environment is maintained that provides privacy and security of confidential information in a cloud environment. Security standards are based on a set of key principles intended to protect this type of trusted environment. Messaging standards, especially for security in the cloud, must also include nearly all the same considerations as any other IT security endeavor. The following protocols, while not exclusively specific to cloud security, merit coverage here. In the next few sections, we explain what they are and how they are used in the cloud environment.

7.6.1   Security (SAML OAuth, OpenID, SSL/TLS)

A basic philosophy of security is to have layers of defense, a concept known as *defense in depth*. This means having overlapping systems designed to provide security even if one system fails. An example is a firewall working in conjunction with an intrusion-detection system (IDS). Defense in depth provides security because there is no single point of failure and no single-entry vector at which an attack can occur. For this reason, a choice between implementing network security in the middle part of a network (i.e., in the cloud) or at the endpoints is a false dichotomy.[8]

No single security system is a solution by itself, so it is far better to secure all systems. This type of layered security is precisely what we are seeing develop in cloud computing. Traditionally, security was implemented at the endpoints, where the user controlled access. An organization had no choice except to put firewalls, IDSs, and antivirus software inside its own network. Today, with the advent of managed security services offered by cloud providers, additional security can be provided inside the cloud.

Security Assertion Markup Language (SAML)

SAML is an XML-based standard for communicating authentication, authorization, and attribute information among online partners. It allows businesses to securely send assertions between partner organizations regarding the identity and entitlements of a principal. The Organization for the Advancement of Structured Information Standards (OASIS) Security Services Technical Committee is in charge of defining, enhancing, and maintaining the SAML specifications.[9] SAML is built on a number of existing standards, namely, SOAP, HTTP, and XML. SAML relies on HTTP as its communications protocol and specifies the use of SOAP (currently, version 1.1). Most SAML transactions are expressed in a standardized form of XML. SAML assertions and protocols are specified using XML schema. Both SAML 1.1 and SAML 2.0 use digital signatures (based on the XML Signature standard) for authentication and message integrity. XML encryption is supported in SAML 2.0, though SAML 1.1 does not have encryption capabilities. SAML defines XML-based assertions and protocols, bindings, and profiles. The term SAML Core refers to the general syntax and semantics of SAML assertions as well as the protocol used to request and transmit those assertions from one system entity to another. SAML protocol refers to what is transmitted, not how it is transmitted. A SAML binding determines how SAML requests and responses map to standard messaging protocols. An important (synchronous) binding is the SAML SOAP binding.

SAML standardizes queries for, and responses that contain, user authentication, entitlements, and attribute information in an XML format.

---

8. Bruce Schnier, http://www.schneier.com/blog/archives/2006/02/security_in_the.html, 15 Feb 2006, retrieved 21 Feb 2009.

9. The reader is encouraged to consult http://www.oasis-open.org/committees/ tc_home.php?wg_abbrev=security.

This format can then be used to request security information about a principal from a SAML authority. A SAML authority, sometimes called the asserting party, is a platform or application that can relay security information. The relying party (or assertion consumer or requesting party) is a partner site that receives the security information. The exchanged information deals with a subject's authentication status, access authorization, and attribute information. A subject is an entity in a particular domain. A person identified by an email address is a subject, as might be a printer.

SAML assertions are usually transferred from identity providers to service providers. Assertions contain statements that service providers use to make access control decisions. Three types of statements are provided by SAML: authentication statements, attribute statements, and authorization decision statements. SAML assertions contain a packet of security information in this form:

```
<saml:Assertion A...>
    <Authentication>
    ...
    </Authentication>
    <Attribute>
    ...
    </Attribute>
    <Authorization>
    ...
    </Authorization>
</saml:Assertion A>
```

The assertion shown above is interpreted as follows:

```
Assertion A, issued at time T by issuer I, regarding subject
S, provided conditions C are valid.
```

Authentication statements assert to a service provider that the principal did indeed authenticate with an identity provider at a particular time using a particular method of authentication. Other information about the authenticated principal (called the authentication context) may be disclosed in an authentication statement. An attribute statement asserts that a subject is associated with certain attributes. An attribute is simply a name–value pair. Relying parties use attributes to make access control decisions. An authorization decision statement asserts that a subject is permitted to perform action A on resource R given evidence E. The expressiveness of authorization decision statements in SAML is intentionally limited.

A SAML protocol describes how certain SAML elements (including assertions) are packaged within SAML request and response elements. It provides processing rules that SAML entities must adhere to when using these elements. Generally, a SAML protocol is a simple request–response protocol. The most important type of SAML protocol request is a query. A service provider makes a query directly to an identity provider over a secure back channel. For this reason, query messages are typically bound to SOAP. Corresponding to the three types of statements, there are three types of SAML queries: the authentication query, the attribute query, and the authorization decision query. Of these, the attribute query is perhaps most important. The result of an attribute query is a SAML response containing an assertion, which itself contains an attribute statement.

Open Authentication (OAuth)

OAuth is an open protocol, initiated by Blaine Cook and Chris Messina, to allow secure API authorization in a simple, standardized method for various types of web applications. Cook and Messina had concluded that there were no open standards for API access delegation. The OAuth discussion group was created in April 2007, for the small group of implementers to write the draft proposal for an open protocol. DeWitt Clinton of Google learned of the OAuth project and expressed interest in supporting the effort. In July 2007 the team drafted an initial specification, and it was released in October of the same year.

OAuth is a method for publishing and interacting with protected data. For developers, OAuth provides users access to their data while protecting account credentials. OAuth allows users to grant access to their information, which is shared by the service provider and consumers without sharing all of their identity. The Core designation is used to stress that this is the baseline, and other extensions and protocols can build on it.

By design, OAuth Core 1.0 does not provide many desired features (e.g., automated discovery of endpoints, language support, support for XML-RPC and SOAP, standard definition of resource access, OpenID integration, signing algorithms, etc.). This intentional lack of feature support is viewed by the authors as a significant benefit. The Core deals with fundamental aspects of the protocol, namely, to establish a mechanism for exchanging a user name and password for a token with defined rights and to provide tools to protect the token. It is important to understand that security and privacy are not guaranteed by the protocol. In fact, OAuth by itself *provides no privacy at all* and depends on other protocols such as SSL to accomplish that. OAuth can be implemented in a secure manner, however. In fact, the specification includes substantial security considerations that must be taken into account when working with sensitive data. With Oauth, sites use tokens coupled with shared secrets to access resources. Secrets, just like passwords, must be protected.

OpenID

OpenID is an open, decentralized standard for user authentication and access control that allows users to log onto many services using the same digital identity. It is a single-sign-on (SSO) method of access control. As such, it replaces the common log-in process (i.e., a log-in name and a password) by allowing users to log in once and gain access to resources across participating systems.

The original OpenID authentication protocol was developed in May 2005 by Brad Fitzpatrick, creator of the popular community web site LiveJournal. In late June 2005, discussions began between OpenID developers and other developers from an enterprise software company named NetMesh. These discussions led to further collaboration on interoperability between OpenID and NetMesh's similar Light-Weight Identity (LID) protocol. The direct result of the collaboration was the Yadis discovery protocol, which was announced on October 24, 2005.

The Yadis specification provides a general-purpose identifier for a person and any other entity, which can be used with a variety of services. It provides a syntax for a resource description document identifying services available using that identifier and an interpretation of the elements of that document. Yadis discovery protocol is used for obtaining a resource description document, given that identifier. Together these enable coexistence and interoperability of a rich variety of services using a single identifier. The identifier uses a standard syntax and a well-established namespace and requires no additional namespace administration infrastructure.

An OpenID is in the form of a unique URL and is authenticated by the entity hosting the OpenID URL. The OpenID protocol does not rely on a central authority to authenticate a user's identity. Neither the OpenID protocol nor any web sites requiring identification can mandate that a specific type of authentication be used; nonstandard forms of authentication such as smart cards, biometrics, or ordinary passwords are allowed. A typical scenario for using OpenID might be something like this: A user visits a web site that displays an OpenID log-in form somewhere on the page. Unlike a typical log-in form, which has fields for user name and password, the OpenID log-in form has only one field for the OpenID identifier (which is an OpenID URL). This form is connected to an implementation of an OpenID client library. A user will have previously registered an OpenID identifier with an OpenID identity provider. The user types this OpenID identifier into the OpenID log-in form.

The relying party then requests the web page located at that URL and reads an HTML link tag to discover the identity provider service URL. With OpenID 2.0, the client discovers the identity provider service URL by requesting the XRDS document (also called the Yadis document) with the content type **application/xrds+xml,** which may be available at the target URL but is always available for a target XRI. There are two modes by which the relying party can communicate with the identity provider: **checkid_immediate** and **checkid_setup.** In **checkid_immediate,** the relying party requests that the provider not interact with the user. All communication is relayed through the user's browser without explicitly notifying the user. In **checkid_setup,** the user communicates with the provider server directly using the same web browser as is used to access the relying party site. The second option is more popular on the web.

To start a session, the relying party and the identity provider establish a shared secret—referenced by an associate handle—which the relying party then stores. Using **checkid_setup,** the relying party redirects the user's web browser to the identity provider so that the user can authenticate with the provider. The method of authentication varies, but typically, an OpenID identity provider prompts the user for a password, then asks whether the user trusts the relying party web site to receive his or her credentials and identity details. If the user declines the identity provider's request to trust the relying party web site, the browser is redirected to the relying party with a message indicating that authentication was rejected. The site in turn refuses to authenticate the user. If the user accepts the identity provider's request to trust the relying party web site, the browser is redirected to the designated return page on the relying party web site along with the user's credentials. That relying party must then confirm that the credentials really came from the identity provider. If they had previously established a shared secret, the relying party can validate the shared secret received with the credentials against the one previously stored. In this case, the relying party is considered to be stateful, because it stores the shared secret between sessions (a process sometimes referred to as persistence). In comparison, a stateless relying party must make background requests using the **check_authentication** method to be sure that the data came from the identity provider.

After the OpenID identifier has been verified, OpenID authentication is considered successful and the user is considered logged in to the relying party web site. The web site typically then stores the OpenID identifier in the user's session. OpenID does not provide its own authentication methods, but if an identity provider uses strong authentication, OpenID can be used for secure transactions.

SSL/TLS

Transport Layer Security (TLS) and its predecessor, Secure Sockets Layer (SSL), are cryptographically secure protocols designed to provide security and data integrity for communications over TCP/IP. TLS and SSL encrypt the segments of network connections at the transport layer. Several versions of the protocols are in general use in web browsers, email, instant messaging, and voice-over-IP. TLS is an IETF standard protocol which was last updated in RFC 5246.

The TLS protocol allows client/server applications to communicate across a network in a way specifically designed to prevent eavesdropping, tampering, and message forgery. TLS provides endpoint authentication and data confidentiality by using cryptography. TLS authentication is one-way—the server is authenticated, because the client already knows the server's identity. In this case, the client remains unauthenticated. At the browser level, this means that the browser has validated the server's certificate—more specifically, it has checked the digital signatures of the server certificate's issuing chain of Certification Authorities (CAs).

Validation does not identify the server to the end user. For true identification, the end user must verify the identification information contained in the server's certificate (and, indeed, its whole issuing CA chain). This is the only way for the end user to know the "identity" of the server, and this is the only way identity can be securely established, verifying that the URL, name, or address that is being used is specified in the server's certificate. Malicious web sites cannot use the valid certificate of another web site because they have no means to encrypt the transmission in a way that it can be decrypted with the valid certificate. Since only a trusted CA can embed a URL in the certificate, this ensures that checking the apparent URL with the URL specified in the certificate is an acceptable way of identifying the site.

TLS also supports a more secure bilateral connection mode whereby both ends of the connection can be assured that they are communicating with whom they believe they are connected. This is known as mutual (assured) authentication. Mutual authentication requires the TLS client-side to also maintain a certificate. TLS involves three basic phases:

1. Peer negotiation for algorithm support

2. Key exchange and authentication

3. Symmetric cipher encryption and message authentication

During the first phase, the client and server negotiate cipher suites, which determine which ciphers are used; makes a decision on the key exchange and authentication algorithms to be used; and determines the message authentication codes. The key exchange and authentication algorithms are typically public key algorithms. The message authentication codes are made up from cryptographic hash functions. Once these decisions are made, data transfer may begin.

7.7   Chapter Summary

In this chapter we have discussed some of the more prevalent standards used in cloud computing. Although we have not analyzed each standard in depth, you should now have a feel for how and why each standard is used and, more important, an understanding of why they have evolved. Standards are important, to be sure, but most of these standards evolved from individuals taking a chance on a new innovation. As these innovative techniques became acceptable to users and implementers, more support for the technique followed. At some point, enough support was present to make the innovation be considered a "standard," and groups formalized protocols or rules for using it. Such a "standard" is used until more new innovation takes us elsewhere.

Chapter 8

End-User Access to Cloud Computing

8.1 Chapter Overview

Rishi Chandra, a product manager for Google Enterprise, outlined in an interview[1] what he believes are key trends that will drive movement toward cloud-based enterprise applications. Chandra cited consumer-driven innovation, the rise of power collaborators (those who embrace and take collaboration to very high levels), changing economics, and a lowering of barriers to entry as the chief reasons why the cloud model is being so widely adopted. Innovation behind the success of cloud services ultimately depends on the acceptance of the offering by the user community. Acceptance of an offering by users changes the economics considerably. As more users embrace such innovation, economies of scale for a product allow implementers to lower the costs, removing a barrier to entry and enabling even more widespread adoption of the innovation.

In this chapter, we will present some of the applications that are proving beneficial to end users, enabling them to be "power collaborators." We will take a look at some of the most popular Software-as-a-Service (SaaS) offerings for consumers and provide an overview of their benefits and why, in our opinion, they are helping to evolve our common understanding of what collaboration and mobility will ultimately mean in our daily lives. We will be examining four particularly successful SaaS offerings, looking at them from both the user perspective and the developer/implementer perspective. Looking at both sides of these applications will give you a much better understanding of how they are truly transforming our concept of computing and making much of the traditional desktop-type software available to end users at little to no cost from within the cloud.

---

1. Paul McDougall, "The Four Trends Driving Enterprise Cloud Computing," http://www.informationweek.com/cloud-computing/blog/archives/2008/06/the_four_trends.html, 10 June 2008, retrieved 26 Feb 2009.

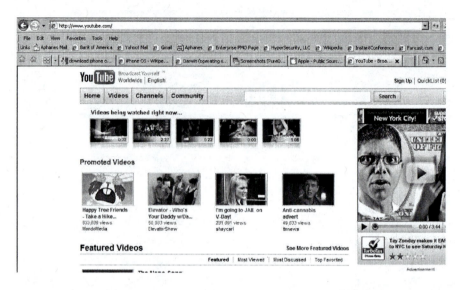

Figure 8.1   YouTube's home page. (Source: http://www.youtube.com.)

In the following sections, we will look at YouTube, Zimbra, Facebook, Zoho, and DimDim.

8.2   YouTube

YouTube is the leader in online video, and a premier destination to watch and share original videos worldwide across the Internet through web sites, mobile devices, blogs, and email. YouTube allows people to easily upload and share video clips on the YouTube web site.[2] Figure 8.1 shows YouTube's home page.

On YouTube, people can view first-hand accounts of current events, find videos about their hobbies and interests, and discover the quirky and unusual—all from videos shared by other subscribers. Founded in February 2005, YouTube received funding from Sequoia Capital and was officially launched in December 2005. Chad Hurley and Steve Chen were the first members of the YouTube management team and currently serve as chief executive officer and chief technology officer, respectively. Within a year of its launch, in November 2006, YouTube was purchased by Google in one of the most talked-about acquisitions to date. Since then, YouTube has struck partnership deals with content providers such as CBS, the BBC, Universal

---

2.   http://www.youtube.com.

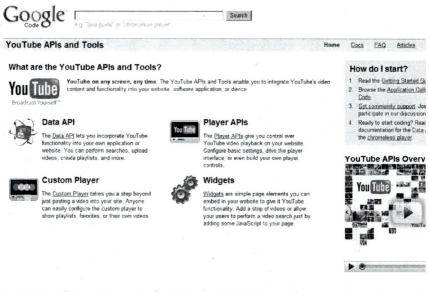

Figure 8.2   The starting point for YouTube APIs. (Source: http://code.google.com/apis/youtube/overview.html.)

Music Group, Sony Music Group, Warner Music Group, the NBA, and many more.

YouTube has become so popular that it now provides a set of development application programming interfaces (APIs) to enable developers to integrate YouTube functionality into their web sites. The YouTube APIs and tools allow programmers to bring the YouTube experience to their web pages, applications, and devices. This open-minded approach has paid huge dividends and helped to further propagate the enormous popularity of the site. In the next section, we will provide a short overview of the APIs. Figure 8.2 shows the starting point for using YouTube APIs.

8.3   YouTube API Overview

The YouTube APIs and tools enable site developers to integrate YouTube's video content and functionality into their web site, software applications, or devices.[3] First, developers need to decide which APIs and tools best meet their needs. For those familiar with HTML but not so familiar with JavaScript, consider looking at the Widgets and custom player. If the development team is comfortable with JavaScript and/or FlashPlayer, they should

---

3.   http://code.google.com/apis/youtube/overview.html.

examine the Player APIs. For those who are programming a device or developing server-side logic for a web site, look at the Data API.

8.3.1   Widgets

Widgets are simple page elements that developers can embed in a web site to give it YouTube functionality. Simply adding a strip of videos or allowing users to perform a video search on your web site can greatly enhance usability and acceptance from those users. All of this can be done just by adding a few lines of JavaScript to a web page. Widgets are JavaScript components that developers can place in a web page to enhance it with YouTube-based content. However, unlike the custom player, which does not require programming skills to use, these widgets are for people who are familiar with development using HTML and JavaScript but who may not be familiar with server-side programming. Two widgets are currently available, the Video Bar and Video Search Control.

The Video Bar

The Video Bar is a simple way to integrate a strip of video thumbnails into your site. Just clicking on a thumbnail opens a floating player for playing video locally. For integration teams, YouTube provides a simple wizard to help jumpstart the process. A Programming Guide[4] is also available to help developers get the most out of the functionality provided and leverage even more from the Video Bar.

The Video Bar is implemented using the Google AJAX Search API. It is designed to let you easily add a strip of playable videos to web pages and blogs. Control is highly customizable, allowing developers to specify the orientation of the video bar, the number of videos displayed, the size of the thumbnails, the location and size of the video player, the list of search expressions that drive the video bar, etc. The locally developed web page controls the selection of videos displayed in the Video Bar. It is very easy to add the Video Bar to a web page. Start with the Video Bar Wizard, which steps through a few simple customization steps and automatically generates all of the code to imbed in your web page.

Video Search Control

The Video Search Control also uses the Google AJAX Search API. It provides the ability to search through massive amounts of YouTube content.

---

4.   http://www.google.com/uds/solutions/videobar/reference.html.

Each Video Search Control search box is preconfigured with a set of HTML tags that define and display thumbnails for the video results obtained from the search. Clicking on a thumbnail of video search results will play it without leaving the page. Like the Video Bar, you can use a wizard to get started; read the Programming Guide[5] for how to customize the player or search automatically based on site links. The Video Search Control is highly customizable, allowing you to configure the initial set of video search terms, the size and location of the player, the number of results, color schemes, etc. Your web page can manipulate the control through the supplied search form or through preselected search terms. You can also save user searches for future use.

8.3.2   YouTube Player APIs

The Player APIs let you control the YouTube player using JavaScript or ActionScript.[6] There is a basic embedded player (which is most often used), and there is also a "chromeless"[7] player that lets you create your own player controls. The Player APIs allow you to establish how users can control YouTube video playback on your web site. By simply configuring some basic settings for the player interface, you can build a highly customized player control. The player APIs provide mechanisms that enable you to control how YouTube videos will look on your site.

It is important to distinguish between the two types of players, the normal "embedded" player you most likely have already seen on the Internet, and a second, chromeless player, which is just a video box without controls. The chromeless player is intended to be implemented by experienced web programmers who want to design a customized video player for their users. Both players have the same API, which is exposed via JavaScript and/or ActionScript. The following sections discuss each option in further detail.

Embedded Player

The embedded player is the simplest way to place YouTube videos on a web page. To customize the behavior and color of the player, developers can use well-documented embedded player parameters. The code needed to display

---

5.   http://www.google.com/uds/solutions/videosearch/reference.html.

6.   ActionScript is a scripting language based on ECMAScript. It is used primarily for development of web sites and software using Adobe Flash Player (in the form of embedded SWF [Shockwave Flash] files).

7.   Chromeless is a term used by developers to refer to a basic player without buttons, gadgets, or menu controls—essentially, the stuff usually found in the silver (or chrome) part of a dialog or window. When those are not present, the control is said to be chromeless.

the embedded player and preconfigured parameters can be quickly generated using a wizard. This makes it possible to find a video by leveraging the Data API and subsequently displaying it using the embedded player. Once the embedded player has been added to a web page, it can be controlled using JavaScript. If you are embedding the player in an Adobe FlashPlayer application, you would use ActionScript instead of Javascript. Using either scripting language, you can create actions similar to what a user could do by clicking on the familiar control buttons—pause the video, seek forward or backward, mute sound, etc. You can use either scripting platform to poll the status of the player and to check for the occurrence of specific events.

Chromeless Player

Interface elements and controls (such as toolbars and buttons) placed around content are sometimes referred to as "chrome," so a chromeless player is, by definition, a YouTube video player without such controls. This makes it easy to customize a player used within a Flash or HTML environment. The chromeless player exposes the same JavaScript and ActionScript APIs as the embedded player.

8.3.3   The YouTube Custom Player

The custom player goes even further than just using scripted API calls to paste videos into your site. Developers can easily configure the custom player to show playlists, favorites, or custom, locally available videos. Sometimes it's nice to have control over your web site without having to edit it. Many web sites benefit from having video content, but updating this content can be difficult. The YouTube custom player allows you to customize a YouTube player and populate it with videos you specify. Once the custom player is on your site, you can easily update the appearance or content by logging into your YouTube account and clicking on Custom Video Players. In creating a custom player, you can choose from a number of themes for the player. The videos that a custom player displays can be all of the videos on your YouTube channel, all of your favorite videos, or any custom playlist you have created. By creating playlists and hooking them up to a custom player, you can easily control what is displayed on your web site without ever leaving YouTube!

8.3.4   YouTube Data API

The YouTube Data API lets you incorporate YouTube functionality into your own application or web site. You can perform searches, upload videos, create playlists, and more. It is possible to search for videos, retrieve standard feeds, and see related content. A program can also authenticate as a user to upload videos, modify user playlists, and more. The Data API is primarily for developers who are used to programming in server-side languages. It is useful for sites or applications that want deeper integration with YouTube. This integration might be a web application to allow users to upload video to YouTube, or a device or desktop application that brings the YouTube experience to a new platform. The Data API gives you programmatic access to the video and user information stored on YouTube. With this, you can personalize your site or application with users' existing information as well as perform actions on their behalf (such as commenting on and rating videos.) If you are curious about how the Data API works at the basic level using XML and HTTP, you can read the Protocol Guide.[8] This guide details the requests and responses that the YouTube API servers expect and return. To learn more about the structure of these requests and responses, read the Reference Guide. This guide defines the API's feed types, HTTP request parameters, HTTP response codes, and XML elements. You may also want to read about the Google Data Protocol[9] and the Atom Publishing Protocol,[10] which are the standards on which the Data API is built. To make working with the API easier, there are a number of client libraries that abstract the API into a language-specific object model. These client libraries are open source and can be used and modified under Apache License 2.0. There are Developer's Guides for Java, .NET, PHP, and Python as well as sample code.

8.4   Zimbra

On September 17, 2007, Yahoo! announced that it had entered into an agreement to acquire Zimbra, Inc., a company specializing in web-based email and collaboration software, for approximately $350 million. The Zimbra email and calendar server is available for Linux, Mac OS X, and virtualization platforms. Zimbra can synchronize with smartphones (such as iPhone and BlackBerry) and desktop clients (such as Outlook and Thunderbird).

Yahoo! Zimbra Desktop[11] is a free, open source email and calendar client which runs on any Windows, Apple, or Linux desktop computer. It

---

8.   http://code.google.com/apis/youtube/2.0/reference.html.
9.   http://code.google.com/apis/gdata.
10.   http://googledataapis.blogspot.com/2008/07/intro-to-atom-publishing-protocol.html.
11.   http://www.zimbra.com.

works online and offline, and it works with any POP or IMAP email account, such as Yahoo! Mail, Zimbra Mail, Hotmail, Gmail, AOL, Microsoft Outlook, or any other work or personal email account that uses POP or IMAP. Zimbra provides software for email and collaboration, including email, group calendar, contacts, instant messaging, file storage, and web document management.

Zimbra can be deployed on-premises or as a hosted email solution and imposes no limit on the size of email storage. Advanced web technology adds Conversation Views and Message Tags to automatically highlight important emails in all your email accounts. The visual Search Builder makes it easy to quickly find important pictures, documents, or messages from people you care about. Yahoo! Zimbra Desktop also manages your Contacts and has a Calendar, Document editor, Task list, and Briefcase for storing all your attachments. Zimbra Desktop uses Web 2.0 AJAX technology and is designed to handle several email accounts with multigigabyte storage (there are no 2-GB mailbox limits!). Zimbra also features archiving and discovery for meeting regulatory compliance guidelines. The Yahoo! Zimbra desktop is shown in Figure 8.3.

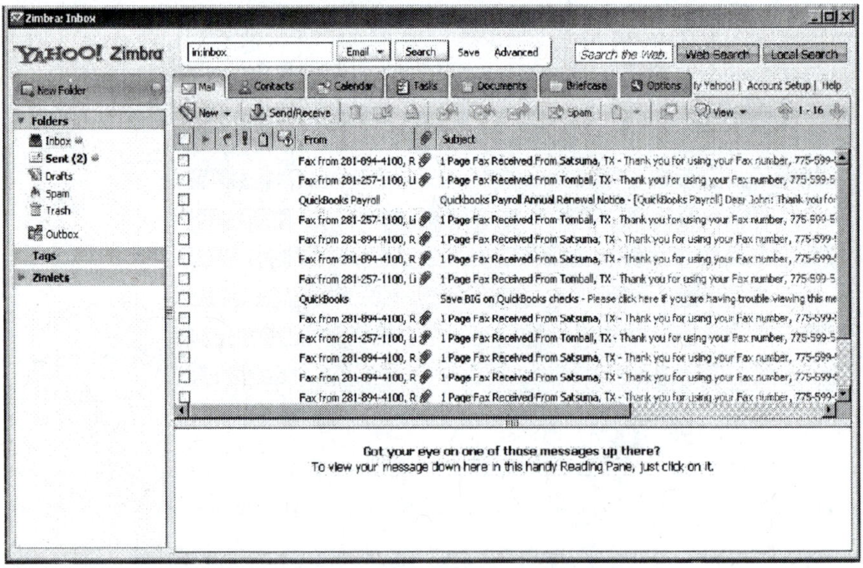

Figure 8.3   The Yahoo! Zimbra desktop.

8.4.1   Zimbra Collaboration Suite (ZCS)

ZCS version 5.0 is a modern, innovative messaging and collaboration application. Ajax-based web collaboration is core to ZCS 5.0. The web client integrates email, contacts, shared calendar, VoIP, and online document authoring into a browser-based interface. Open source Zimlet technology makes it easy to include custom mash-ups in the ZCS web client.

ZCS 5.0 includes an Ajax-based administration interface and scripting tools to use with the ZCS server. Full support is provided for standards-based APIs (IMAP/POP/iCal/CalDAV) as well as MAPI and iSync. This approach enables compatibility with third-party clients such as Microsoft Outlook, Apple desktop suite, and Mozilla Thunderbird. Zimbra also offers Zimbra Mobile, which provides over-the-air push synchronization to smartphones and supports BlackBerry Enterprise Server via a Connector. The Zimbra solution also has a set of security features including antispam and antivirus scanning. Zimbra also features archiving and discovery services as an optional component to save and search email for various compliance issues.

8.5   Facebook

Facebook, Inc., is a leading engineering company located in the heart of Silicon Valley. Facebook was formerly called Thefacebook and is a free-access social networking web site that is operated and privately owned by Facebook, Inc. While he was a student at Harvard University, Mark Zuckerberg founded Facebook with his roommates, Dustin Moskovitz and Chris Hughes, fellow computer science majors at Harvard. Initially, site membership was limited to Harvard students. Later, membership access was expanded to other colleges in the greater Boston area, the Ivy League, and Stanford University. It later expanded to include any university student, then to any high school student, and, finally, to anyone 13 years old and over. Getting onto Facebook is easy. First you create a sign-on identity and provide your email address, as shown in Figure 8.4. A simple three-step process is all it takes to establish an account.

Once you have completed the account creation process, you are taken to your home page, where you can customize it to suit your interests. Figure 8.5 shows a home page as it looks before customizing.

Figure 8.4   Finding friends on Facebook.

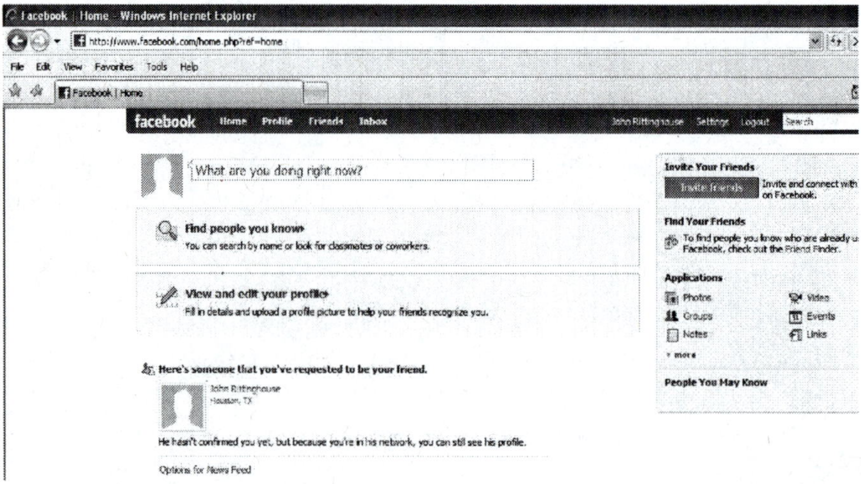

Figure 8.5   The Facebook default home page.

The Facebook web site currently has more than 175 million active users worldwide. Users can join networks organized by city, workplace, school, and region to connect and interact with other people. People can also add friends and send them messages, and update their personal profiles to notify friends about themselves. The web site's name refers to the paper facebooks depicting members of a campus community that some U.S. colleges and preparatory schools give to incoming students, faculty, and staff as a way to get to know other people on campus.

Facebook serves up over 50 billion page views a month while employing fewer than 200 engineers. It is the second most-trafficked PHP hypertext preprocessor site in the world (Yahoo is number 1), and it is one of the world's largest MySQL installations, running thousands of databases. In terms of total photo page views, Facebook exceeds all of the next-largest photo sites combined. It is the largest photo-sharing site in the United States, with over a billion photos. Facebook is the fourth most-trafficked web site in the United States, and Facebook users upload more than 14 million new photos every day. It is also the largest user in the world of **memcached,** an open source caching system originally developed by LiveJournal. It is obvious from these statistics that the engineering team at Facebook is pushing the limits of IT engineering. They have created a custom-built search engine capable of processing millions of queries a day, completely distributed and entirely in-memory with real-time updates.

8.5.1 Facebook Development

Facebook provides anyone the ability to create Facebook applications. A user can get a basic application up and running in minutes. To create a Facebook application, you should be well versed in PHP or some other coding language such as Ruby on Rails, JavaScript, or Python. It is preferable to know one that already has a client library for the Facebook API. You will need to have a basic understanding of the Internet, SSH, MySQL, and Unix.

8.6 Zoho

Zoho is an office productivity suite from AdventNet, Inc., which was founded in 1996. The Zoho product is supported by over 120 developers. To date, Zoho has launched 15 different applications, and more are in the works. When you first go to the Zoho web site, you see the page shown in Figure 8.6.

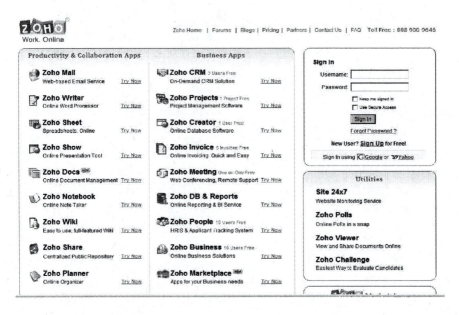

Figure 8.6   The Zoho home page. (Source: wwwzoho.com.)

From the home page you can create an account or sign in. After signing into Zoho, quite a few options are available to you. For example, signing into Zoho Mail, as shown in Figure 8.7, provides you with a rich set of features.

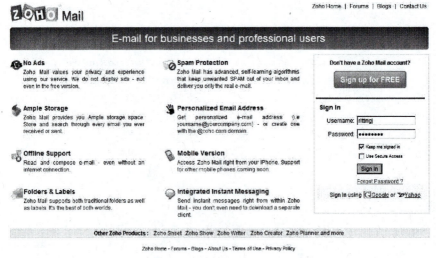

Figure 8.7   Zoho Mail home page.

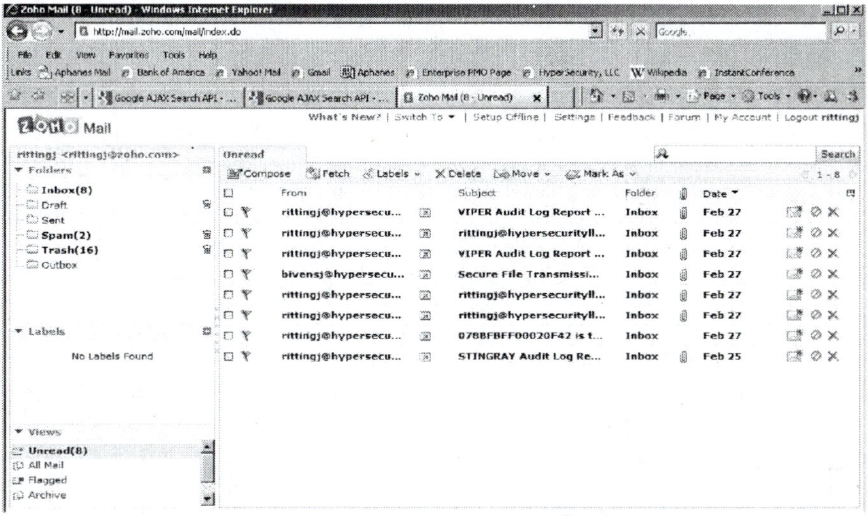

Figure 8.8   The inbox for Zoho mail.

Zoho Mail provides ample storage space. You can store and search through every email you have ever sent or received, and it offers offline support so you can take your mail with you. You can read and compose emails without an active Internet connection and send them out once you are connected. Zoho Mail supports both traditional folders as well as labels. A label is a type of folder that you can customize by both name and color.

Zoho Mail offers advanced, self-learning algorithms that keep unwanted spam out of your inbox and deliver only legitimate emails. Using Zoho, you can have a personalized email address or create one using the zoho.com domain. Also, there is support for mobile users. Zoho Mail can be read from an iPhone, and support for other mobile phones is expected this year. Integrated instant messaging (IM) is available, so you can send instant messages from within Zoho Mail and, best of all, you don't need to download a separate client.

8.6.1   Zoho CloudSQL

CloudSQL is a technology that allows developers to interact with business data stored across Zoho Services using the familiar SQL language. Unlike other methods for accessing data in the cloud, CloudSQL encourages developers to leverage the years of experience they have with the SQL language. CloudSQL allows businesses to connect and integrate the data and applications they have in Zoho with the data and applications they have in-house, or even with other SaaS services. This leads to faster deployments and easier integration projects. CloudSQL is offered as an extension to the existing Zoho web API. It is meant to be used by developers, not end users. Cloud-SQL supports multiple database dialects (e.g., ANSI, Oracle, Microsoft SQL Server, IBM DB2, MySQL, PostgreSQL, and Informix). The main purpose of the SQL Interpreter component is to translate SQL statements that are executed by a third-party application into a neutral dialect that can be understood by any of the individual Zoho services. The federation layer understands and handles service-specific query delegation and result aggregation. The federation layer enables a query to span across multiple Zoho services to fetch data in an aggregated manner, thus virtualizing different Zoho services so they appear as a single service.

Each of the specific Zoho services (i.e., Zoho CRM, Zoho Creator, Zoho Reports) comprises the last layer of the CloudSQL architecture. They collect, store, and mine business data consumed by Zoho users and developers. The services execute the query against their data store and pass the results back to the CloudSQL middleware. The services take care of authorizing each query to verify whether the user who is executing the query has permission to access or manipulate the data on which the query is executed.

8.7   DimDim Collaboration

Dimdim[12] invested more than 15 person-years of engineering development into making a product to support complex web meetings. This free service lets anyone communicate using rich media in real time. Unlike competing web conference products, Dimdim does not require users to install software on their computers in order to attend a web meeting. Users can start or join meetings using only a few mouse clicks.

Dimdim is available as open source software, and it already integrates with CRM and LMS software so it can be extended easily. It is extremely flexible, available in hosted and on-site configurations, and easily customizable. Dimdim Open Source Community Edition v4.5, code named "Liberty," is meant for developers and highly technical enthusiasts, and for use in noncritical environments. It has nearly all of the features touted by the commercial version of Dimdim (Enterprise) and is based on open source streaming and media components. Dimdim Enterprise is based on commercial streaming and media components (Adobe Flash Server) and runs on top

---

12.   http://www.dimdim.com.

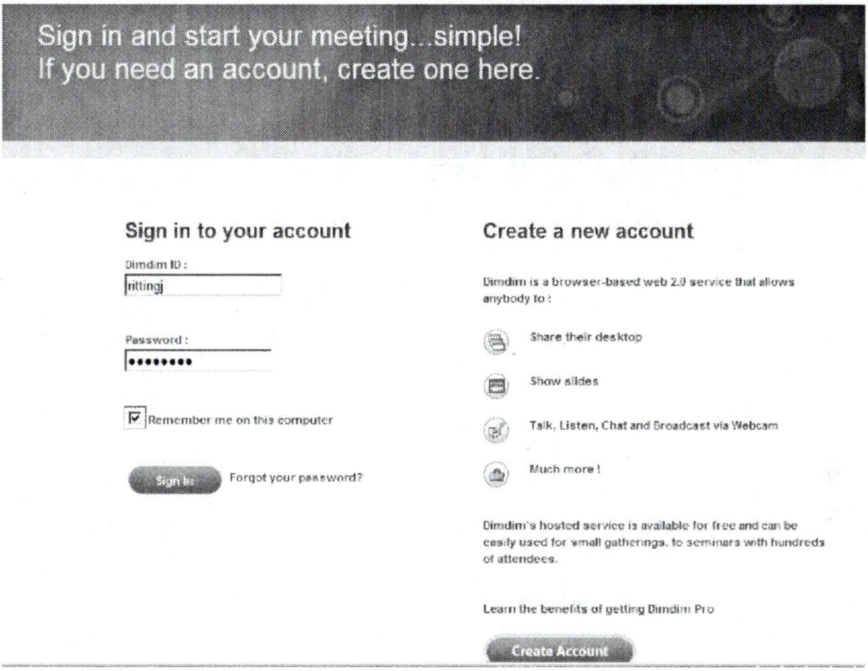

Sign in and start your meeting…simple!
If you need an account, create one here.

Sign in to your account

Dimdim ID :

[rittingj]

Password :

[••••••••]

☑ Remember me on this computer

[Sign In]   Forgot your password?

Create a new account

Dimdim is a browser-based web 2.0 service that allows anybody to :

Share their desktop

Show slides

Talk, Listen, Chat and Broadcast via Webcam

Much more !

Dimdim's hosted service is available for free and can be easily used for small gatherings, to seminars with hundreds of attendees.

Learn the benefits of getting Dimdim Pro

[Create Account]

Figure 8.9   The Dimdim sign-in page. (Source: http://www.dimdim.com.)

of their SynchroLive Communication Platform. The open source community supports the Open Source Community Edition.

Dimdim has a simple user interface that is easy for presenters and attendees to learn. Meeting hosts and attendees do not have to install anything to broadcast audio or video, because all that is needed is a very tiny plug-in (which is required only if you want to share your desktop.) The free version is not a limited-feature trial product. Dimdim Free boasts a powerful feature set that allows anyone to host meetings with up to 20 people simultaneously using diversified platforms such as Mac, Windows, and Linux. Signing up to use Dimdim is easy, as shown in Figure 8.9: Simply go to the web site and fill in the requested information.

If you already have an account, you can just use your existing information. Otherwise, you can create one in a few clicks and sign in. Once you sign into Dimdim, you will see the home screen, which will look like Figure 8.10.

To start a meeting with Dimdim, simply click the Host Meeting button, as shown in Figure 8.11. Provide a name for the meeting and an agenda and then enter the email addresses of the attendees. Next, choose a key to

Figure 8.10   The Dimdim home screen. (Source: http://www.dimdim.com.)

use as Host and one for the attendees to gain access to the meeting and click
the Start button.

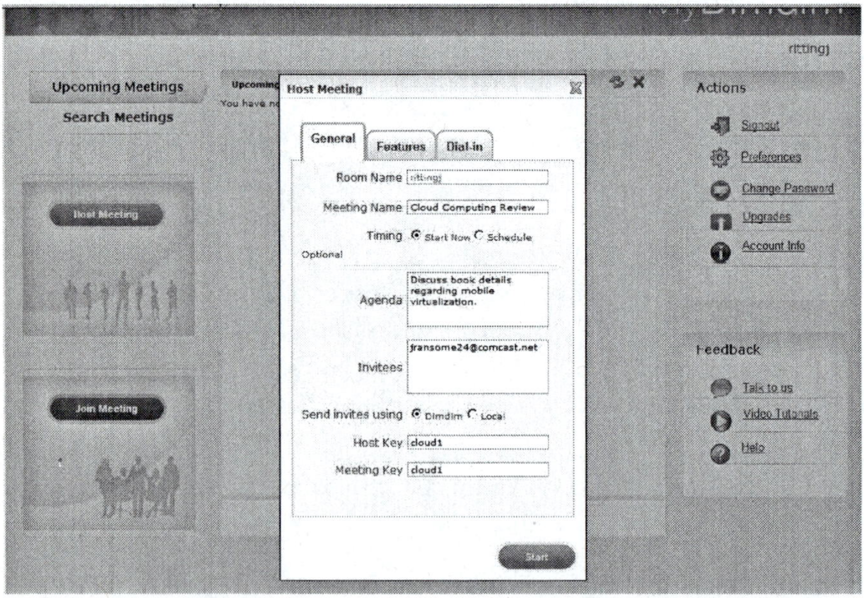

Figure 8.11   Dimdim Host Meeting screen. (Source: http://www.dimdim.com.)

Schedule Meeting   ✕

General   Features   Dial-in

Room Name rittingj

Meeting Name Cloud Computing Review

Timing ○ Start Now ● Schedule

Room URL http://webmeeting.dimdim.com:8
0/portal/JoinForm.action?confKe
y=rittingj

Click on the URL to copy it to
Clipboard.

Optional

Agenda Discuss book details
regarding mobile
virtualization.

Repeat Option Once Only ▼

Start Date March 02, 2009

End Date March 02, 2009

Invitees jransome24@comcast.net

Start Time 3 ▼   00 ▼   PM ▼

Timezone GMT-05:00 Eastern Time ▼

Send invites using ● Dimdim ○ Local

Host Key cloud1

Meeting Key cloud1

Schedule

Figure 8.12   Dimdim Schedule Meeting screen. (Source: http://www.dimdim.com.)

In the example shown in Figure 8.11, the meeting will begin immediately. If you want to schedule a meeting for a future time, click Schedule on the Timing option. This brings up the screen shown in Figure 8.12.

In the Schedule Meeting screen, enter the start and end dates and the start time. The time zone you select should represent the time zone where the meeting will be hosted. Click the Schedule button to bring up the dialog box shown in Figure 8.13.

Meeting Scheduled   ✕

A meeting Cloud Computing Review is scheduled. All
the participants have been notified via email. Would
you like to schedule another meeting?

Yes   No

Figure 8.13   Meeting Scheduled dialog box. (Source: http://www.dimdim.com.)

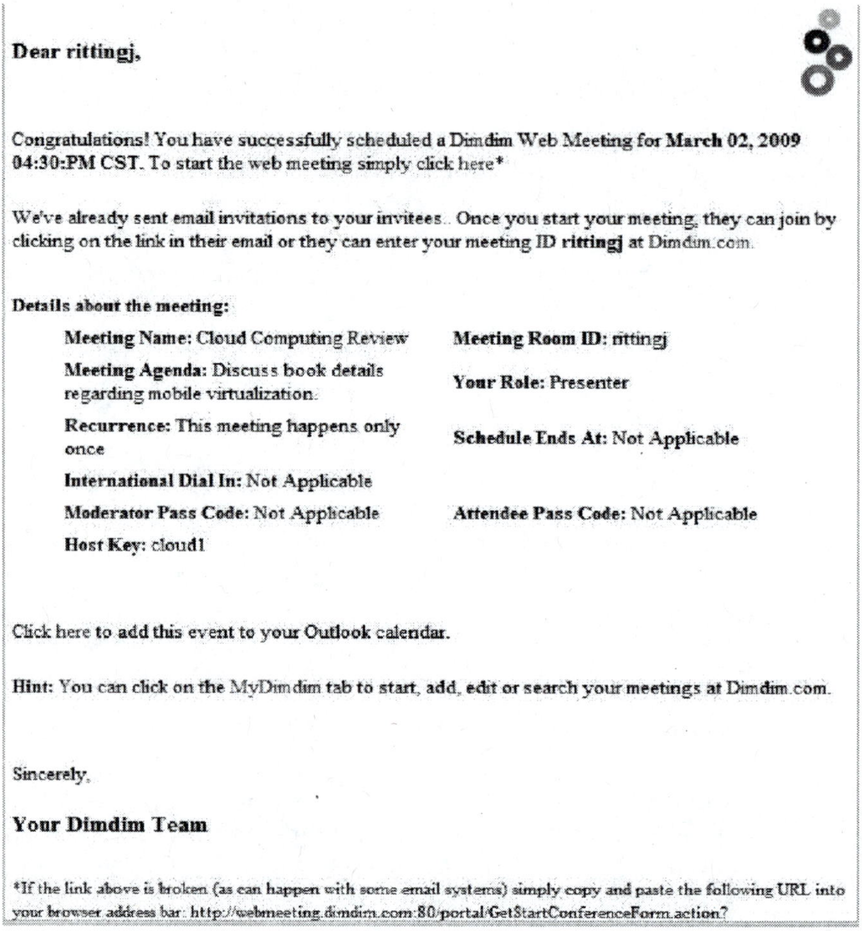

Dear rittingj,

Congratulations! You have successfully scheduled a Dimdim Web Meeting for **March 02, 2009 04:30:PM CST**. To start the web meeting simply click here*

We've already sent email invitations to your invitees.. Once you start your meeting, they can join by clicking on the link in their email or they can enter your meeting ID **rittingj** at Dimdim.com.

Details about the meeting:

Meeting Name: Cloud Computing Review   **Meeting Room ID:** rittingj

Meeting Agenda: Discuss book details   **Your Role:** Presenter
regarding mobile virtualization.

Recurrence: This meeting happens only   **Schedule Ends At:** Not Applicable
once

International Dial In: Not Applicable

Moderator Pass Code: Not Applicable   **Attendee Pass Code:** Not Applicable

Host Key: cloud1

Click here to add this event to your Outlook calendar.

Hint: You can click on the MyDimdim tab to start, add, edit or search your meetings at Dimdim.com.

Sincerely,

Your Dimdim Team

*If the link above is broken (as can happen with some email systems) simply copy and paste the following URL into your browser address bar: http://webmeeting.dimdim.com:80/portal/GetStartConferenceForm.action?

Figure 8.14   An email confirming the meeting invitation extended via DimDim.

You and your attendees will all receive an email similar to the one shown in Figure 8.14.

A single click starts your meetings, as shown in Figure 8.15.

A single click shares PPTs, PDFs, whiteboards, even your entire desktop. A click is all it takes to pass control of the meeting to any attendee. Pass the mic or webcam around with a single click. The attendees at a meeting can see the presenter's live video and desktop while hearing multiple voices-over-IP (VoIP). For larger meetings, you can use the free teleconference service. All attendees can simultaneously annotate a presentation, mark up a whiteboard, send instant messages, and broadcast their audio and video if permitted by the host. In Figure 8.16, the Whiteboard is being used.

Figure 8.15   Dimdim Web Meeting opening screen. (Source: http://www.dimdim.com.)

Figure 8.16   Using the Whiteboard in a Dimdim meeting. (Source: http://
www.dimdim.com.)

Dimdim has a fully integrated web browser, which allows you to take your audience to various web sites and show them specific features live on the Internet. Figure 8.17 is an example of showing your audience the web site.

Figure 8.17   Showing your audience a web site. (Source: http://www.dim-
dim.com.)

Dimdim is a powerful tool for collaboration in the cloud. Connectors
for open source software such as SugarCRM,[13] coupled with Dimdim's web
conferencing software, means that users, developers, and partners have
cloud-based access to advanced browser-based collaboration features that
allow them to easily interact with groups large or small across multiple geographies, while simultaneously recording the activity in their SugarCRM
application.

Online support[14] for Dimdim includes a complete collection of tools
designed specifically to improve the Dimdim experience. First, you can use
Forums, where you can join the discussion group relevant to your topic and
learn from others in the Dimdim community. Dimdim employees also use
the forums to gain better understanding of customer issues. There is an
online knowledgebase that is connected to the support database. It is constantly updated and is a great place to get self-help. Dimdim uses an issue
tracker and keeps it updated so you can check the status of an issue or view
issues for all users. Tools are available to help you check your system, bandwidth, and even test your webcam before you conduct meetings. You can
also download any plug-ins if necessary. Other support resources such as

13.   http://www.sugarcrm.com/crm/download/sugar-suite.html.
14.   http://www.dimdim.com/support/dimdim_help.html.

product and API documentation, videos, Dimdim support policies, supported platforms, and open source support links can also be found on the support site.

8.8   Chapter Summary

This chapter provided an overview of end-user access to cloud computing. We first talked about key trends we believe will drive collaboration further into the cloud environment. We chose five significant entities to present you with an overview of the types and levels of capability available in the cloud today—things you can use now. YouTube, an online video repository, has an amazing hold on the global audience. Collaboration suites such as Zimbra both enhance mobility and allow you to maintain a virtual office in the cloud. Social networking with Facebook has become very popular, especially in academic settings. Zoho is a SaaS vendor to watch. Backed by Google, Zoho offers something for everyone. Finally, for presentations and online sharing, Dimdim is a good choice. With the vast amount of free, open source software available from the cloud, is it any wonder technology is outpacing our ability to keep up? In the next chapter, we will discuss how the new mobile virtualization technologies are improving our ability to interact at all levels.

Chapter 9

Mobile Internet Devices and the Cloud

9.1 Chapter Overview

A December 2008 Informa Telecoms & Media study[1] estimated that there are over 4 billion connections to mobile devices worldwide—an astounding number when you realize that this figure represents 60% of the global population today. Of course, this does not mean that two out of every three people on Earth have a mobile phone. It is common in more than 60 countries, however, for one person to have two or more devices, even while there are no phones at all in some parts of the globe. In some countries, millions of people are now experiencing connectivity to the world for the first time through wireless technologies. It is changing their economic, social, and political fortunes forevermore.

The number of wireless users on 3G services continues to rise daily. Informa estimates that there are nearly 415 million 3G subscriptions to date, with 77% share of the 3G market on UMTS/HSPA1 networks or 320 million connections, and the remaining 95 million subscribed to the older CDMA EV-DO2 technology. The number of commercial UMTS/HSPA networks has risen to 258 in more than 100 countries, including 41 networks in 20 countries in the Latin America and Caribbean region. It is a foregone conclusion that HSPA and HSPA+3 will compete with all prevailing mobile wireless technologies available today. Telstra's recent commercial launch of HSPA+,reports peak theoretical downlink speeds of 21.6 Mbps. The 3G technology is more than capable of delivering the high-speed bandwidth that customers demand.[2]

If the cloud is becoming increasingly pervasive and mobile browsers are getting better every day, you may be asking yourself if you need anything

---

1.   http://www.unstrung.com/document.asp?doc_id=169641.
2.   http://www.unstrung.com/document.asp?doc_id=169641.

more on your mobile device beyond a browser that can access the cloud. Can browser widgets provide enough functionality that you don't need applications on your device? What if you could get everything you need accomplished using simple widgets that leverage your mobile device-based browser to access the cloud? The potential impact on enterprise mobility is huge. While organizations are deploying more and more Software-as-a-Service (SaaS) applications, there is no reason mobile workers can't access those applications from their mobile devices, assuming they have enough bandwidth (i.e., 3G- or 4G-capable devices). All that is really required beyond such bandwidth is a browser that can actually handle all of the various SaaS-associated web standards. Imagine a future environment in which mobile device manufacturers will partner with multiple SaaS vendors to provide enterprises complete cloud-based computing solutions that work anywhere.

9.2   What Is a Smartphone?

The definition of a smartphone is not standardized and varies depending on who you ask. For most users, the consensus is that a smartphone is a mobile device that offers advanced capabilities beyond those offered by a typical mobile phone. Modern versions come with PC-like functionality. Many of the newer models have customized operating systems and associated software that provides a standardized interface. Nearly all smartphones have advanced features such as email, Internet access, instant messaging, etc. Smartphones are much more than just another cell phone. They provide instant access to the web, which translates into immediate collaboration capability. Whether you are researching financial news to predict the stock market or looking for the perfect golf course to treat your client, it's on the Internet. Most smartphones allow you to sync data with your desktop computer. You can store and work on documents from your smartphone, and you can receive and reply to emails as they arrive in your inbox using real-time push email.

Smartphone applications may be developed by the manufacturer of the device or by any other third-party provider or developer capable of accessing the open source operating system. Other functionalities might include an additional interface such as a miniature QWERTY keyboard on the touch screen, built-in video and camera features, contact management, built-in navigation software, office document processing capability, and software for playing music and viewing video clips. Such smartphone capabilities transform the common cell phone into a mobile multimedia platform for your entertainment. They can store and display pictures, videos of friends and family, or even play live broadcasts of sports or movies.

9.3   Mobile Operating Systems for Smartphones

Many regard the smartphone as a minicomputer with a phone. Most smartphones use an identifiable and open source operating system, often with the ability to add user applications. This is a major factor differentiating smartphones from traditional mobile phones, which only support dedicated, proprietary applications. In the next few sections, we will take a look at several popular mobile devices and the operating systems used with them.

9.3.1   iPhone

The Apple iPhone uses 3G technology, and its operating system (OS) is based on the Darwin OS. Darwin forms the core set of components on which both the Mac OS X and iPhone OS are based. Darwin is compatible with Single UNIX Specification version 3 (SUSv3) and POSIX UNIX applications and utilities. The iPhone touts features such as Global Positioning System (GPS) mapping, support for enterprise applications such as Microsoft Exchange, the new App Store, etc. The iPhone is a wide-screen mobile device very much like the iPod. It provides users a rich interface with HTML email and an outstanding web browser. The iPhone home screen is shown in Figure 9.1.

The iPhone lets you customize your home screen with applications and web clips of your choosing. You can arrange the icons any way you want or even create as many as nine home screens, each customizable to your needs. For example, if you check the same web site every day, you can create a web clip to access it directly from your home screen using a single tap of a finger. You can always press the home button to go back to your main home screen. iPhone supports rich HTML email which allows you to see email attachments in their original format. The iPhone supports more than a dozen file and image formats, including PDF, Microsoft Word, Excel, PowerPoint, and iWork attachments. Support for Microsoft Exchange Active-Sync gives you push email that arrives automatically to your inbox, as shown in Figure 9.2.

9.3.2   Google (Android)

Android is a software platform and operating system for mobile devices that is based on the Linux kernel. It was originally developed by Google and

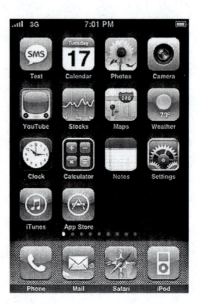

Figure 9.1   The iPhone home screen.

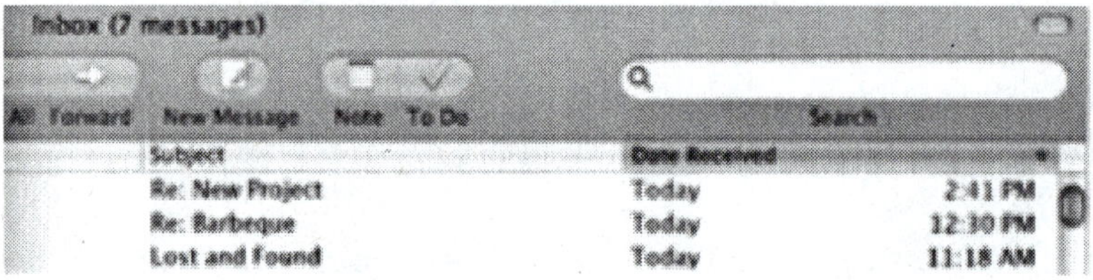

Figure 9.2   The message inbox for iPhone.

later with the Open Handset Alliance (which is a group of more than 30 technology and mobile companies). The Android operating system is the first complete, open, and free mobile platform. An Android Software Development Kit is available to help developers get started on new applications. Android allows developers to write managed Java code to control a mobile device. Developers can distribute their applications to users of Android mobile phones. There is a marketplace called Android Market that enables developers to easily publish and distribute their applications directly to users of Android-compatible phones. The T-Mobile G1, shown in Figure 9.3, is one of the better-known commercial offerings using Android.

Figure 9.3   The T-Mobile G1.

Google has now released most of the Android code under the Apache license, a free software and open source license. Figure 9.4 shows the major components of the Android operating system.

Android developers have full access to the same framework application programming interfaces (APIs) used by the core applications. The architecture is designed to simplify reuse of components, so any application can publish its capabilities and any other application may then make use of those capabilities (subject to security constraints enforced by the framework). This same mechanism allows framework components to be replaced by the user. Underlying all applications is a set of services and systems, including:

1.   A rich, extensible set of views that can be used to build an application (i.e., lists, grids, text boxes, buttons, and an embedded web browser)

2.   Content providers that allow applications to access data from other applications or to share their own data

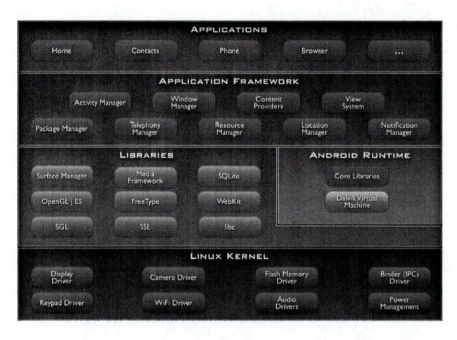

Figure 9.4   Major components of the Android operating system. (Source: http://
d.android.com/guide/basics/what-is-android.html.)

3.   A resource manager to manage access to noncode resources such
     as localized strings, graphics, and layout files

4.   A notification manager that enables all applications to display
     custom alerts in the status bar

5.   An activity manager to manages applications and provide a com-
     mon navigation stack

Every Android application runs in its own process, with its own
instance of the Dalvik virtual machine (VM). The Dalvik virtual machine
is a major piece of Google's Android platform for mobile devices. It runs
Java platform applications which have been converted into a compact Dalvik Executable (.dex) format suitable for systems that are constrained in
terms of memory and processor speed.[3] Dalvik has been written so that a
device can run multiple VMs efficiently. The Dalvik VM relies on the
Linux kernel version 2.6 for underlying functionalities such as threading,
low-level memory management, and core system services such as security,

3.   "Dalvik Virtual Machine," Wikipedia, retrieved 8 Mar 2009.

memory management, process management, network stack, etc. The kernel acts as an abstraction layer between the hardware and the rest of the software stack.

9.3.3 Blackberry

The BlackBerry solution consists of smartphones integrated with software that enables access to email and other communication services. Developed by the Canadian company Research In Motion (RIM), the BlackBerry is a wireless handheld device originally introduced in 1999 as a two-way pager. In 2002, RIM released their version of the smartphone, named BlackBerry. It supported push email, mobile telephony, text messaging, internet faxing, web browsing, and other wireless information services. BlackBerry first made progress in the commercial marketplace by concentrating on enterprise email. The BlackBerry has a built-in QWERTY keyboard, optimized for "thumbing" (the use of only the thumbs to type). System navigation is primarily accomplished by a scroll ball in the middle of the device (older devices used a track wheel on the side). Their current solution gives mobile users access to email, phone, data, applications, games, and the Internet from a state-of-the-art smartphone, as shown in Figure 9.5.

The BlackBerry offers an end-to-end encryption solution with two transport encryption options, Advanced Encryption Standard (AES) and Triple Data Encryption Standard (Triple DES) for all data transmitted between their BlackBerry Enterprise Server and licensed BlackBerry smartphones. Private encryption keys are generated in a secure, two-way authenticated environment and are assigned to each BlackBerry smartphone user. Each secret key is stored only in the user's secure enterprise email account and on the user's BlackBerry smartphone. Data sent to the BlackBerry is encrypted by the BlackBerry Enterprise Server using the private key retrieved from the user's mailbox. Next, the encrypted information is transported securely across the network to the smartphone, where it is decrypted using the key stored on the smartphone. Data remains encrypted in transit and is never decrypted outside of the corporate firewall.

9.3.4 Windows Mobile

Windows Mobile is a compact operating system offering a set of basic applications commonly found on mobile devices. It is based on the Microsoft Win32 API. Devices that run Windows Mobile include pocket PCs, smartphones, portable media centers, and on-board computers for certain automobiles. Windows Mobile is designed to appear similar to desktop versions

Figure 9.5   The Blackberry.

of Microsoft Windows. The platform supports third-party software development. Originally, Windows Mobile appeared as the pocket PC 2000 operating system, then known as Windows Compact Edition (CE). Since then, Windows Mobile has been updated several times. The next planned release, Windows Mobile 7.0, is slated for the latter part of 2009. Figure 9.6 shows what it is expected to look like.

Microsoft had projected in 2008 that it would see an increase of devices shipping with Windows Mobile from 11 million to 20 million units. It missed its initial goal, selling only 18 million licenses, but even that number indicates the phenomenal growth of this market. Microsoft attributed the shortfall in its prediction to the delayed launch of some smartphone devices. Since then, Windows Mobile's market share as an operating system for smartphones worldwide has fallen from 23% in 2004 to 12% in 2008.[4] Windows Mobile now has a worldwide smartphone market share of 14%. It is interesting to note that Microsoft licenses its Windows Mobile platform

Figure 9.6   Windows Mobile

to four of the world's five largest mobile phone manufacturers—a strong testament to its popularity in the marketplace.

9.3.5   Ubuntu Mobile Internet Device (MID)

Ubuntu MID Edition is designed specifically for mobile internet devices (MIDs). Ubuntu MID is based on the popular Linux distribution Ubuntu. Ubuntu MID is highly flexible and customizable. It is an open source platform that is best suited to the kind of product differentiation that reaches target users in the mobile marketplace. MIDs generally have the following common features and attributes:

1.   Small size/form factor, typically a 4- to 7-inch touch screen

2.   Physical and/or virtual keyboard

3.   Wi-Fi, 3G, Bluetooth, GPS, WiMAX

4.   2- to 8-GB Flash or disk storage

---

4.   Prince Mclean, "Microsoft Plans "Skymarket" Apps Store for Windows Mobile 7 in 2009," http://www.roughlydrafted.com/2008/09/01/microsoft-plans-%E2%80%9Cskymarket%E2%80%9D-apps-store-for-windows-mobile-7-in-2009, Rough-lyDrafted Magazine, San Francisco, CA, 1 Sept 2008, retrieved 9 Mar 2009.

5. 256 to 512 MB RAM (the more the better)

Figure 9.7   Clutter user interface.

6. OpenGL 3D graphics support

7. USB, camera, headphone jack, speakers, microphone

8. Customizable (Flash or Clutter[5]-based) user interface (see Figures 9.7 and 9.8).

Ubuntu MID Edition has a suite of applications that work seamlessly to meet the needs of mobile users. Web applications such as Facebook, MySpace, YouTube, and Dailymotion are easily supported. Ubuntu MID needs no stylus—you navigate using a touchscreen. Just tap the screen or drag a finger for navigation and control. To launch applications, tap the application icon with your finger or tap menus and buttons to use them. You can swipe a web page to pan up, down, or sideways, and you can swipe a video, photo, song, or thumbnail page to move to the next or the previous one. Figure 9.9 shows the home screen of Ubuntu MID.

In the next few pages we highlight some of the applications found in the default distribution of Ubuntu MID, to give you a feel for what capabilities exist on modern mobile devices and how they can enhance daily life, simply by facilitating collaboration via the Internet. When you first get the device running, it is important to set preferences such as time and date (see Figure

---

5.   Clutter is an open source software library for creating fast, visually rich, and animated graphical user interfaces.

Figure 9.8   Flash user interface.

Figure 9.9   Ubuntu MID home screen.

9.10) and to perform any system updates to bring the version current with any releases or updates since your particular version was made available.

To update your system, simply tap the System menu and select the Update Manager. The application will start and display the "Starting Update Manager..." message as shown in Figure 9.11.

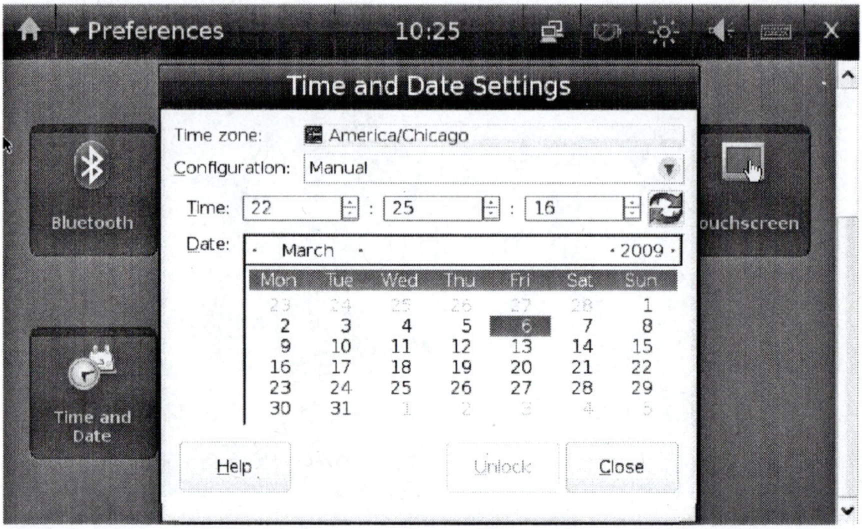

Figure 9.10   Setting the time and date on Ubuntu MID.

Figure 9.11   The Ubuntu MID Update Manager.

Once the update manager starts, it will use your existing Internet connection and check with the update server to determine which applications on your system may need to be updated. You can even update the system itself using this tool. After checking with the server to see what may have changed, you will be presented with the screen shown in Figure 9.12.

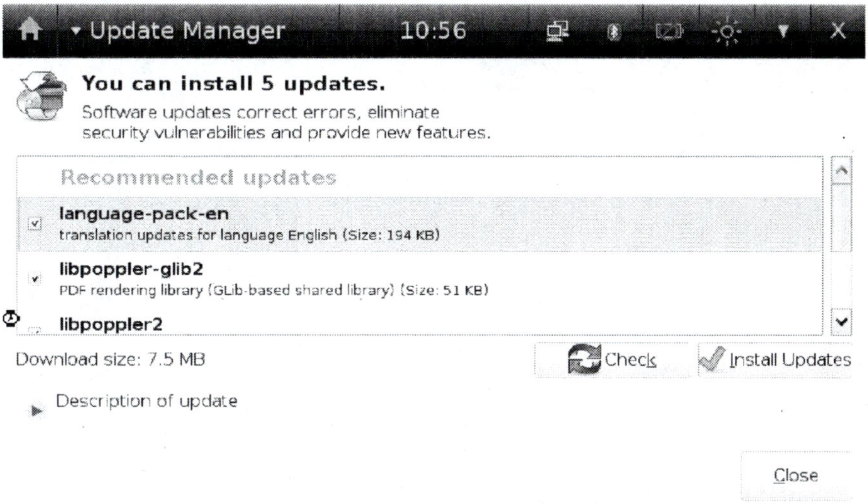

Figure 9.12 Installing updates.

Simply click the green checkmark button to install updates. For the example in Figure 9.12, five updates will be installed. The first part of the installation downloads the updates, as shown in Figure 9.13.

The download will proceed and, depending on your connection speed, may take anywhere from a few seconds to minutes to complete. After the downloads complete, installation proceeds automatically. You may be asked to reboot the device to complete the install process.

Mobile users deal with office documents on a daily basis. Ubuntu MID offers an office document reader to read various document types such as .doc, .pdf, .xml, etc. The reader is shown in Figure 9.14 displaying a .pdf file.

For users who need more than a read-only display of a document, Ubuntu MID also offers a complete mobile office solution, OpenOffice version 2.4 (see Figure 9.15), which allows you to build presentations, spreadsheets, documents, etc. It is a very popular solution in the open source community.

Figure 9.16 shows the editing of an .html document using OpenOffice. OpenOffice is the leading open source office software suite for word pro-

Figure 9.13   Downloading updates.

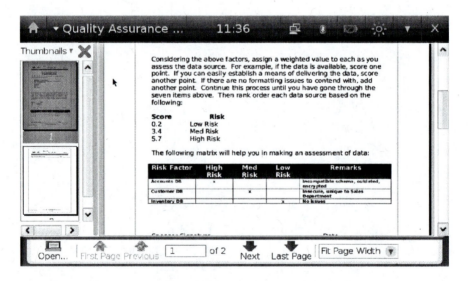

Figure 9.14   The Ubuntu MID document reader.

cessing, spreadsheets, presentations, graphics, databases, etc. It is available in many languages and works on all common computer platforms. It stores data in an international open standard format, the ISO-approved Open Document Format (ODF), and it can read and write files from other common commercial office software packages. It can be downloaded from the official web site[6] and used completely free of charge for any purpose.

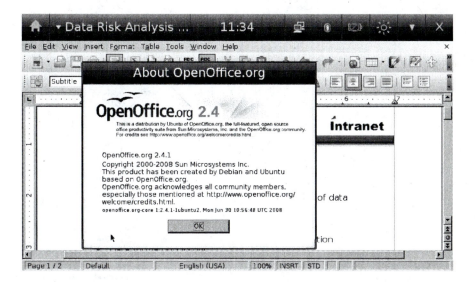

Figure 9.15   Ubuntu MID OpenOffice.

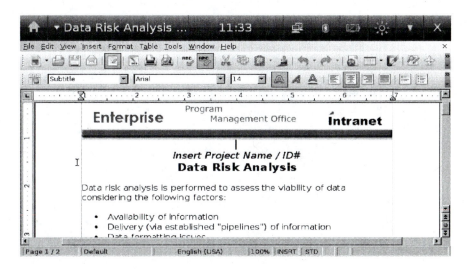

Figure 9.16   Editing a document using OpenOffice.

The most recent versions of OpenOffice (version 3.0 and later) provide support for integrated email and calendaring, using Thunderbird 2.0 for email and Lightning for calendaring. Both of these products are available

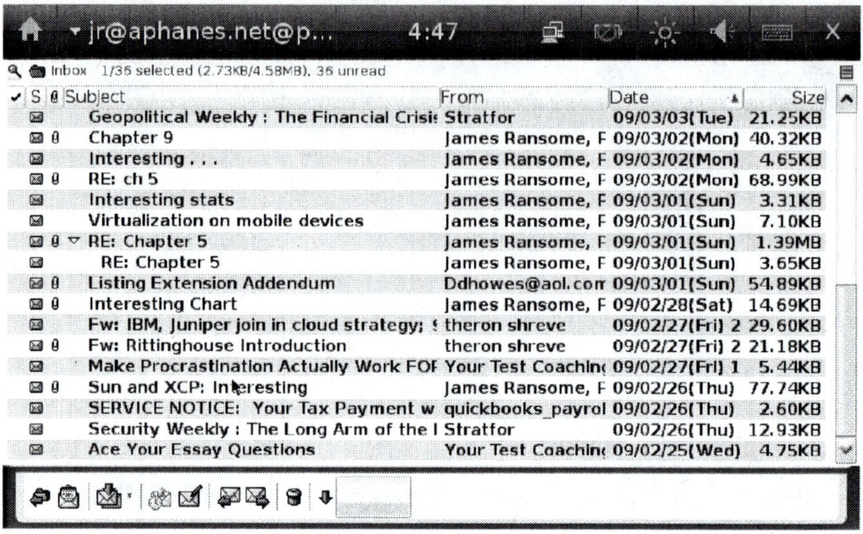

Figure 9.17   OpenOffice email in Ubuntu MID.

from mozilla.org and are also open source. Figure 9.17 shows an inbox in OpenOffice email.

For mobile users, traveling often involves downtime, sitting on a plane or in an airport or hotel lobby. FBReader is an ebook reader included with Ubuntu MID. FBReader works on Linux, Windows XP/Vista, FreeBSD, and various other Linux-based mobile operating systems. FBReader is distributed under the terms of the GNU GPL. It supports many ebook formats, such as fb2 ebook format, HTML, CHM, plucker, Palmdoc, zTxt,TCR, RTF, OpenReader, and plain text format. Direct reading from tar, zip, gzip, and bzip2 archives is also supported. FBReader can perform automatic library building, and automatic language and character encoding detection is also supported. Other features include:

1.   Automatically generated contents table

2.   Embedded images support

3.   Footnotes/hyperlinks support

4.   Position indicator

5.   Keeps the last open book and the last read positions for all opened books between runs

6. List of last opened books

7. Automatic hyphenation

8. Text search and full-screen mode, including screen rotation by 90, 180, and 270 degrees

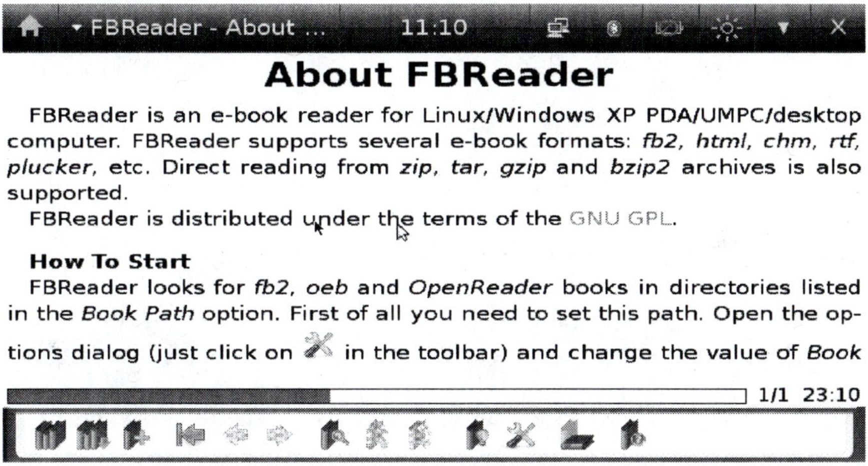

Figure 9.18 FBReader.

An FBReader screen is shown in Figure 9.18.

For those more inclined to chat using instant messaging, a full-featured IM client is provided, as illustrated in Figure 9.19.

If you cannot find anyone to chat with, you can always use the Internet browser to visit your favorite web sites, listen to the radio, or watch videos on YouTube, Hulu, etc. The browser is very capable, supporting the most recent standards for a rich user interface. See Figure 9.20.

9.4 Mobile Platform Virtualization

Smart phones with rich and open operating systems are growing in popularity, resulting in a market that is undergoing tremendous innovation and change. The pressure to reduce development costs and get phones to market faster has increased competitive pressure to deliver feature-rich phones to market faster and to migrate from proprietary operating systems to open operating systems without compromising the security of trusted services.

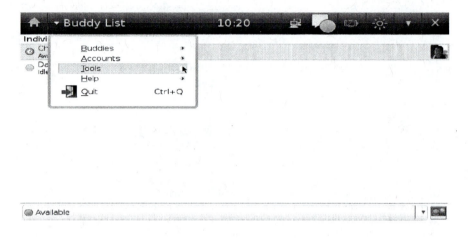

Figure 9.19   Ubuntu MID instant messenger.

Figure 9.20   Internet browsing on Ubuntu MID.

As mobile phones have become more powerful, beyond their basic phone functionality, phones now offer music, video, cameras, and built-in GPS capabilities. Rich applications are being built every day by a vibrant developer community utilizing the open operating systems. As these capabilities have been developed, the mobile phone user's ability to include applications, pictures, videos, music, emails, bank and credit card information, and personal information management (PIM) have all been combined to provide a much richer and more valuable experience into a persona that is portable and can be transferred seamlessly when upgrading to a new phone. The ability to protect and migrate personas will become an important purchasing decision. The risk of not securing and managing employee-owned devices if they contain confidential information is significant, and managing a wide variety of devices is complex in terms of both cost and security. Virtualization is a key enabling technology to address these issues.

Security is a serious issue for mobile handsets running an open source operating systems. There are already a significant number of known viruses, and their numbers are growing fast for mobile phones but still lag far behind the number of known PC viruses. The mobile handset user is a roving agent in a wireless IT world, and security is every bit as important as it is in the fixed-wire IT world. The frequent emergency security upgrades and patches common in the PC world, however, would be unacceptable to the average user of a mobile handset. Such an approach to security could stall the proliferation of smart and feature phones. Consequently, security must be designed in from day one of the handset's life cycle. Real-time virtualization solutions offer robust security via hardware-enforced memory isolation of partitions, isolating each operating system from the others and preventing cross-corruption. In addition, specific partitions may be added and used to execute secure applications in small certifiable environments protected from the larger open environment or real-time operating system (RTOS) executing in other partitions. Security cannot be an afterthought.

A virtualization solution may be used to ease introduction of smart phone software functionality to an existing feature phone hardware platform, with minimal effort and cost. Virtualization-based solutions open up the phone software architecture to bring added functionality to both feature phones and smartphones in terms of service availability, security, and device management. Two examples of virtualization software being used on smartphones are discussed in the following.

9.4.1   KVM

Kernel-based Virtual Machine (KVM) is open source software that is a full virtualization solution for Linux on x86 hardware containing virtualization extensions (Intel VT or AMD-V). KVM consists of a kernel module, kvm.ko, which provides the core virtualization infrastructure, and a processor-specific module, kvm-intel.ko or kvm-amd.ko, depending on the CPU manufacturer (Intel or AMD). KVM also requires a modified QEMU,[7] although work is underway to get the required changes upstream. Multiple virtual machines running unmodified Linux or Windows images can can be run using KVM. . A wide variety of guest operating systems work with KVM, including many versions of Linux, BSD, Solaris, Windows, Haiku, ReactOS, and the AROS Research Operating System. Each virtual machine has private virtualized hardware: a network card, disk, graphics adapter, etc. The kernel component of KVM is included in Linux, as of the 2.6.20 kernel version.

KVM's performance is good, but not as good as that of some of the more mature products, such as VMware or VirtualBox. For example, network and graphics speeds are noticeably slower with KVM. In general, KVM performance can offer near-native speed, thanks to its use of Intel VT or AMD-V extensions. As an open source product, it is being very actively developed and is constantly improving.

9.4.2   VMWare

VMware Mobile Virtualization Platform (MVP) is a thin layer of software that is embedded on a mobile phone to separate the applications and data from the underlying hardware. It is optimized to run efficiently on low-power, low-memory mobile phones. MVP is planned to enable handset vendors to bring phones to market faster and make them easier to manage.[8] VMware inherited the MVP software when it bought Trango Virtual Processors in October 2008. The technology serves much the same function as VMware's flagship server product, adding a flexible software layer onto hardware and making it easier to move applications from device to device.[9] MVP currently supports a wide range of real-time and rich operating systems, including Windows CE 5.0 and 6.0, Linux 2.6.x, Symbian 9.x, eCos, μITRON NORTi, and μC/OS-II.

VMware MVP benefits end users by being able to run multiple profiles (e.g., one for personal use and one for work use) on the same phone. Increasingly, handset vendors and carriers are migrating from proprietary operating systems to rich open operating systems so that their customers can choose from the widest selection of applications. With this transition to open operating systems, however, protection of trusted services such as digi-

---

7.   According to Wikipedia, "QEMU is a processor emulator that relies on dynamic binary translation to achieve a reasonable speed while being easy to port on new host CPU architectures," QEMU, Wikipedia, http://en.wikipedia.org/wiki/QEMU, retrieved 9 Mar 2009.

8.   http://www.vmware.com/company/news/releases/mvp.html.

9.   http://bits.blogs.nytimes.com/2008/11/10/vmware-lends-virtual-hand-to-mobile-phone-crowd.

tal rights management, authentication, billing, etc., is becoming of increasing concern. VMware MVP allows vendors to isolate these important trusted services from the open operating system and run them in isolated and tamper-proof virtual machines so that even if the open environment is compromised, the trusted services are not affected.

With VMware solutions, desktop and IT security administrators get the control and visibility they need to protect mobile data and prevent malicious code intrusion, while end users get the freedom and flexibility of "anytime, anywhere" access to their own familiar desktop environment. For virtual teams and telecommuters with a steady Internet connection, VMware View (formerly VMware Virtual Desktop Infrastructure, VDI) can be used to deliver remote access to server-based virtual desktop PCs through a secure network connection. Using VMware View, an organization can keep desktop images and sensitive information stored on servers behind the corporate firewall, eliminating the risk of a security breach as a result of laptop theft, allow remote access through a Web browser for maximum flexibility, or keep access limited to PCs with VMware View client software installed for maximum control, and can prevent data leakage and network intrusions with strong encryption, multifactor authentication, and access control policies for client-side USB devices.[10]

Mobile users with intermittent access to the Internet can use VMware ACE to deploy "assured computing environments" (ACEs) that workers can use on corporate-owned laptops, employee-owned PCs, or even iPods and USB memory sticks without putting sensitive corporate information at risk. VMware ACE clients are encapsulated inside a single file or "package," and ACE packages can be secured with strong encryption to protect the entire virtual desktop environment, not just specific files and folders. Administrators can set and enforce granular policies governing the lifespan of each ACE client package, the networks it can access, and the peripheral devices that can interface with it, with Active Directory integration for unified user authentication. The result is a scalable solution that helps enhances the mobility of users while protecting access to valuable corporate information assets.[11]

---

10.   http://www.vmware.com/solutions/desktop/mobile.html.
11.   http://www.vmware.com/solutions/desktop/mobile.html.

9.5   Collaboration Applications for Mobile Platforms

The growing popularity and power of mobile devices and the demand for business solutions and collaboration tools on mobile devices, along with Web 2.0 as a new platform for developing interactive applications across devices, has ushered in a new era for collaboration technologies—as can be seen in the advent of devices such as the Apple iPhone, the BlackBerry Storm touchphone, and the Google phone. The adoption of mobile collaboration services is not just a matter of design but also depends on factors such as mobile network coverage and pricing structures, all of which have been leveraged by these three phones, and others are on the way.

Mobile phones have evolved rapidly in the past few years, from specialized devices for voice communication to a general-purpose computing devices that are able to run a rich variety of data applications. The latest mobile phones also provide a variety of networking options such as cellular, Bluetooth, Wi-Fi, and WiMAX, which serve a range of coverage and bandwidth requirements. Mobile phones have now become the device of choice for people to keep in touch with family members, friends, and business partners. Current mobile phones allow people not only to make telephone calls but also to access email and short messages, play games, share information, run video conferences, and coordinate business actions. Mobile phones are now equipped with faster processors, larger memory, and longer-life batteries. Many mobile phones today come with integrated position-tracking and camera features. Many of the software tools previously available in personal digital assistants (PDAs), tablets, laptops, and desktop PCs have been ported to mobile phones, such as office and multimedia applications. Today, many collaboration technologies are widely used, such as email, instant messaging, data conferencing, workflow, wiki, and social networking systems.

Collaboration technologies based on mobile phones have unique advantages over laptops and desktop systems because they are lightweight and can fit into pockets or purses. They are truly mobile and can be connected all the time, which means you can take your desktop with you: Collaboration software on mobile hand-held devices provides the ability to be productive wherever you are. In this new era of mobile computing, the next generation of collaboration technologies on mobile phones is being developed to enable consumers to collaborate anytime, anywhere, using just their mobile phones. Although mobile collaboration technologies are still in their infancy and there is still significant room for progress, there

have been several significant recent developments, such as the Cisco
WebEx collaboration software, which currently has over 60% of the web
collaboration conferencing software market,[12] being ported over to the
iPhone[13]; the IBM Lotus Notes Traveler being extended to support a range
of S60-based Nokia mobile phones built on the S60 third edition of the
Symbian operating system and providing a major alternative to Windows
Mobile device support[14]; and Unison Technologies recently announcing its
free unified communications software offering in a direct challenge to
industry giants Microsoft and Google.[15]

9.6   Future Trends

The real value of cloud computing is that it makes software and data available transparently and everywhere—include the mobile environment. Consumers of cloud computing services purchase computing capacity on
demand and need not be concerned with the underlying technologies used
to achieve server capabilities. Computing resources are being accessed which
are typically owned and operated by a third-party provider on a consolidated basis in data center locations. This stateless model facilitates much
greater scalability than conventional computing and can be used in conjunction with virtualization to achieve maximum data center and computing resource utilization. One of the key elements of a stateless computing
environment is a networked storage system that enables ubiquitous availability of software, making the cloud the ideal environment to enable
mobile smartphone users to access its powerful computing power remotely.

Each day, more and more users connect to the Internet using their
mobile devices. The mobile operating system as an extension to the cloud is
emerging as a value-added alternative to sophisticated and complex operating systems such as Windows. New players such as Apple and Google are
developing their mobile operating systems to challenge Symbian and Windows Mobile. Mobile device hardware is currently too weak to run fully
capable hardcore software such as Adobe Photoshop or Microsoft Office
natively on a smartphone, which is why cloud computing will likely be the
future model for of mobile computing. Cloud computing may prove to be

---

12.   http://www.pcmag.com/article2/0,4149,1418533,00.asp.
13.   http://www.webex.com/iphone.
14.   http://www.itwire.com/content/view/21856/1154.
15.   http://www.channelinsider.com/c/a/Messaging-and-Collaboration/Unisons-Free-Unified-
       Communications-Software-Challenges-Microsoft-and-Google.

an ideal strategy for reaping the full benefit of mobile devices, by allowing companies to essentially push their IT environment out to employees, rather than employees having to get access to the IT environment. In the future, cloud computing will also reduce the need for unnecessary full application overhead by using the mobile smartphone as a "dumb terminal" to leverage the powerful computing power of the cloud.

9.7   Chapter Summary

Cloud computing for mobile devices is taking off with the expansion of high-speed wireless networks around the world. Mobile devices take data out of homes and offices and put them in our pockets, increasing the attractiveness of cloud computing as a model to connect end users with more than just the Internet and email while they roam. This means that much of your vital data will be available not just at home, at the office, or in your wallet, but can easily be accessed by hooking up to the huge memory of the Internet cloud with a mobile device. Consumers are beginning to demand not only access to hotel and restaurant directions, airline reservations, weather reports, social networking sites, personal email and instant messaging, but also full and secure access to their business applications at work or a business partner's site as well.

The cloud is becoming increasingly pervasive and mobile browsers are getting better every day, providing the ability to access the cloud and its applications Organizations are deploying more and more SaaS-based applications and, assuming they have enough bandwidth, there is no reason that mobile workers cannot access those applications on their devices with a browser that can actually fully handle web and cloud standards. In this chapter we described the mobile smartphones platforms, their operating systems, virtualization of these platforms, mobile collaboration applications, and future trends.

9.8   Closing Comments

Cloud computing is in a period of strong growth, but cloud technology is still somewhat immature and will take another few years to mature. Development will probably be dominated by a select group of vendors, mostly technologically aggressive application development organizations. There will likely be proliferation of new vendors and then subsequent consolidation as cloud computing becomes appealing to more mainstream development organizations. As with any other technology going through a period of rapid growth, the stronger small players will survive and the weaker players will be driven out of the market. In the meantime, demand for interoperability and integration will likely drive a widely supported fabric of "intracloud" application programming interfaces that will be developed to link cloud-based systems across vendor platforms. This consolidation and integration, along with improved security, privacy, and governance enhancements, will broaden the appeal of cloud computing while building the trust of consumers, who will increasingly offload large portions of their IT infrastructure to third parties such as the SaaS providers described throughout this book. The cloud is going to be the hot topic in the next few years and probably beyond, and it is not just IT personnel who will need to understand the benefits of cloud computing, but personnel across the entire business continuum. Many consumers and companies are missing out on the benefits of cloud computing because they do not fully grasp the concept of cloud computing; we hope this book has improved your grasp.

Appendix A

Virtualization Practicum (Linux)

A.1 Overview

In this practicum, we will once again use the Sun VirtualBox product that you downloaded in Chapter 4. This time, we will show you how to install and configure it using a Linux-based .vdi operating system. Figure A.1 shows the Sun operating system named OpenSolaris running on top of Windows XP via VirtualBox. In this appendix, we will walk you through setting up a similar environment.

We will begin by starting the Sun xVM VirtualBox product. You may remember that for Microsoft Windows-based systems, the installer created a group called VirtualBox in the Programs folder of the Start Menu, which

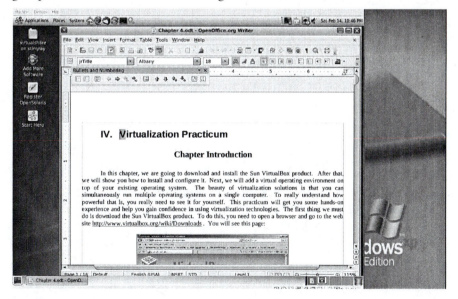

Figure A.1   OpenSolaris running on top of Windows via VirtualBox.

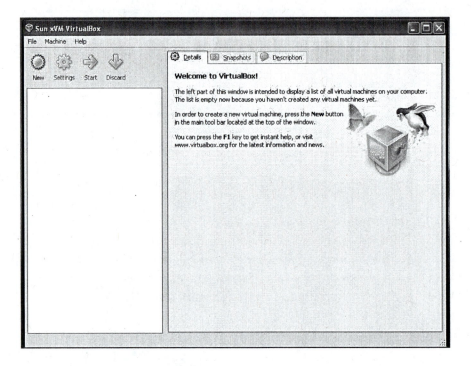

Figure A.2   VirtualBox opening screen.

allows you to launch the application and access its documentation. Figure A.2 shows what the opening screen looks like after you have started Virtual-Box. If you have already installed the FreeDOS product as described in Chapter 4, your opening screen may look slightly different.

A.2   Adding a Linux-Based Guest Operating System to VirtualBox

As we pointed out in Chapter 4, VirtualBox allows you to run guest operating systems using its own virtual computer system, which is why it is called a *virtual machine* (VM). The operating system (OS) we will be working with is Sun Microsystems OpenSolaris, which is an open source product most often distributed under an approved open source license. The version of OpenSolaris we will be using in this practicum is OpenSolaris 2008.11, which offers technical support from Sun Microsystems. This release includes a network-based package management system, the GNOME desktop, and LiveCD technology supported on AMD64, Pentium, and Xeon

EM64T platforms. More information on OpenSolaris can be found at http://opensolaris.org.

A.3   Downloading OpenSolaris as a Guest Operating System

In order to add OpenSolaris to our host machine as a guest OS, we must first download it from the Internet. Minimize the VirtualBox application for now and open a web browser. Go to the site

```
http://virtualbox.wordpress.com/images
```

Once your browser has brought up the site, your screen should look similar to Figure A.3. You will see a list of virtual operating systems, with the sponsoring web site for each OS shown in parentheses.

Toward the bottom of the page you will find the entry for Indiana under the GNU/OpenSolaris heading. You should go to the web site for each operating system in which you are interested, and check it out before downloading a file.

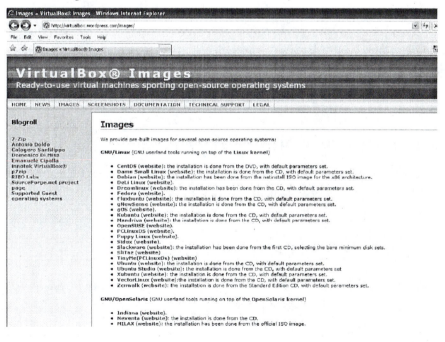

Figure A.3   VirtualBox Images page.

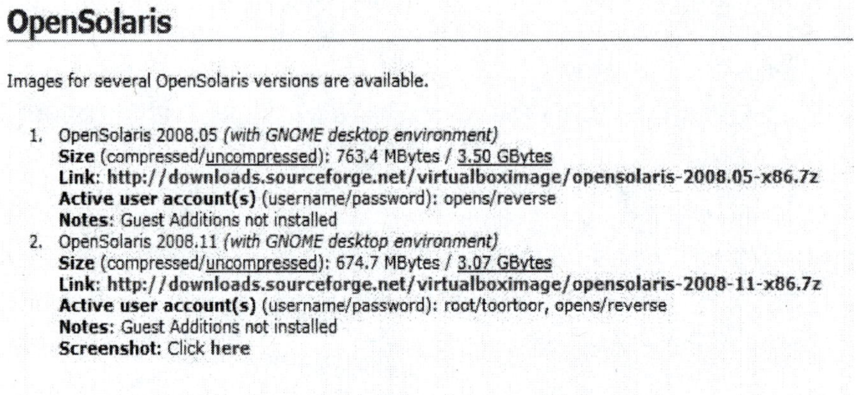

OpenSolaris

Images for several OpenSolaris versions are available.

1. OpenSolaris 2008.05 *(with GNOME desktop environment)*
   Size (compressed/<u>uncompressed</u>): 763.4 MBytes / <u>3.50 GBytes</u>
   Link: http://downloads.sourceforge.net/virtualboximage/opensolaris-2008.05-x86.7z
   Active user account(s) (username/password): opens/reverse
   Notes: Guest Additions not installed
2. OpenSolaris 2008.11 *(with GNOME desktop environment)*
   Size (compressed/<u>uncompressed</u>): 674.7 MBytes / <u>3.07 GBytes</u>
   Link: http://downloads.sourceforge.net/virtualboximage/opensolaris-2008-11-x86.7z
   Active user account(s) (username/password): root/toortoor, opens/reverse
   Notes: Guest Additions not installed
   Screenshot: Click here

Figure A.4   OpenSolaris image options.

Click on the **Indiana** entry to start the download process. When you click on any of the operating system links, you will be taken to that system's download page. There you will be given the choice of which architecture (32-bit or 64-bit) you want to install. For almost every operating system displayed on this page, it is important to *write down the passwords for root user and default user.* An example of what you will see is shown in Figure A.4.

Next, click the link to download the image (in our case, link 2 in Figure A.4) and save it to a location you will remember—later in this practicum you will need to unzip this file and extract the images. We recommend that you save the files on a drive with plenty of space available, since it will take up at least 650 megabytes just to save the file.

A.4   Using the 7-Zip Archive Tool

Next, we will need to use the open source product named 7-zip (which works on both Linux and Windows platforms), which we downloaded in Chapter 4. If you have removed it, it can be obtained again from this location:

```
http://www.7-zip.org/download.html
```

Once the download is complete, perform the following steps *in order:*

1. Pick a drive with plenty of spare room on it and locate (or create) the folder named VirtualGuests.

2. Download the 7-zip file to the VirtualGuests folder and install it using the standard options.

3. Once you have installed 7-zip, find the OpenSolaris file you downloaded previously.

4. Highlight the file and right-click on it—choose the 7-zip extraction option to extract files.

5. Extract the files to the VirtualGuests folder.

6. The VirtualGuests folder will now contain two folders, Machines and VDI. The VirtualBox image for OpenSolaris will be in the VDI folder.

A.5   Adding the OpenSolaris Guest OS to Sun xVM VirtualBox

Now, we will add the OpenSolaris guest operating system to our VirtualBox host. We start by clicking on the **New** button. The New Virtual Machine Wizard dialog will appear, as shown in Figure A.5.

The wizard is an easy-to-follow guided setup for installation of your guest operating system. Click **Next >** to continue and you will be presented with the Virtual Machine Name and OS Type dialog shown in Figure A.6.

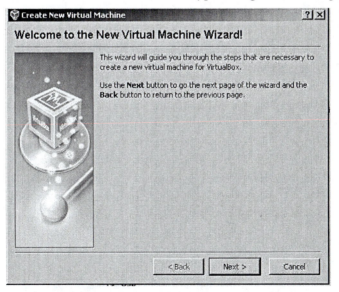

Figure A.5   The New Virtual Machine Wizard dialog.

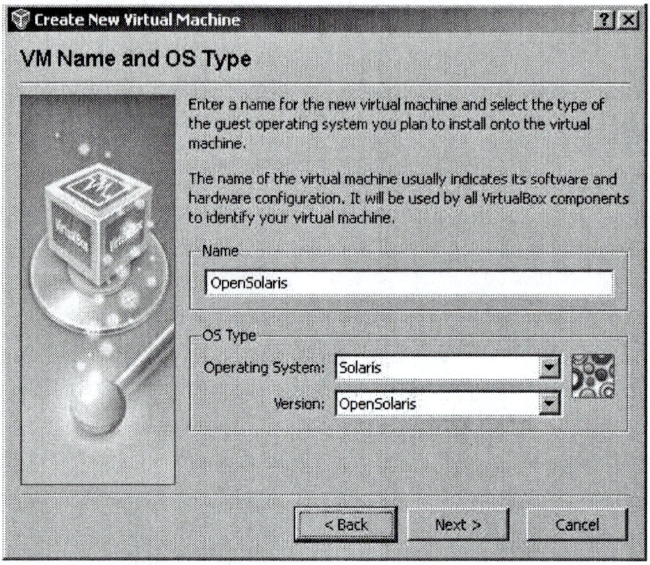

Figure A.6   The VM and OS Type dialog.

Type **OpenSolaris** in the Name field. Select **Solaris** for the Operating System, and for the Version, choose **OpenSolaris.** Click **Next >** to continue with to the dialog to choose a memory configuration. In this part of the wizard, as shown in Figure A.7, you have the option to increase or decrease the amount of memory that will be used for the guest operating system. For our purposes, the default, 512 megabytes of memory should be fine.

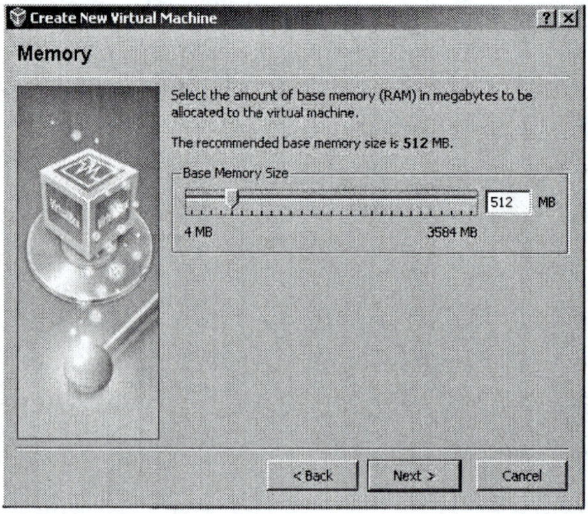

Figure A.7   Choosing memory size.

Figure A.8   The Virtual Hard Disk dialog.

Click **Next >** to proceed to the next section of the wizard, the Virtual Hard Disk dialog, which is shown in Figure A.8.

The Virtual Hard Disk dialog allows you to select the virtual device image file (.vdi file) that you previously downloaded and saved to the VirtualGuests folder. What you see displayed in Figure A.8 is the name of the last image that was added. In this case, it was an image of Damn Small Linux (dsl). If no images have been installed on the host, the default selection would look similar to the one shown in Figure A.9.

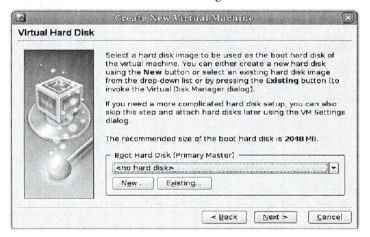

Figure A.9   Default display in the Virtual Hard Disk dialog.

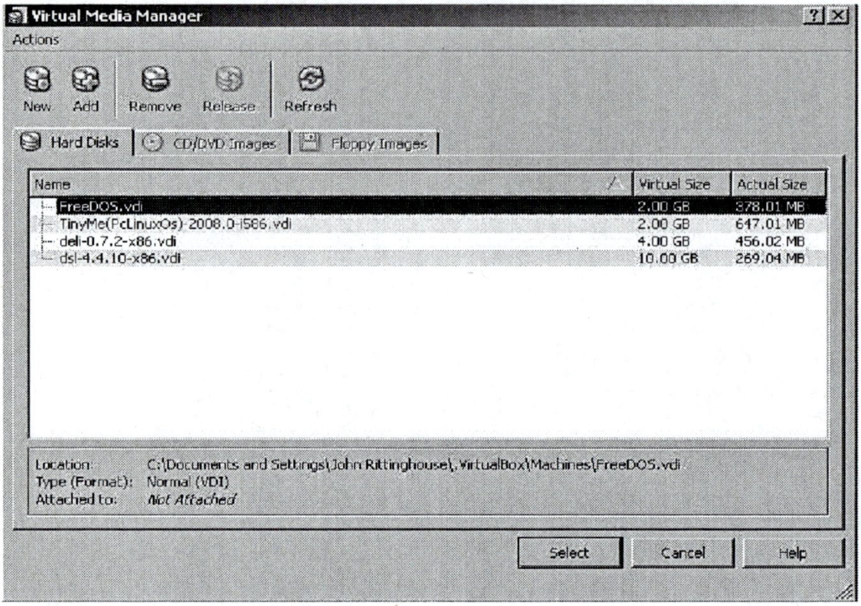

Figure A.10   The Virtual Media Manager.

If you previously created any virtual hard disks which have not been attached to other virtual machines, you can select from among those using the drop-down list in the Wizard window. Since we have downloaded and extracted a new image of OpenSolaris, it will not be included in the list. Click on the **Existing...** button to continue on to the Virtual Media Manager, as shown in Figure A.10. In this figure, OpenSolaris is not listed as an available selection. Since it is not listed, we need to add it by clicking on the **Add** button at the top of the dialog.

The Virtual Media Manager keeps an internal registry of all available hard disk, CD/DVD-ROM, and floppy disk images. This registry can be viewed and changed in the Virtual Disk Manager, which you can access from the File menu in the VirtualBox main window. The Disk Image Manager will show you all images that are registered with VirtualBox, grouped in three tabs for the three supported formats.

These are hard disk images, either in VirtualBox's own Virtual Disk Image (VDI) format or in the widely supported Virtual Machine DisK (VMDK) format. CD and DVD images in standard ISO format are also supported. There is support for floppy images in standard RAW format. As shown in Figure A.11, for each image, the Virtual Disk Manager shows the

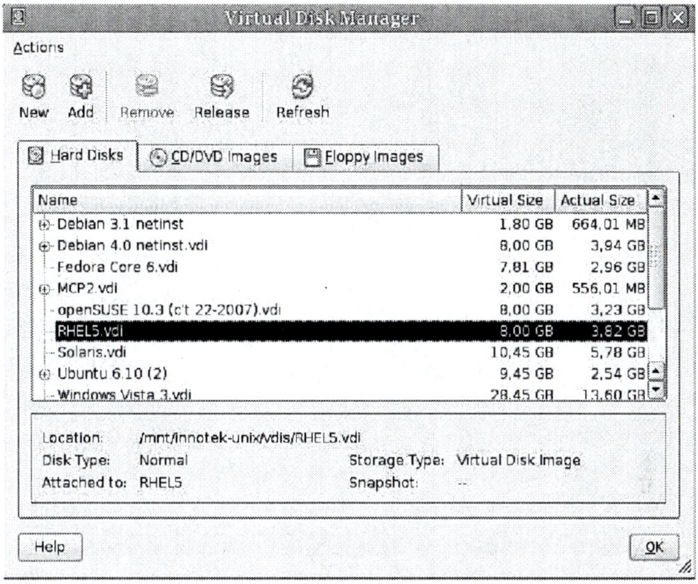

Figure A.11

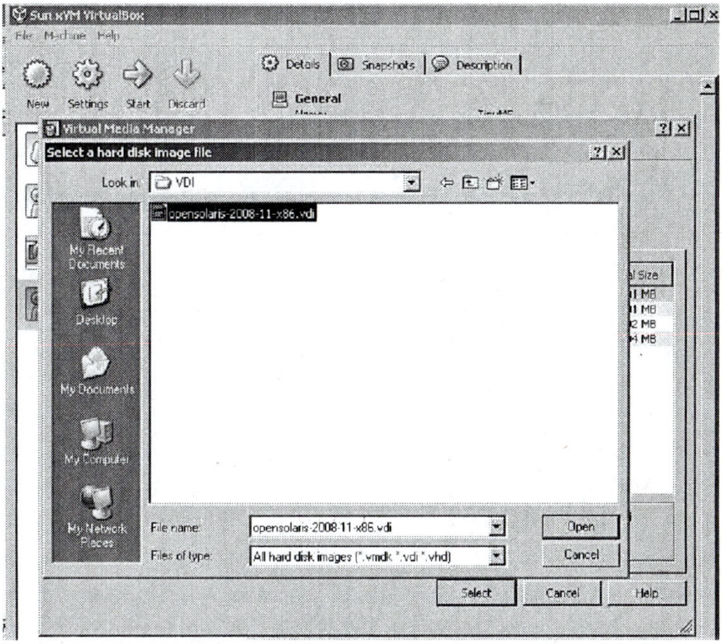

Figure A.12   The **Select a hard disk image** file dialog.

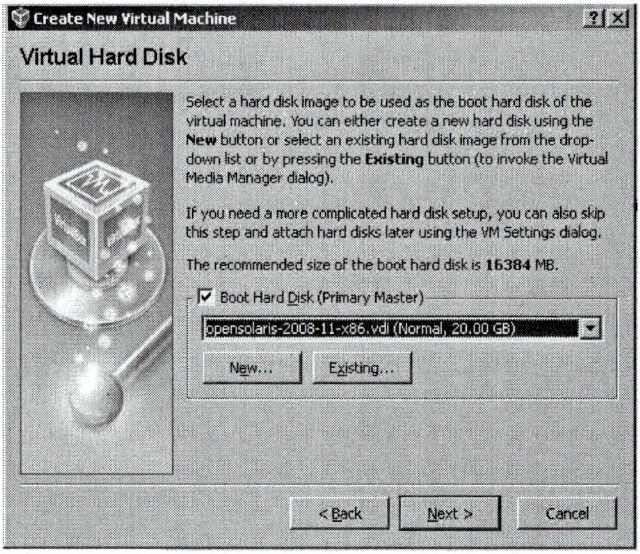

Figure A.13   Back to the Virtual Hard Disk dialog.

full path of the image file and other information, such as the virtual machine to which the image is currently attached, if any.

Clicking the **Add** button will bring you to the **Select a hard disk image file** dialog, as shown in Figure A.12. Use this file dialog to navigate to the VirtualGuests folder.

In the VirtualGuests folder, open the **VDI** folder and highlight the **OpenSolaris.vdi** file. Once you have highlighted it, simply click on the **Open** button to continue. You will be returned to the Virtual Hard Disk dialog where you earlier clicked on the **Existing...** button (see Figure A.13).

Click **Next >** to complete the addition of the OpenSolaris virtual image. A summary screen will appear, as shown in Figure A.14.

Now, simply click the **Finish** button and you will be returned to the Sun xVM VirtualBox main display. OpenSolaris should be displayed in the left panel (it should be the only entry on your system), as in the list shown in Figure A.15.

Since you have just created an empty VM, the first thing you will probably want to do is make a CD-ROM or a DVD-ROM available to use with your guest operating system. In the main menu, click on **Settings** and then **CD/DVD-ROM,** which will bring up the screen shown in Figure A.16. Here you can tell the VM to access the media in your host drive, and you

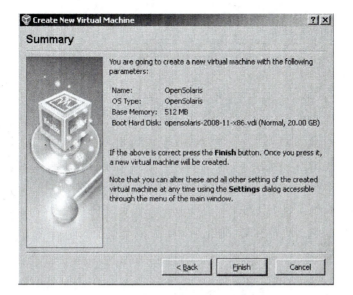

Figure A.14   Summary screen for the Create New Virtual Machine wizard.

Figure A.15   VirtualBox main display.

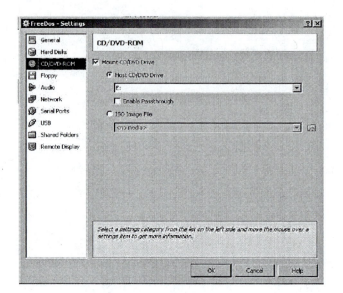

Figure A.16

Figure A.17   Starting OpenSolaris.

can proceed to install from there. Check the box in the CD/DVD section if you want to use an optical device.

For now, that is all you need to do in Settings to prepare to run your virtual image. The next part of this practicum will take you inside the virtual guest system to use and see for yourself that it is a real, functioning environment. Returning to the main menu, highlight the entry in the selections panel and click on the green **Start** arrow, as shown in Figure A.17, to start OpenSolaris.

When you first start OpenSolaris, you will be presented with a "loader" menu. Usually, the default selection best for your system is highlighted automatically. Choose the default option as shown in Figure A.18 and press **Enter** (or just let the timer expire).

Once OpenSolaris completes the initial loading process, you will be presented with the Username screen to log onto the system. The default

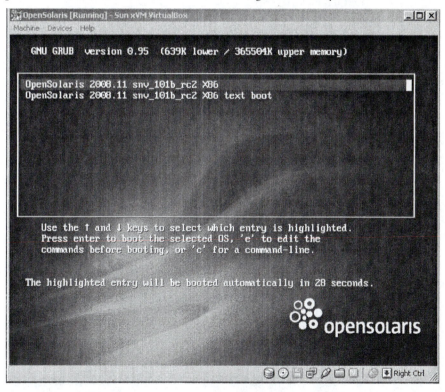

Figure A.18   The OpenSolaris "loader menu."

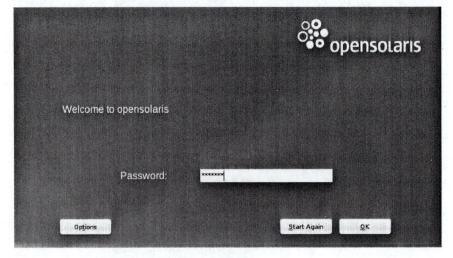

Figure A.19   The OpenSolaris Username screen.

Username is **opens,** so for your first time, type that into the box as shown in Figure A.19.

Next, the password (which is **reverse**) is required. Go ahead and fill that in, as shown in Figure A.20.

Since the operating system in the virtual machine does not "know" that it is not running on a real computer, it expects to have exclusive control over your keyboard and mouse. This is not actually the case, however, since,

Figure A.20   The OpenSolaris Password screen.

Figure A.21   OpenSolaris running on a Windows XP installation.

unless you are running the VM in full-screen mode, your VM needs to share the keyboard and mouse with other applications and possibly other VMs on your host. This will be evident if you look at Figure A.21, which shows OpenSolaris running on a Windows XP installation.

Only one OS—either the VM or the host—can "own" the keyboard and the mouse at any one time. You will see a second mouse pointer, which will always be confined to the limits of the VM window. Basically, you activate the VM by clicking inside this window. To return ownership of the keyboard and mouse to the host operating system, VirtualBox reserves for itself a special key on the keyboard, called the **Host Key.** *By default, this is the* ***Control*** *key on the right lower part of your keyboard.* You can change this default in the VirtualBox Global Settings if you wish. In any case, the current setting for the Host Key is always displayed at the bottom right of your VM window in case you may have forgotten which key to use. If needed, click the mouse in the virtualized window to gain focus in the guest system. Press the Host Key to give focus back to the host.

OpenSolaris comes with a basic set of applications, but to have a fully functioning office capability, you must use the Package Manager and

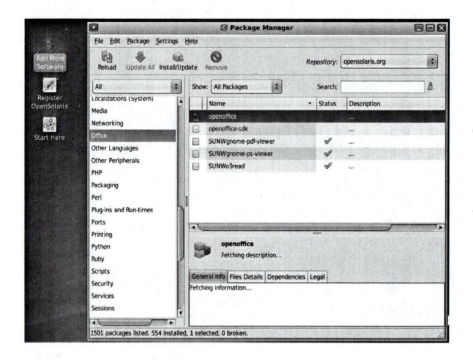

Figure A.22   The Package Manager.

install your product on the new system. We will install OpenOffice 3.0 in the OpenSolaris environment to show you that it is a fully functioning virtualized platform. In the OpenSolaris desktop, click on the **Add More Software** icon. The Package Manager will open up as shown in Figure A.22. All the software distributed by Sun as part of OpenSolaris is released in package format.

Packages are the preferred way of distributing software on OpenSolaris specifically because it enhances uniform package installation and removal interfaces and provides users with the ability to see exactly which versions of a package are installed (pkgchk -l). The ability to verify the integrity of the contents of the package (pkgchk -p -l) and to specify package dependencies and/or incompatibilities (depend, compver) is a also significant benefit. Being able to specify additional space requirements for a package (space) or to create custom, dynamic package installation and removal scripts is also a significant feature that makes package distribution very popular.

On the left side of the Package Manager, scroll down to the **Office** section, where you will see which office applications are available for downloading and installation on the right side of the display. Choose **Office**, as

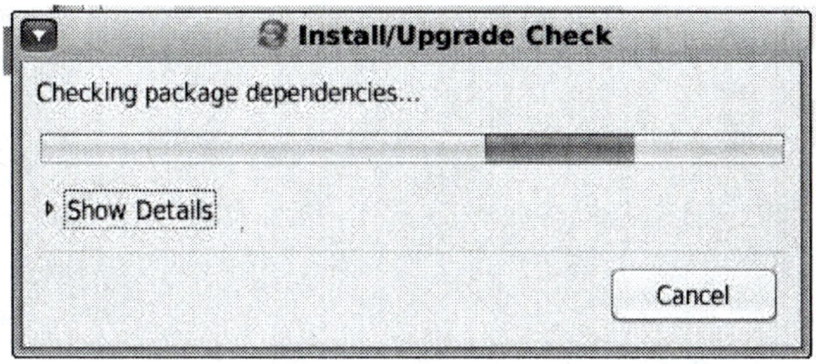

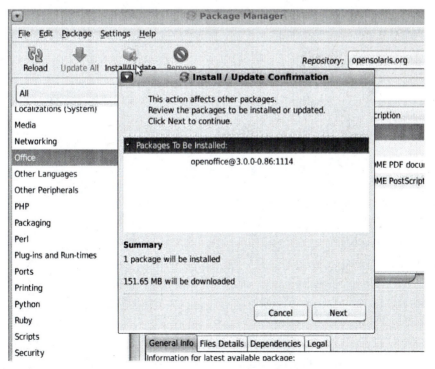

Figure A.23   The Install/Upgrade Check screen.

shown in Figure A.22, and check the box for **OpenOffice** on the right side. Next, click on the **Install/Update** button to continue. This action will bring up the screen shown in Figure A.23.

The process may take a minute or two to complete. Once dependency checks have completed, you will see the Install/Update Confirmation dialog shown in Figure A.24, which will inform you that installing the selected package may affect other packages (and usually will). Simply click on **Next** to continue.

Figure A.24   The Install/Update Confirmation dialog.

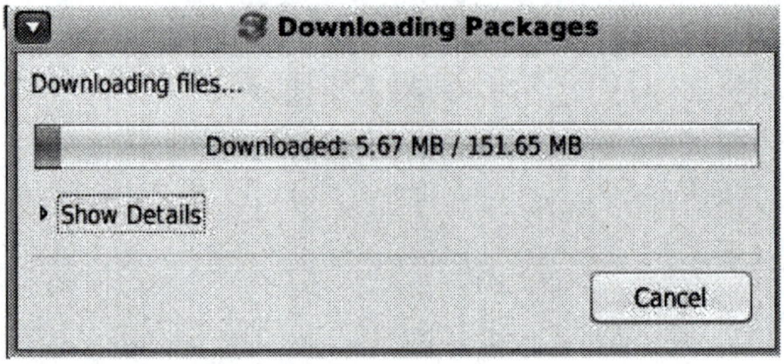

Figure A.25   The Downloading Packages dialog.

You should then see the dialog box shown in Figure A.25, informing you that downloading has started.

Once the download has completed, package installation will begin automatically. You should see the screen shown in Figure A.26.

Figure A.26   Installing packages.

When the install phase has completed, a package index will be created, as indicated in Figure A.27.

Figure A.27 ˙ Creating packages index...

When the process has been completed, you will be returned to the Package Manager main screen. Now all you need to do is click on the **Close** button in the upper right corner and you will be back to the Open-Solaris desktop.

Next, we will go to the **Applications** menu at the very top left of the desktop, select the **Office** menu, and choose the submenu item

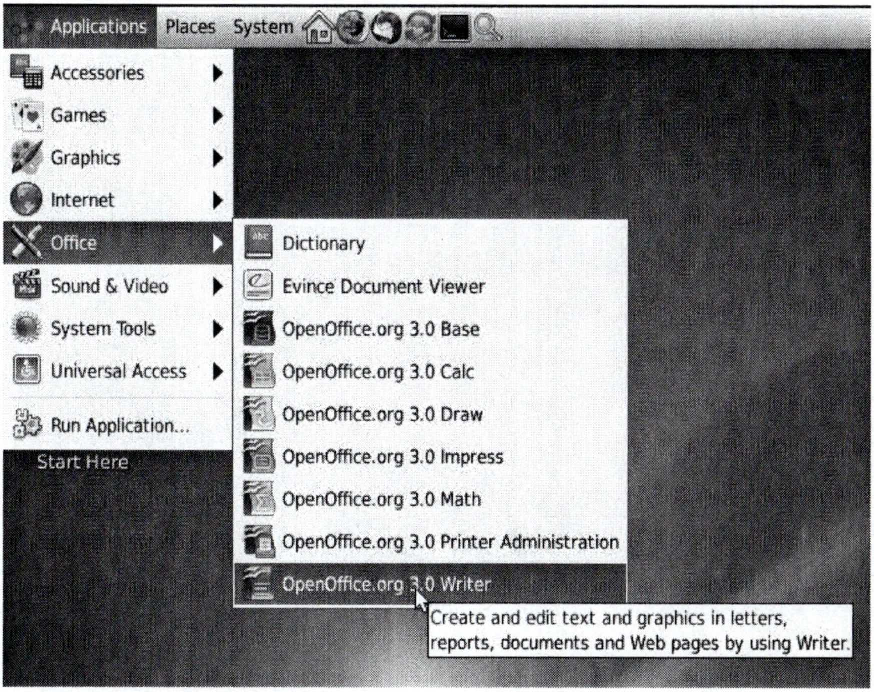

Figure A.28   Getting to OpenOffice Writer.

OpenOffice.org 3.0 Writer, which is the word processing application in OpenOffice. See Figure A.28.

The splash screen for OpenOffice appears, as shown in Figure A.29.

Figure A.29   Splash screen for OpenOffice.

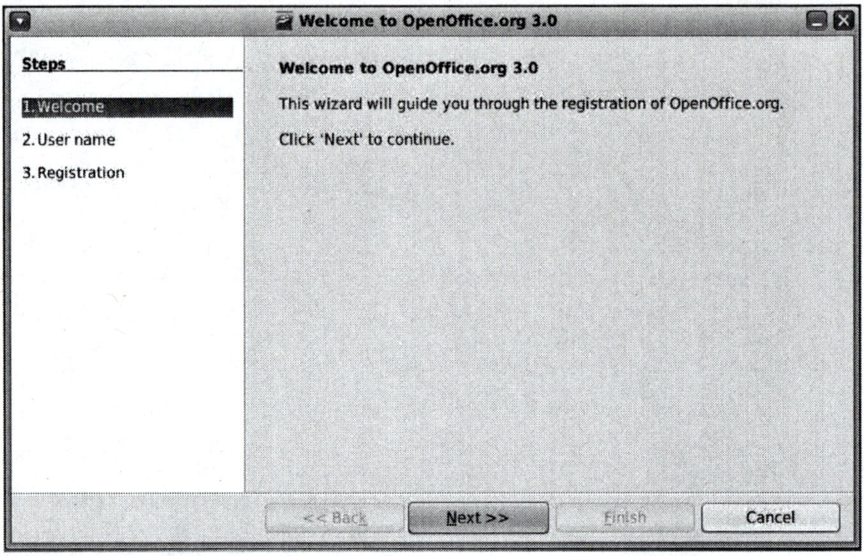

Figure A.30   Registering OpenOffice: step 1.

Since this is the first time OpenOffice is being invoked, you will be asked to complete a simple, three-step registration process. Figure A.30 shows the first screen. Click **Next** to continue.

You will advance to the second screen, shown in Figure A.31, where you can fill in your personal information.

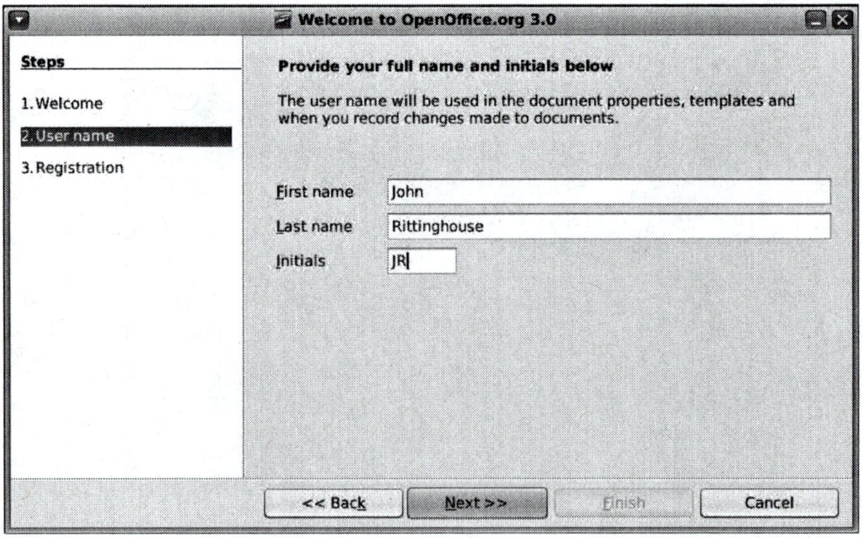

Figure A.31   Registering OpenOffice: step 2.

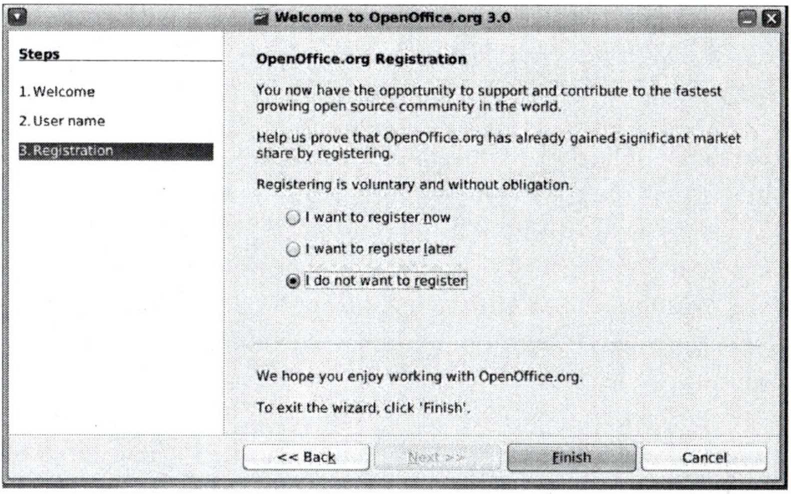

Figure A.32   Registering OpenOffice: step 3.

Click **Next** to continue. The final screen, shown in Figure A.33, will ask you to register your product. For now, click on the "I do not want to register" radio button and click **Finish**. You can always register your product later if you so choose.

The OpenOffice Writer desktop, shown in Figure A.33, will appear.

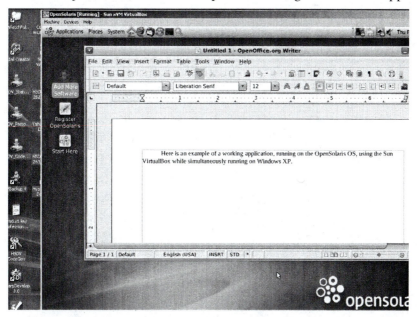

Figure A.33   The OpenOffice Writer desktop.

That's it; you can now start working in Writer.

A.6   Summary

This practicum has walked you through setting up another instance of a virtual operating system using the Sun xVM VirtualBox. The process for installing any .vdi file is nearly identical. You should, by now, have enough confidence in using the VirtualBox to install any or all of the files that are available for download from the VirtualBox web site at http://virtual-box.wordpress.com. We encourage you to try some other operating systems to get an appreciation for what each may be able to provide in terms of setup and management of a virtual environment. The ability to virtualize can go from a single host running multiple operating systems to a cluster of hosts being managed through a single front-end product. Clustering pools of resources (forming computing grids) enables more efficient use of physical assets, increasing the overall computing availability for users and providing resources that would otherwise not be available. So, you may be asking, what next? How do I use this VirtualBox in a realistic setting?

There are several cloudlike ("Infrastructure-as-a-Service") technologies, such as Eucalyptus or Globus Nimbus, that expose remote interfaces for provision of virtual machines with customized software environments. These components provide open source alternatives to commercial interfaces such as Amazon EC2. One such product is OpenNebula,[1] an open source distributed VM manager that enables the dynamic placement of VMs on a pool of physical resources. OpenNebula extends the benefits of virtualization platforms from a single physical resource to a pool of resources, decoupling the server from the physical infrastructure and the physical location where it resides. OpenNebula is focused on the efficient, dynamic, and scalable management of VMs within data centers (i.e., private clouds) that involve a large number of virtual and physical servers. OpenNebula can interface with a remote cloud site, being the only tool able to access on demand to Amazon EC2 in order to scale out a locally managed infrastructure. OpenNebula is collaborating with the most relevant cloud projects in order to promote its integration as an alternative cloud back-end product.[2]

---

1.   http://www.opennebula.org/doku.php?id=start.
2.   Ibid.

OpenNebula's latest release, version 1.2, supports Xen and KVM virtualization platforms and also features support for image transfers, cloning, and virtual network management. The OpenNebula web site provides additional information about tools for extending the functionality provided by OpenNebula, such as the Haizea[3] lease management system. Haizea is a product that, in combination with the OpenNebula virtual infrastructure manager (VIM), can be used to manage a Xen or KVM[4] cluster, allowing you to deploy different types of leases that are instantiated as virtual machines. KVM allows you to run multiple virtual machines (running unmodified Linux or Windows images), where each virtual machine has private virtualized hardware (a network card, disk, graphics adapter, etc).

Another open source product, libvirt,[5] supports the management of virtual machines, virtual networks and storage. libvirt is a toolkit that is used to interact with the virtualization capabilities of recent versions of Linux (and other operating systems). It provides remote management using TLS encryption and x509 certificates, supports user authentication with Kerberos and SASL, manages local access control using PolicyKit, supports zero-conf[6] discovery using Avahi multicast-DNS,[7] and touts a portable client API for Linux, Solaris, and Windows. We hope you take time to explore these solutions further.

---

3.   http://haizea.cs.uchicago.edu.
4.   http://kvm.qumranet.com/kvmwiki.
5.   http://libvirt.org/index.html.
6.   Zero configuration (zero-conf) is a set of techniques that automatically creates a usable IP network without configuration or special servers. The specifications for zero-conf are managed by the IETF.
7.   Avahi is a free zero-conf implementation, including a system for multicast DNS/DNS-SD service discovery. It allows programs to publish and discover services and hosts running on a local network with no specific configuration.

Appendix B

Executive Scenario for Cloud Migration

This narrative discussion will help you to understand the decisions that must be made by members of a corporate executive team when considering a move to cloud-based operations. In our scenario, consider a situation which the Acme Widgets company has increased production from $12M in revenue to $120M over the past five years. Facing a projected growth of 20% in sales ($144M in the next year), the company infrastructure has been stretched to the limits of capacity and there are demands for more from both internal users and from external clients and vendors.

Susan, the CEO, has been lauded for bringing the company phenomenal growth. Increasing a company's revenue stream 10-fold over a five-year period gets notice from a lot of people, especially shareholders. The board of directors has been very generous, so keeping up the growth has made the CEO feel like the proverbial duck swimming on a calm pond—no one sees how fast the feet below the water line are moving to keep the duck afloat. Susan knows from conversations with each of her team members that the company is at a point where it cannot continue without making some changes, and she has assembled the executive team to discuss how to proceed with a proposal made by Jim, the CIO, to reduce operational costs by using cloud services.

Murray, the CFO, knows that administrative costs, labor, and accounts payable and receivable are struggling to keep up, expenses are lopsided and far too high on the sales side, and there is not enough staff to do the job without having people stay until 9 or 10 p.m. every night. Trying to balance profitability, cost of sales, and management of operational costs has become Murray's favorite daily exercise. Making a cut that may impact the flow of revenue could cause a burp in the system that the company cannot afford, so any changes are made only after lots of study and meetings, when a general consensus has been reached among the management team that it is the right course of action. Murray realizes that something needs to change.

Danny, who is Executive Vice President for Sales, truly believes that he has succeeded in every facet of his role and in bringing home the business. He doesn't care what it takes to make the deal—as long as the deal is booked and his sales team gets compensated for the sale, he gets his spiff and demands that the rest of the company support him, regardless of the internal struggles it may take to keep customers happy and buying widgets. Spending money for advertising and marketing is part of the cost of making the sale, just like travel, lunches, dinners, hotels, conventions, etc. These are necessary costs of business to get the widgets into the hands of customers. Customer support, service-level agreements, cost of goods sold, delivery, maintenance, and installation costs are all things that are taken care of by someone else. Danny believes that nothing needs to change on his watch, since sales are doing so well.

Linda, the Vice President for Human Resources, has during the last five years gone from a job that was almost boring to one with not enough hours in the day. She is swamped with paperwork, and the state mandates many documentation requirements. She could certainly use more staff to help her, but the budget does not allow for non-revenue-generating head counts that are not absolutely essential for operations. Human Resources is also responsible for the population and data maintenance of directory services (Active Directory and Lightweight Directory Access Protocol), and she has to battle for everything with Murray, the CFO, to get something done. As a result, Linda has become afraid to ask for much. She has resigned herself to taking lots of work home at night and on the weekends to catch up, and focuses mostly on recruiting and hiring processes during the normal workday.

Jim, the CIO, has seen the IT department become a 24/7 operation. Customer support requirements now demand that continuous operations be supported, and company growth has outpaced the technology being used. While the company has grown from 25 people in the first year to 700 currently, only one-fifth of the technology used company-wide is less than one year old. There is not enough staff to do the job without having people stay late and work well beyond their normal work shift. Most of the computers are three to fours old and are recycled from desktop machines to be used as file or print servers and in the customer support center as vendor and customer access data stores. Some have been converted from Windows-based platforms to Linux servers to save costs. The cost of replacing obsolete machines and buying new equipment amounts to about 15% of the total IT budget. Costs for telephone-related equipment, support, and networking are about 20% of the budget.[1] Corporate software licensing accounts for about 30% of this budget. Labor accounts for most of the remainder of the budget, leaving only a very small discretionary fund for use by IT to optimize operations. Jim knows that something needs to change.

Following is a transcript of the executive team meeting.

Susan: Ok, folks—let's get the meeting started. Please take a seat and let's begin. We have a few other things to cover today, but I want to start with a proposal Jim brought to my attention that may be useful in cost cutting and helping us keep our numbers from falling back.

Danny: All they do is go up on my watch ...<grin>

Susan: Jim, why don't you tell everyone what you are proposing?

Jim: Sure. I think we can make some changes that will help us in nearly every area. By getting rid of our data center and outsourcing the services and equipment from the cloud, we can save a lot of money. I have been researching how moving away from desktop licenses for software could impact our budget, and I believe we can get the same features for a lot less money and have the same capabilities provided. There are many areas to cover, so I thought we should start first with customer-facing solutions, as they have the most impact soonest.

Murray: That sounds very interesting. I believe I heard some scuttlebutt about how one company did that and cut operational costs by more than half.

Susan: Jim, what areas did you have in mind?

Jim: Well, to start, the way we manage customer data is not very efficient.

Danny: Well, I'm not going to have customers see any negative effects of a change. I have to deal with those, and my

---

1.   Advances in VoIP, VoWLAN, softphones, and dual-mode cellular/wifi phones are coming to the rescue here, as costs go down and mainstream production goes up.

team will have to be convinced this is something really good if we're going to go along with it.

Susan: Danny, none of us want to see customers view us in a bad light. Go on, Jim.

Jim: For every customer, the sales guys use the contact management software to enter the customer data into their laptop. That data gets synchronized to our central customer database when they connect through our dedicated VPN lines back to the office. They sync that data and we have data scrubbing software that performs integrity checks. That data is used by the marketing department for reaching out to current customers, new customer prospects, and even former customers.

The contact management software licenses for 150 sales team members amounts to about 75K per year in license fees and maintenance costs. The cost of maintaining a dedicated VPN line is about 6K per month, or 72K per year. The cost of maintaining a staff to manage 24/7 the database servers and network servers for the VPN and database amounts to an average cost of 120K per year for each IT contractor, totaling 8 bodies for those functions, or 960K.

By replacing the contact management software and the database back office, we can save over $1M a year by using a cloud-based CRM product called sugarCRM. We wouldn't have recurring license fees, no cost for the software to run it on, the back-office staff to run the contacts database can be released, and the rest of my team can function without them. The dedicated VPN line won't be necessary, since we can secure a connection over normal Internet for using this product, and the data would still be housed with us on site.

Murray: You really think we could shave $1M in costs just by dumping the contacts software? Jim, in my former CFO roles I've seen many problems with the risk factors associated with IT systems, because they're notorious for failing to deliver their promised benefits, and a large percentage of projects end up scrapped due to poor user acceptance. How will this be different?

Jim: Absolutely. Good points Murray—that's precisely why we're exploring cloud computing. The use of cloud computing matches cash flow to system benefits more appropriately than the packaged software use model. In the old way of doing things, a large investment is made early in the project, prior to system build-out, and well before the business benefits, presumably financial in some shape or form, are realized. This model is even more troubling given the risk factors associated with IT systems that you've highlighted. In contrast, cloud computing is a pay-as-you-go or, as we call it in our shop, pay-by-the-drink, an approach in which a low initial investment is required to get going, and additional investment is incurred only as system use increases. This way, cash flows better match total system cost.

Murray: That's interesting, Jim, but doesn't this concept use open source software?

Jim: Yes. it does. What I described mirrors the use of open source software versus proprietary software— and, in fact, that's no accident. Cloud computing infrastructures are built, by and large, from open source components. After all, the cloud providers don't want to make large investments upfront without knowing the financial outcomes, either. One might say that cloud computing is a proxy for end-user open source adoption, since it acts as a middleman to "civilize" open source for end users.

Murray: Ok, but do you really want to take the risk of outsourcing our critical resources to a third-party provider?

Jim: Not at all, Murray. Cloud computing provides a way to outsource noncritical applications to organizations that are better suited to run them, which will allow our IT department to focus on critical applications. This should be very attractive to you from a cost perspective, and this concept has already been applied throughout companies in many different areas.

Murray: You do realize that if we found a cloud provider that we could really trust, and hold them to their SLA, and they are as efficient and responsive as IT, then from a cost/benefit perspective, I may want to modify IT in this company and move our infrastructure ownership and control over resources to a cloud provider.

Jim: Of course. This is actually called a "shadow IT" organization, but it won't happen overnight. First we need to find a provider that we can trust with our noncritical data, and then asses over time whether we want to go the next step. There isn't a single C-level executive with fiduciary responsibility to his or her company and shareholders that would make a commitment of this magnitude without meeting the providers, doing a deep dive to separate reality from roadmaps of future promises, and establishing a true partnership for success. Frankly, with the limited number of staff I currently have, we can become the governance arm of this relationship. Another value-add that we can leverage is to have the cloud providers provide security and privacy compliance services, avoiding the cost of expensive personnel, hardware, and software to do it. This is very similar to what was provided by MSSPs before the dot-com bust. Murray, I believe you were around then and understand the value; in fact, if I remember correctly, don't you go back to the Commodore days?

Murray: Yes, I certainly do, Jim. There's some value to having a gray-hair on this board. If you start attending a few more of my staff meetings, you might even start to learn something other than your gear-head stuff.

All: <Chuckle.>

Danny: All my team knows our current product—do you know how much time it will take for them to learn a new product and what makes it better?

Jim: Danny, the new product can do so much more for you—things like pipeline forecasting, executive dashboards, global views by customer category, etc. The learning curve isn't that steep, and we could help you by providing brown-bag seminars and sessions that show them essential skills first, to get this moving quickly.

Linda: Jim, is this software limited just to customer data? What can it do for HR?

Jim: Linda, that's the best part. While HR abounds with SAAS providers, there aren't many that fit the cloud model. Most HR service providers today simply don't have the well-defined APIs yet. Today, much integration among HR systems is brute-force replication and synchronization of data. In some ways, the proliferation of various best-of-breed SAAS offerings has simply increased the extent of data replication across systems. In a full-blown version of cloud computing for HR, employee and HR data would stay in place, perhaps even apart from any particular HR service provider. In this idealized version of HR cloud computing, data is integrated or "mashed up" on an on-demand basis. This is a key difference from today's SAAS offerings. Cloud computing implies that data is available from cloud-based data stores, which can be read, updated, subscribed to, and maintained by various authorized HR services—enrollment, performance management, learning, compensation, etc. It doesn't mean that there would be a single HR cloud database for an employer's entire HR function. There likely would be a single cloud database for HR master data and separate stores for data owned or controlled by ecosphere partners. Examples of the latter might be competency content or candidate profile data. Suffice it to say, though, that the version of cloud computing I'm talking about here is not how HR services are provided today. Full-blown cloud-computing for HR is likely a few years away, and skepticism is warranted. However, it merits watching. End users should neither lump it in with SAAS and ASP offerings, nor tolerate loose claims from vendors about providing services from the cloud. This software allows us to customize it so we can have part of it used for managing internal employees as well as customers. We can create automated reports to help you, and it costs no more to do that. This could help streamline the processes you have and, with the project management and task features, it can be useful to everyone.

Susan: What exactly is this cloud you talk about, and where do you think it will be next year?

Jim: Well, the Internet is the cloud, and we have a choice of hosting it ourselves since we already own the equipment, or we could outsource all of it. The thing about outsourcing all of it is that those providers will want to collect a monthly recurring charge for providing the equipment and the service. When we ran the numbers for us to outsource the equipment and the service, it didn't pan out as well as for us to continue using our own investment in hardware and hosting the software out of the box. As for next year, it's not going away anytime soon.

Murray: How long would it take to set up something like this?

Jim: We have a sandbox set up with it now. We've been playing around with it for about three weeks, testing what it can and cannot do, and I'd be happy to show you all how we can benefit from taking this approach.

Danny: I'd like to see this before making a decision.

Murray: Jim, as the CFO, I'm also responsible for privacy risk and compliance. I'm very concerned about what I've been hearing about a cloud provider's ability to protect or PII and our ability to keep our SAS 70, and ISO 17799 attestation if we go with a third party.

Jim: First of all, we've prepared for this by gaining an understanding of what your risk and what compliance requirements really are and how we currently address them on our internal systems. Before anybody asserts that cloud computing isn't appropriate because of risk and not having an answer to "How do we handle that today?," we wanted to be prepared in order to avoid embarrassment. My security operations and engineering manager Mike and I briefed you on our requirements last month in preparation for this meeting.

Murray: Yes you did—it was an excellent approach, by the way. Go on. . . .

Jim: Of course we also explained our risk assessment mechanism to define levels of risk and make it part of the system development life cycle. Without our preparation in this regard, it would be impossible for us to evaluate whether a given system is a good candidate for operating in the cloud and to assess your potential cloud hosting operators for their risk management practices. With this completed, our projects can have their risk assessments mapped against the cloud provider and a decision can be reached about whether cloud hosting is appropriate for this system. Our cloud hosting risk assessment should be treated as a dynamic target, not a static situation. Since cloud computing is developing rapidly, our current evaluation will probably not be accurate in six months and we'll have to continue the assessment. As part of the external assessment, we'll also assess the cloud provider's compliance with SAS 70, ISO 17799/27001, PCI, and other appropriate standards for our business, and most important, the effect on our continued compliance with these standards.

Susan: I agree. Big decisions should take time, to ensure we get it right. We'll set that up later. Jim, was that it?

Jim: No. For the finance folks, there's a similar solution for expense reporting and payments. For helping the customer, there's a solution that ties to the contact solution to provide customer support and track customer history. There are a lot of ways we can improve, but I recommend taking one step at a time. We should change one area and see the improvements before trying to change another area. This gives us flexibility to adjust along the way. I do think we can make all of this happen within six months, and if we shave a couple of million in expenses along the way, that's not a bad thing!

Susan: Let's do a deeper dive on our security risk in going with a cloud provider. I read recently that, along with PII protection, this is the biggest concern of organizations and individuals using these services.

Jim: As I said before, it's all about assessing the capabilities and integrity of the provider that we choose, in addition to ensuring that they have the security staff and privacy control and protection expertise that can be leveraged to make up skill sets and security hardware and software that either we currently don't have or can reduce if we are using a third party. As a recent Gartner report stated, there are seven primary focus areas that we need to address with the cloud vendor that we chose: privileged user access, as I mentioned earlier, regulatory compliance, data location, data segregation, recovery, investigative support, and long-term viability. Of course, there are also many other items that we have to address with a prospective vendor, which we have included in our assessment report—I can email it to all of you right after this meeting adjourns.

Danny: Come on, Jim, are you going to try to tell me that you've accounted for the virtualization security challenges?

Jim: Actually, yes, I have, Danny. Of course, as security experts warn, all the vendor activity in the world won't help a company that dives headlong into the cloud without thinking through the risks first, and as long as companies fail to grasp the nuts and bolts of virtualization, dangers remain. As Murray will attest to, we have done our homework in this regard. You must realize that security in a virtual server environment is different, and you have to think differently and use different tools to achieve the same level of security and risk management you had in the past. Operationally and technically, there's a lot more integration and tightening that have to occur. There are even solutions that protect both physical and logical infrastructure, and that can provide application-aware firewalling, inter-VM flow visibility and analytics, application policy control, and intrusion-prevention capabilities.

Susan: All right, I've heard enough. You've caught my interest about this cloud computing initiative. Murray and Jim, I'll have my admin set up a follow-on meeting of the three of us, and I want a draft proposal put together along with answers to further questions that I have that will follow with the invite. Does anyone else have anything they want to contribute to this discussion? If not, I think we should move on this as Jim has proposed. Danny and Jim should take some time to go over the sandboxed solution and make sure it can do what we need before we jump in.

Danny: Yeah, I'd like to see this dashboard thing as soon as possible.

Murray: Any savings we can get in cost cutting will help—believe me.

Jim: Thanks, everyone. I'll set it up and send each of you an email to coordinate a showing after Danny and I have had a walk-through with it.

And so it goes, all across corporate America. The point of this Appendix is to show you that the same kinds of questions you would ask are the ones the execs in the board rooms also ask. No person likes change for the sake of change, least of all when it can have a impact on employees and revenue streams. With nearly fifty years of combined management experience between the authors, we can assure you that this meeting only opened the door. The proof of the pudding will be when Jim and Danny have the sit-down and Danny sees how good or bad the proposed solution actually is. Jim knows that Danny won't give carte blanche to a solution without trying to get what he sees as the best he can for his team. Just corporate politics, folks.

Jim knows that Linda walked away from the meeting feeling great hope because he knows how backlogged her department is and how useful this solution can be. Jim thinks this might be a good time to visit her office later today and circle wagons. Murray is easy—if it saves money, he'll go for it. As long as profits go up and costs go down, he'll be happy. After the quarter ends, Susan will be pleased with the savings showing real numbers. That's shareholder value, and the board of directors likes to see such positive changes. Jim knows all of this and has held back the best part of this solution—it's only the tip of the iceberg, and more savings can be had from the cloud solution. He thinks to himself, "Wait till I spring VoIP on them!"

Index